Hollywood's New Deal

In the series *Culture and the Moving Image,*
edited by Robert Sklar

Hollywood's New Deal

GIULIANA MUSCIO

Temple University Press
PHILADELPHIA

Temple University Press, Philadelphia 19122

Published 1996

Printed in the United States of America

⊖ The paper used in this publication meets the requirements of the
American National Standard for Information Sciences—
Permanence of Paper for Printed Library Materials, ANSI Z39.48–1984

Text design by Robert Freese

Library of Congress Cataloging-in-Publication Data

Muscio, Giuliana.
    Hollywood's New Deal / Giuliana Muscio.
       p.   cm.
    Includes bibliographical references and index.
       ISBN 1–56639–495–3 (alk. paper).—ISBN 1–56639–496–1 (pbk. :
    alk. paper)
       1. Motion pictures—Political aspects—United States.   2. New
    Deal, 1933–1939.   3. Motion pictures—Economic aspects—United
    States.   I. Title.
    PN1995.9.N47M87   1997
    302.23′43′0973—dc20   96-34525

For Alessandro and Francesca

Contents

Acknowledgments

This project has many "fathers": Nick Browne, who directed the Ph.D. dissertation at the origins of this work; Gian Piero Brunetta, who supported the Italian version of the research; Lary May and Robert Rosen, who have generously contributed their historical knowledge; and most of all, Robert Sklar, who has always stimulated my studies and who encouraged the (long) process of completing this book.

Vito Zagarrio and the conferences of the Retrospettiva Internazionale of the Mostra of Pesaro allowed me to develop arguments and elements of this project and periodically confront the state of the art in the international and American studies of the mode of production. Analogously I also feel indebted to the Biennale of Venice and to Patrizia Pistagnesi for giving me the responsibility and the great opportunity of working on the retrospective *Prima dei Codici*.

I thank Adriano Aprà, Tino Balio, Janet Bergstrom, Bruno Cartosio, Guido Fink, Michael Friend, Jane Gaines, Miriam Hansen, Lea Jacobs, Richard Jewell, Richard Maltby, Nick Roddick, Lynn Spiegel, Bill Uricchio, Charles Wolfe, and especially Steven Ricci and Giuliana Bruno, for many hours of thought-provoking discussions. I also thank Giorgio Bertellini, Larry Bird, Tom Cripps, David Ellwood, Thomas Elsaesser, James Hay, Julia Mickenberg, Kathryn Kish Sklar, and Brian Taves for all their help.

I very much appreciate the competence and cooperation of Elaine Mejstrik of the Antitrust Division of the Justice Department in Washington, D.C., and the personnel of the Roosevelt Library at Hyde Park, New York, in allowing me access to the documents that were essential to this research. I also thank the personnel of the Archivio Storico of the Foreign Affairs Ministry in Rome, the Academy Library and the RKO Archives in Los Angeles, and Leith Adams of the Warners Collection at the University of Southern California library, Los Angeles, Patrick Sheehan of the Motion Pictures Division of the Library of Congress, and Bill Murphy at the Motion Picture Branch of the National Archives in Washington, D.C.

I thank Janet Francendese for her firm but relaxed editorial attention, and Debby Stuart for the collaborative and patient copyediting.

Acknowledgments

I thank also Paola Golinelli, Sandra Sfara, Monica Crepaldi, Teresa Catena, Dario Minutolo, and Davide Marangon, who have given me, in their own specific and special way, a support necessary in the writing of this book.

A final consideration goes to my family: to Norberto, early companion in this adventure and, in spite of all, in his way still part of the team; and to Alessandro and Francesca, who participatd in all this studying and traveling always making my life brighter and actually less tiring.

Hollywood's New Deal

Introduction

The interaction (or, more precisely, the reciprocal attraction) between politics and communication in the 1930s is at the core of this work.[1] In the thirties, the function and methodology of politics were modified by their contact with modern systems of communication. Politics transformed its "public" into "spectators" at the same time cinema transformed its spectators into a public—especially through the implementation of the self-censorship guidelines of the Hays Code. The mechanical description of the phenomenon, however, does not imply a mechanistic historical interpretation. On the contrary, in re-articulating the analysis of the decade, I stress the temporal processes: there is a Depression and a New Deal; there is a pre-code cinema and a self-censored cinema; and there is symbolic coincidence in the traditional periodization, which positions 1933 as a watershed for both. This coincidence requires investigation, but with the understanding that there was no linear process in the economy and society from the hard times of the Great Depression to the happy days of the New Deal,[2] and the Hays Code was not simply a form of repression that cleaned up the Hollywood product once and for all.[3] Delays and contradictions help historical explanation as much as regularity and orderly data. Skeptical of deterministic interpretations, I focus on the interstices of the events, through a complex model of explanation.[4]

In this instance, advances in technology did not determine the change of political practices in the thirties, and the battle over control of the Hollywood screens was not about economic control but about the continuous ideological distrust of commercial cinema by civic groups and reformers. Discussing the interaction between politics and communication, between Washington and Hollywood, I refer to the notion of hegemony in Raymond Williams's reconceptualization: "A lived hegemony is always a process. It is not, except analytically, a system or a structure. . . . It has continually to be renewed, recreated, defended, and modified. . . . It is also continually resisted, limited, altered, challenged by pressures not at all its own."[5]

1

INTRODUCTION

The argument of this book differs substantially (and polemically) from the common practice of projecting culture onto a historical background to demonstrate how society is *reflected* by the popular culture of a period.[6] Media production in the 1930s did not just work as a conveyor-belt from economy and politics to society, instead, it was one of the factors that changed political participation and sociocultural perceptions of the economy. I argue in fact that there was a similar ideological function, and an interchange, between politics and communications in the thirties. Both the New Deal and cinema had a stabilizing effect on society that was strengthened and sustained by a re-interpretation of the idea of Americanism, such that the thirties have been identified with the desire for a "new national vision of popular culture and the country."[7]

The ahistorical definition of "Hollywood classical cinema" comes under discussion too, as I argue that American cinema of the thirties could be productively re-interpreted as a *national* cinema, in that it performed a crucial role in the national organization of cultural distribution,[8] and in the re-elaboration and articulation of national identity. Like the cultural politics of the New Deal, Hollywood cinema of the thirties revitalized the idea of Americanism in the depressed country.

This cinema favored the adaptation of the confused citizen to the new needs of society, elaborating reassuring interpretations of socioeconomic reality, stressing the typical American virtues of faith, courage, pragmatism, and individual action, and adjusting conflicts with the imposition of an optimistic ritual happy ending.[9] Hollywood cinema did not simply reflect or transmit this ideological project. It negotiated it with the representatives of dominant culture, the political establishment, and its audience.[10]

American cinema offered more than "escapist entertainment": it articulated ideological contradictions, for example, by personalizing conflict and diversifying the ideological structure of film genres. Furthermore, if we compare the history of film exhibition and film going in the thirties with the profile of the textually inscribed spectator emerging from the films of that period, we note signs—sometimes weak traces, sometimes evident marks—of an unreconciled social reality: devastating representations of forgotten men, lynch mobs, and unstable expressions of sexuality, before and *after* the code. There appears to be no homogeneity in the racial, class, and sexual characteristics of the spectators of Hollywood cinema of the 1930s. This is particularly evident if we consider not only the average product but also the B movies,[11] or if we remember the segregation of black audiences, the important role of the local exhibitor, and the consumeristic impact of the give-aways in film theaters.

Between 1929 and 1941, the Depression, innovative federal programs, precarious economic conditions, and widespread social unrest challenged the sociocultural organization of the United States, within a crisis that encouraged a variety of responses from dominant social forces. The strategies ranged from the implementation of state-endorsed federal relief programs to sponsorship of cultural activities (Works Progress Administration, Federal Theater, etc., and the intellectual work elaborated by private foundations), encouraging a redefinition of the role of popular culture, particularly cinema, as well as attempts to maintain national unity through the dissemination of shared cultural values. In a transitional stage, between 1929 and 1934, the American film industry, through the implementation of the Hays Code, differentiated its product from expressive forms that were associated with marginalized social formations, while seeking legitimation within mainstream mass culture, through the "better films" program, suggested by Will H. Hays. By the end of the decade, changes in film expression, economic organization, exhibition outlets, and audience composition worn over some of the groups that had castigated moving pictures for their (supposedly negative) influence on working-class and poor filmgoers.

I agree with recent historiography on the interpretation of the New Deal as a "conservative" program, an attempt to "save" the socioeconomic system after its collapse in the Depression.[12] But, I would add, it was also a new social alliance of modern economic forces and modern labor organizations, characterized by an innovative political practice that included efforts by President Franklin D. Roosevelt to involve the people in its reforms. Thus the New Deal was a powerful *modernizing* mechanism that conserved the economic system but, in the end, produced a new sociopolitical configuration, which is still operative today.

Although radical and revisionist historians point out that this enlarged political constituency did not include marginal social groups (Barton Berstein), and that the New Deal's effect was mainly psychological (Warren Susman), I believe that the New Deal qualitatively changed the relationship between political leadership and the public, and that this transformation was not limited to the traditional area of political history. The thirties in fact saw what the cultural historian Warren Susman describes as "the crucial and perhaps climactic stage of the [twentieth-century] battle" between Puritan-capitalist culture and the "culture of abundance."

> One of the fundamental conflicts of twentieth-century America is between two cultures—an older culture, often loosely labeled Puritan-republican, producer-capitalist culture, and a newly emerging culture of abundance. If twentieth-century American politics rarely carries the burden of ideological conflict, there was nonetheless a significant and profound clash between different moral orders.[13]

This concept requires us to focus on the specific characteristics of this "battle" in the 1930s and allows us to discuss politics in terms of communications and vice versa, within the field of cultural history. This analysis makes it necessary to consider cinema *within the system* of communications of that period. But we must not simply take into account the histories of other media such as radio or press in the 1930s, or the eventual relationship between the cinema and the other media, as if these stories were running parallel to our account and needed to be referred to only when they meet tangentially. We must examine communications as a system, seeing it as a whole, as a culture, in the sense of Susman's definition of "culture of abundance" and "communications revolution" as two interchangeable and interdependent aspects of socioeconomic life in the 1930s that were neither entirely overlapping nor fully independent. Within this system, cinema was the dominant medium of the time.

In reexamining the institutional history of Hollywood cinema against a socioeconomic background, I argue that this is the history of a monopoly of discourse (i.e., the domination of a worldwide, collective fantasy), as well as the history of an economic monopoly. This interdependence was embodied by the Motion Picture Producer Distributor Association (MPPDA), the trade organization that also controlled the system of self-censorship.

The *Paramount* case, an antitrust suit filed in 1938 by the Antitrust Division of the U.S. Justice Department against eight film companies, is both the conclusion of a narrative history of the film industry in the period and an important interpretative element that sheds light on the relationship between industry and government, as well as on the New Deal's sophisticated understanding of the relationship between economic structure and cultural expression.[14] This is why, throughout the book, I repeatedly refer to the work of Thurman Arnold.[15] He was a crucial personality in the New Deal reelaboration of the symbolic relationship between political institutions and society in the thirties, and as the main "trust buster," he played a significant role in the filing of the *Paramount* case.

The book is divided into three parts, Chapters 1 and 2 cover politics and communications in the thirties, Chapters 3 and 4 American cinema in the thirties, and Chapter 5 the *Paramount* case.

Politics and Communications in the Thirties

In recent years, historians have synthesized the traditional view of the New Deal as either an economic program or an ideological reaction. The New Deal is now seen as an operation of socioeconomic reform, characterized by a specific ideological and political project.

Warren Susman, Richard Pells, Barton Bernstein, and Gabriel Kolko, and other radical and revisionist historians tend to stress the continuity of the

New Deal, with, for instance, the progressive movement. Therefore, they argue for the implicit conservatism of the New Deal, which was "farsighted enough to grasp what was required to save capitalism for itself."[16] Labor and black historians have further developed this interpretation, demonstrating how New Deal reforms reacted to the pressures of organized groups (business, labor, agriculture) but never created an authentic "equality" or addressed the socioeconomic situation of groups marginalized by the basic structures of American capitalism.[17]

The New Deal reacted to the Depression through a series of reforms on both the economic level and the political-institutional level. It strengthened the role of the federal government, politically enforcing the tendency developed by the economy to go "national" and centered, mostly through the transformation of distribution. At the same time, the New Deal decentralized its experimental projects through new local agencies and institutions, responding to the demands of different interest groups and diverse social subjects, often co-opting their organizations, and at times even adopting their interpretations of social problems.[18] In so doing, the New Deal enlarged the representation and increased the participation of these groups in the Democratic party, and in the wider political arena. By mediating between different groups and producing new institutions to meet newly perceived socioeconomic needs, the New Deal was able to "suture" intense social conflicts and create a new "social pact." This had a stabilizing effect that helped to preserve and update the deeply rooted socioeconomic foundations of American society.[19]

The most recent historiography of the New Deal (best represented by the work of Gary Gerstle, Lizabeth Cohen, Steve Fraser, and Thomas Ferguson) has dramatically revised these views. Ferguson, for example, analyzes the New Deal as "a whole in the light of industrial structure, party competition, and public policy," arguing that "what stands out is the novel type of political coalition that Roosevelt built."At the center of this coalition was "a new 'historical bloc' [Antonio Gramsci's phrase] of capital-intensive industries, investment banks, and internationally oriented commercial banks."[20]

The New Deal found its allies in the newer industries and economic agencies with reformist roots, under modern management that was oriented toward a consumer economy. These industries were comparatively less labor-intensive, or less antagonistic toward labor, and involved in the study of a "scientific" approach to the question of labor. These industries also supported foundations such as the Taylor Society, the Industrial Relations Counselors, and Filene's Twentieth-Century Fund, where the social sciences found fertile soil, where many future New Dealers developed and practiced their theories, and where important legislative projects on social security and industrial relations were elaborated.

5

INTRODUCTION

The stagnation of the economy in the 1930s was due in large part to structural problems not at first identified by economists, who theorized that the economy had reached the stage of "mature economy" and argued that economic expansion was not limitless. The frontier, they said, had been reached: "No new sectors capable of matching railroads, steel, and automobiles as engines of expansion were likely to emerge."[21] But the problem with the 1930s economy was that recovery and investments were applied to sectors with "low shares of national employment . . . [that were] most stimulated by the new patterns of consumer spending at the time," while the traditional, labor-intensive industries were slow to diversify and expand production, and slow to modernize industrial relations.[22] On one hand, therefore, the New Deal by trial and error tried different prognoses and different therapies for an economy that seemed unable to recover. On the other hand, because of mutual interests, the more modern industrialists were able to attract the attention of the New Dealers and were more inclined to support the government's policies.

These business supporters of the New Deal also controlled (directly or through financial interests) the means to inform and influence public opinion, such as foundations and media (newspapers, magazines, radio, and film), and were among the constant users of advertising. The inextricable link between economics, politics, and communications is here particularly marked. The supporters of social reform represented "a set of newer, mass-consumption-oriented industries—mass merchandisers like Filene's and Macy's; urban real estate developers like the Greenfield interests in Philadelphia; newer investment banks that underwrote the mass consumer sector like the Lehman Brothers and Goldman, Sachs; mass-consumer-oriented banks with diversified investments in real estate, fire insurance, furniture, lumber, the movies, agricultural finance, and various consumers services like the Bank of America and the Bowery Saving Bank; industries like clothing, housing constructions and supplies, dry goods, office equipment and supplies, appliances; capital goods suppliers to mass market producers: a wide variety of producer service organizations including management consultants and foundations—all associated with the exponential growth in the size and depth of the urban mass market."[23] This detailed list emphasizes the connection between the business supporters of the New Deal and "the movies": Bank of America, for example, was an early support of the film business; Goldman, Sachs financed Warner Bros. in its escalation toward the status of major studio. (We should consider that the film executives' frequenting of Wall Street and of the business community since the late 1920s might have affected not only their business methods and industrial practices but also their cultural and political integration.)

This "historical bloc," joined by labor, constituted the core of the Democratic party in the 1930s. As the New Deal attracted modern business and industry, it also attracted what Fraser describes as a "new species of worker."

These workers were "quintessentially urban, . . . far more integrated as consumers into the mass market and more influenced by the media of mass culture than their parents."[24]

Compared to the dynamism of the twenties, the New Deal thirties has been perceived as a moment of stall, of economic stagnation, of fear and retrenchment. But, quite the contrary, beneath its apparently incoherent and pragmatic attempts to reform capitalism, the New Deal redefined the characters of political and economic leadership. It was undeniably a key phase of modernization, the starting point of the modern configuration of the welfare state—whose model is always in a process of transformation; and it was the new model of partisan politics that established the traits of the Democratic party and of the liberal tradition in America.[25]

If the New Deal was in the end, conservative, the number and impact of innovative reforms it introduced and the political project that characterized them constituted, indeed, a *new* deal—a breaking point in the chain of the historical reactions to the Great Depression. The New Deal should not be seen as a linear government philosophy or, especially, as a homogeneous economic theory. It was instead, a program masterfully conducted by the pragmatist-idealist Franklin Delano Roosevelt, who through it broadened the legislative action of the presidency. From the point of view of economic theory, the New Deal was a coalition of opposing—at times, even contradictory—views, in which there was no linear movement, no unproblematic progression from planning and cartelization to antitrust, from corporatism, state planning, and trust-busting to the economics of John Maynard Keynes. The New Deal was never anti-capitalistic; but the reformers did change their view about what was wrong with the economic structure and what were the means to change it, always reserving a central position to government intervention.

Given the nonlinear economic philosophy of the New Deal, it is only possible to establish which of several positions predominated at a particular time and how that position could have influenced, for example, the government's interpretation of the film industry. But these positions did not smoothly replace one another throughout the thirties, in a way that might facilitate a neat chronology.

The first phase of the New Deal was characterized by the institution of a series of emergency and relief programs (sponsored and directly financed by the federal government) and by an attempt to rationalize the economic system through the establishment of the National Recovery Administration (NRA) and the Agricultural Adjustment Administration (AAA). The NRA set up codes of fair competition within each industry, in a system of self-regulation, under government supervision, aimed at stabilizing wages and prices and establishing standards of quality. But because of its poor economic results and the uncooperativeness of most industries, "the NRA began to self-destruct almost from the moment it began operations. Free traders fought with protectionists; big firms battled with small competitors; buyers collided with suppliers."[26] The NRA was abolished in 1935 when the Supreme Court declared it unconstitutional.

In 1937 the emerging neopopulist component within the Roosevelt administration started voicing the need for a new economic policy that would enforce the necessary reforms and develop an antimonopoly strategy. But beneath the family antimonopoly rhetoric, the New Dealers were actually not trying to break economic concentrations because of their "bigness," for, as long as their structure was efficient, in both production and distribution, the consumer could benefit. To help revitalize production, legislation passed during this phase of the New Deal expanded the regulatory functions of the state, according to the opinion that "the competitive struggle without effective antitrust enforcement is like a fight without referee."[27]

In 1938 Roosevelt appointed Thurman Arnold as his "referee," that is, director of the Antitrust Division of the Justice Department. Arnold immediately started an intense trust-busting program, while arguing that what Americans needed above all was a "religion of government which permits us to face frankly the psychological factors inherent in the development of organizations with public responsibility."[28] Arnold used antitrust laws to police rather than forestall "bigness." But the effects of such a direction were still to be felt when the political crisis in Europe (and later, the war) reintroduced the need for tighter collaboration between government and industry.

In the late 1930s, it became evident that the economy was too complex for a single economic plan to encompass it all, and, most of all, for the state to be able to solve *all* the problems. Instability and conflict were inevitable. Believing that spending cuts had been responsible for a recession in 1937, the New Dealers started a new program of broad economic intervention. This time, however, spending was not directed at solving specific socioeconomic problems or dealing with emergencies. In accordance with the principles of Keynesian economics, spending was aimed at encouraging employment and redistributing income to promote mass consumption.

World War II dramatically changed the scenario. The necessities of the war effort lessened antipathy toward big business. In addition, the wartime economy demonstrated that capitalism was still able to expand, that perhaps the economy had not yet reached "maturity." Most of all, the democratic war against Nazi-fascist states seemed to demonstrate that a "good" capitalism "represented the best hope for social progress," that vigilant intervention by the state was preferable to strong government intervention as practiced by the totalitarian states. It is necessary to remember that this "accommodation with capitalism" was made possible *because* "the achievements of the New Deal had already eliminated the most dangerous features of the capitalist system."[29]

Traditional historiography has concentrated on the political, institutional, and socioeconomic activities of the New Deal. But the history of the New Deal is also a history of cultural mediation in a social order enfeebled by the Depression and disoriented by the experimental programs of the federal government. This mediation might best be described as the attempt at a synthesis of two cultural and ideological positions that had previously been entirely separate within the history of the American political thought—populism and the "frontier spirit."[30] This improbable synthesis of populism and frontier spirit was essential to both economic growth and social reform because it allowed the New Deal to seemingly reconcile a series of fundamental contradictions innate in American ideology and cultural heritage. Thus, collaboration between "good neighbors" might be merged with dynamic individualism, antitrust with economic realism, decentralization with centralized planning, immigrant America with pioneer America, and regionalism with New York and Washington.[31] On one hand, uniquely populist values (anti-city, anti-politician, anti-intellectual, anti-progressive, anti–big business) would have been unwieldily if not entirely unmanageable in the context of the proposed intensive federal programs. On the other hand, the stockmarket crash had undoubtedly demonstrated the faults of an aggressive frontier spirit of individualism in business.

Populism has traditionally been interpreted as a rebellious but not revolutionary movement, as a conservative and backward movement. But in the past decade the definition of populism has undergone a complex revision.[32] Revisionist scholars have re-evaluated its deep-rooted advocacy for redistribution of power and wealth, stressing its democratic basis, its anti-elitist stance, its continuous challenge to capitalism, and the important political function of its project to redistribute power and resources in a country without an established tradition of socialism. Specifically, the re-interpretation of populism offers the potential for a "subversive" reading of the populist inclinations often attributed to the lower middle class, that is, to an unstable section of the New Dealist constituency, and to a vast segment of film audiences.

Studies comparing the New Deal with German nazism and Italian fascism have emphasized that the three nations, facing similar deep socioeconomic crises, developed similar internal strategies of social organization but with different degrees of cooperation between private industry, the work force, and the political establishment.[33] The concept, common to all three, of a "corporative state" as a rationalization of the capitalist system was an experiment in socioeconomic reform and a phase in the economy of mass production that pointed to a new role for the masses. Social cooperation and nationalism went together, in the name of national identity, of the people, and of national culture.[34]

If we widen the scope of this comparative analysis to include the relationship between politics and communication in these three sociopolitical systems during the 1930s, we would find an extraordinary degree of similarity in the central role played by audiovisual communication in the cultural production of that period. But there were crucial differences among the nations. In Germany, and to a far lesser extent in Italy, the government controlled film production.[35] In the United States, however, although the government ventured into documentary production and, during World War II, tried to influence the Hollywood message through the Office of War Information, it did not manipulate information and produce propaganda in a way even comparable to that adopted by the two totalitarian systems.[36] The role of mass media and, in general, of cultural and ideological production, in these systems was thus crucial, not just in terms of propaganda (of an active use of the media), but in the sense of how mass media—and film in particular—gave the masses a vision of the world. These political systems established a closer contact with the masses, immediately perceiving the importance of the "new" audiovisual media in this action.

Roosevelt was always reluctant to coordinate the communication and information needs of his administration within a single agency. As with the federal agencies he had instituted, often with overlapping fields of action and consequent feuds among the various departments, Roosevelt atomized the system of information gathering and dissemination. There was perhaps a touch of vanity or jealously in his choice of appointing different people and different agencies to collect information and maintain contact with public opinion. But this choice also had the effect of avoiding the creation of an unified and unilateral propaganda machine.

The New Deal attached particular importance to its own representation. What has been described as a general inclination toward documentary and realism in the American culture of the 1930s provided a mode of address for, and coincided with, the government's attempt to reduce the distance between itself (as information agency and as educator), the object of its inquiries (the current state of affairs in Depression America), and its public.[37] The way radio news and newsprint investigation brought its listeners and readers "closer" to current events was echoed by the presence of the social worker, who acted, in the name of the government, on the problems about which he reported. The government's efforts to get close to its public, to be present on the social scene, were symbolized by President Roosevelt's famous fireside chats, the radio addresses direct to the American people.

While the American public was brought face to face with "reality" in the American realist novel, various governmental agencies and congressional committees produced reams of raw data on that same reality. It has been argued that the real American literature of the period is to be found among these administration reports and investigations.[38] Not only were they the basis for much legislation, but also they inspired novels, book of photographs, and documentary films.[39] These data reflected the New Deal administration's "desire to know," just as its directly subsidized cultural programs (such as the WPA Federal Theater and Writers Project) also reflected a desire to be known by its public.

Roosevelt tried to maintain close contact with public opinion.[40] His particularly pragmatic approach include traveling widely,[41] monitoring the press, and reading the mail sent to the White House by common citizens as well as reports and administrative materials. Roosevelt preferred newsreels and radio broadcasts to the traditional medium of the press, which he distrusted and which had, at that time, lost the confidence of the American people.[42] Politics overlapped with communication in Roosevelt's efforts both to know the people and to inform them. In an important essay on the American culture of the thirties, Susman points out that "the newly developed media and their special kinds of appeal helped reinforce a special order rapidly disintegrating under economic and social pressures that were too great to endure, and helped create an environment in which the sharing of common experiences, be they of hunger, dustbowls, or war, made uniform demand of action and reform more striking urgent. . . . Whatever else might be said about the New Deal, its successes and its failures, . . . it was *a sociological and psychological triumph.*"[43] Thus, we might say that the New Deal, mostly, but not exclusively, through the charismatic figure of Franklin Roosevelt, transformed its constituency into an audience, giving new relevance—a more active role—to the "spectators" of political ceremonies and inextricably linking politics and communication.

American Cinema in the Thirties

Since the beginning of the century, the mesmerizing power of movies and advertising had radically modified the urban landscape, creating through signs, symbols, and images what Vachel Lindsay called a "hieroglyphic civilization."[44] In the thirties, the technology of communications induced deep transformations in people's perception as more and more Americans bought radios and filmmakers introduced color and sound in film. The media system absorbed the impact of radio.[45] Voice-over narration of newsreels and documentary was accompanied by narrative experimentations with sound in film and literature. As image and representation slowly replaced real experience, audiences in the 1930s developed a "documentary passion."

Techniques and knowledge from advertising and the social sciences helped to generate a growing interest in behavioral and external aspects of the individual. With the development and influence of the communication

11

system, particularly film, this interest translated into attention to the "image" of a person (or of an institution). But the decisive contribution of film to this cultural transformation was the star system, which intensified the concept of personality, calling into play the techniques and theories of advertising.

In *Screening Out the Past*, Lary May assigns a key role to cinema in this cultural transformation.

> The movies were perhaps the most powerful national institution which offered private solutions to public issues. In other words, movies could not change society, but their form could infuse life with a new instinctual dynamism and provide a major stimulus for generating modern manners, styles and models of psychological fulfillment.[46]

Cinema also played a key role on an emotional level. The dismay provoked by the Crash paralyzed the country. The miraculous cure was to come from a dynamic president in a wheelchair, and from a cinema of movement—a cinema that proposed movement in any sense, from the literal movement of the camera and elliptical editing to storylines involving social mobility.

The traits traditionally attributed to Hollywood classical cinema (the resolution of a series of individually and psychologically rooted moral and social conflicts, the central role of the young couple, the indirect satisfaction of the erotic needs of film viewers, etc.) had an important stabilizing effect in ideological terms, while also confirming the American values system. In these ways cinema maintained a crucial political valence, without transforming itself into manipulation and occult persuasion. These were the years of Fear and Shame—reflections of the Depression on the individual sphere— the years of the nostalgia fantasies like *Gone with the Wind* and of Frank Capra's screwball comedies, the years when the country was singing and whistling "Who's Afraid of the Big Bad Wolf?" to try to exorcise the crisis.[47]

Popular directors of that period such as John Ford, King Vidor, and Capra have been defined as populist.[48] Their Hollywoodian elaboration of the relation between community and the individual, combining traditional values with social themes made them popular with the left, all over the world.

Rationalizing the social, transmitting optimism to the people, vehicling the extreme need for information and contact, the film medium was an essential agent in the great New Deal mediation. Cinema and the New Deal were strongly related in other ways: the Roosevelts were "film fans" and some members of the family even worked within the film industry; some of the President's closest collaborators came from newsreels; Hollywood stars and personalities often visited the White House; many members of the administration has professional and business connections with the film industry. In addition, Roosevelt himself hired a screenwriter as a ghostwriter for his fireside chats, and successfully appeared in the newsreels.[49]

The *Paramount* Case

The studio system was fully realized in the New Deal period. That is, the New Deal was not merely a historical backdrop onto which to set the action but it existed in historically specific relationships with the studio system.

In those years the industry "met" the government on many institutional grounds: in Federal Trade Commission proceedings, and through the NRA code of fair competition, labor disputes, block booking hearings, propaganda hearings, the Temporary National Emergency Committee study, and, most of all, the *Paramount* case. These investigations produced extensive data for the government on the economic structure of the industry and its operations. Because of these investigations, the industry was continuously changing to escape federal regulations affecting film content and its own structure. We thus could say that the New Deal administration not only first sanctioned and later attacked the monopoly of the major studios, but also that it participated in the formation of the historically specific structure the industry assumed in time.

Through this diachronic analysis of the studio system, we can identify the characteristics of this economic and enterpreneurial model, rather than positioning it in an autonomous space, outside the history of American industry and of American culture (in a sense, outside ideology itself).

The "studio system" was the characteristic mode of functioning of the film industry in its "classical" period. Its main element was the industry's vertical integration, that is, a film company could own theaters as well as produce, distribute, and exhibit films—all within an integrated structure. This complete control of the economic life of the film implied also that the studio was able to program its annual output and hire creative and technical personnel on long-term contracts.

Most aspects of the studio system were in place in the twenties, but in my view the complex workings of the integrated structure were fully developed only in the thirties. The introduction of sound and the acquisition of theaters tightened the already existing liasons with the financial world and imposed on the industry more refined enterpreneurial operations. Double billing combined with such trade practices as block booking and blind selling encouraged greater diversification and higher degrees of efficiency in production. The "producer-unit" system had organized the creative division of labor on the set.

In the mid-thirties advertisement and film exploitation became more centralized as the major studios took direct control of the first-run market, excluding the small exhibitor.[50] The writing and enforcement of the Hays Code concluded this process of economic and discourse centralization, leaving the independents at the margins of the market and the major studies dominating the film business.

Any definition of the studio system must take into account its vertically integrated structure and deal with the issue of the consolidation of control over the market, that is, monopoly. Recent literature on the economic structure of the film industry in its classical period tends to define monopoly through a theoretical economic model, or through a comparative study of other industrial models.[51] But there are also historical definitions of monopoly, such as that elaborated by the Antitrust Division of the Justice Department in the *Paramount* case. This definition was applied to the analysis of the structure of the film industry, but also it directly affected this very structure. The New Dealers in the Antitrust Division had to break new ground in determining what constituted a monopoly in the film industry. They were influenced by the changes in legal doctrine that legal realism, the social sciences,[52] and new economic studies had effected. They tended to consider vertical integration and "bigness" insufficient conditions to define a monopolistic control of the market. Within the *Paramount* case, the Antitrust Division attributed the monopolistic control held by the majors not only to their vertical integration (that is, the ownership of film theaters, which closed an economic circuit including production and distribution) but also to the fact that these companies controlled mostly first-run theaters and adopted trade practices related to this privileged position in the market, such as block booking. Thus the New Dealers were interested not only in the size and structure of the industry but also in its behavior in the market.

Instead of ahistorically defining the structure of the film industry as "innate monopolism," we must account for the process by which the majors achieved a high degree of market control. This definition should reconstruct the Antitrust Division's interpretation of the studio system, because the division was the authority that studied and castigated monopoly.

The history of the economic monopoly of the majors is subtly connected to the history of the monopoly of discourse held by Hollywood cinema, that is, the undisputed domination of screens and collective fantasies exercised by the films produced within the studio system. From an institutional point of view, the Hays Office administered both the system of self-censorship and the system of industrial self-regulation, thus materially controlling access to the screens, that is, both the content of films and their commercial circulation. The functioning of censorship itself was guaranteed by the internal homogeneity of the industry, by the arranged standardization of commercial and expressive practices.

Critics of the economic monopoly held by the majors recognized the connection between the monopoly of discourse and the monopoly of the market. Always afraid of the ideological power of cinema, these civic groups and reformers continued to search for ways to control it until they discovered, in the thirties, that they could deal with this concern more directly by attacking the economic monopoly.

14

INTRODUCTION

The role of exhibition within the studio system, the action of pressure groups, block booking hearings, exhibitor's discontent against the majors, changing patterns of film exploitation: the history of the studio system in the mid-thirties inextricably interweaves Hollywood's monopoly of discourse and the major's economic monopoly, on the scene of the *Paramount* case.

Reflection—the history of great men and events, occult persuasion and media manipulation, cinema as either escapist entertainment or representational (and referential) medium: these biased and outdated historiographic models are no longer adequate. The relationship of the New Deal to cinema resembles a game of mirror reflections—a reciprocal production and reproduction. Instead of looking for the one determinant that could explain the entire system, we should adopt a multidimensional historiographic model that allows us to understand the complex interaction of the New Deal and cinema, permitting us to read the history of American cinema of the thirties in the light of New Deal historiography and vice versa to transcode—to read in counterlighting—the New Deal through the history of Hollywood cinema.

1

The New Deal and the Media

"The words, ceremonies, theories, and principles and other symbols which man uses make him believe in the reality of his dreams and thus give purpose to his life," wrote Thurman Arnold in 1935, expressing the urgency of revitalizing the American dream, in the wake of the Depression.[1] A key figure in the history of American thought in the 1930s, Arnold observed and described the pathology of the sociopolitical system, diagnosing in it the cause of the gap created between society and the world of production. He emphasized the need for political institutions to create new "symbols of government" and a new "folklore of capitalism" able to reactivate sociopolitical life, which had been short-circuited by the Crash.[2]

> In order to solve the pressing problems of waste of labor and national resources, new organizations were sorely needed; yet there was no logical place in the mythology of government to which they could be assigned. The social needs were felt by everyone, but the slogans which the new organizations used had a queer sound.[3]

Arnold maintained a pragmatic approach to the problem, identifying the solutions to the crisis, in politics and in a "new class of government, opportunistic, competent and pragmatic," that is, the New Dealers. He distained "high ideals" because they were absolute and therefore not malleable, and he questioned even the ideological differences between parties.[4] He described ideology as not in and of itself false but rather as a dress uniform for "institutions on parade," valid only for its symbolic effectiveness. Arnold questioned the effectiveness of politics and advised politicians to learn from businessmen how to restructure their rapport with society. He pointed to the effective use of public relations, advertising, rhetoric, slogans, and pictures to move people. In other words, Arnold advocated that politicians adapt the practices of mass marketing, the application of spectacularization and mise-en-scène, to the concept of democracy.[5]

> Men are coming to realize that political government is necessarily a dramatic spectacle, that games are really important in the growth and development of institutions, and that these games can be controlled. . . . The most primitive type of such contest is war. The most civilized types are games and judicial trial. . . . It gives us an understanding of the part that football teams play in the growth and traditions of a college, and the similar part that such an institution as the Supreme Court of the United States plays in the growth, tradition, and unity of a nation.[6]

Arnold did not propose, therefore, to dismantle the old symbols of government, but instead he implicitly suggested to the New Dealers that they reappropriate the folklore of capitalism in order to make innovative practices appear "traditional," by formulating associations and analogies, which would supply the "New Organizations" with mythico-symbolic roots and thus reactivate the mechanisms of consensus. Although he wrote about the emotional needs of the people (Arnold preferred the term "people" to "masses") and discussed the "spectacularization" of politics, he was not advocating a manipulation of the consensus or predicting the advent of a charismatic leader who would hypnotize the crowd. Arnold's reaction to the culture of mass production did not constitute a populist escape into the past. On the contrary, he called for the insertion of the new culture into a traditional apparatus, hoping to render it both stable and dynamic. In a sense, he described a process in which he was simultaneously an observer and—as a trust buster and head of the Antitrust Division of the Justice Department—a player.

Arnold is a key figure in my analysis in part because of some interesting similarities between him and Franklin Roosevelt in the way they approach readers and listeners, in their peculiar combination of idealism and pragmatism, in their attention for the construction of consensus. But, most important, my interest in Arnold's ideas is inspired by the precision with which he singled out the mediating role of the New Deal, the dynamic interaction between economy, politics, culture, and communication that characterized the 1930s.

Politics and Communications

Toward the end of the nineteenth century the traditional party system began a slow decline, causing a consistently lowering voter turnout, a toning down of partisan passions, and a weakening of party machines.[7] Accompanying this phenomenon were an incessant reformist criticism and a newly enlarged role for communications. The telegraph, the telephone, and electricity made instantaneous communication possible. To satisfy the demand of an ever-growing public, but one void of specific preparation in political affairs, the popular press began delving into muckraking journalism and developing other new approaches to information, such as the human interest story. "Throughout American history," as Ronald Brownstein notes, "each new tool of mass communication [has] been rapidly fitted for political use."[8]

Theodore Roosevelt was the first President "to become a national icon." During the Cuban campaign in the Spanish-American War, he received some of the greatest battlefield publicity in the history of warfare. (Ever on the lookout for new technology to spread his image, Roosevelt had found a spot for two operators of the new revolutionary Vitagraph motion picture process on the boat to Cuba.)[9]

The press, however, was slow in keeping up with the demand for visual images because of technical problems and its attachment to the traditional form of illustration. The technology for sending photographic images by telegraph did not yet exist, and photographic equipment was too unwieldy to allow working "on the scene" of the action. But after World War I, American newspapers hired full-time photographers to cover Washington and the political scene. In a short time, the ever-more illustrated popular tabloid became the most-read form of newspaper in the country.[10]

Developments in photo journalism and the newsreel late in the nineteenth century had a notable impact on political behavior. "Actualities" shot by D. W. Griffith's cameraman, Billy Bitzer, came out at the height of the electoral campaign for William McKinley, inspiring a demand for actualities of the candidates. The public, accustomed to still pictures of the politicians, wanted now also to observe their gestures. Soon newsreels became an important source of information about the political life and activities of the president. By 1919, Fox, Pathé, Hearst, and Universal were each producing two newsreel issues a week, reaching an average of 40 million people.[11]

At the beginning of the 1920s radio entered the communication field. It was soon launched and legitimated by transmitting the final results of national elections.[12] During the presidential campaign of 1924 the Republicans broadcast electoral propaganda messages within normal radio programming. The decision to broadcast the two party conventions greatly stimulated the sale of radios and enhanced radio programming.

The strengthening link between radio and politics inspired widespread debate about the effect on political speech. Reformists hoped it would eliminate falsehoods and high-sounding rhetoric. Furthermore, with the entrance of women onto the political arena following their winning the right to vote (an event that coincided, in America, with the grand "launch" of radio) political language was transformed, and political discussion within the family enhanced. But despite these crucial transitions in the political culture of the period, Presidents and other politicians did not necessarily develop competence in using the new communication technology. The technology served them and excited their curiosity, but they did not show any control over the communication process.

Beginning in the 1920s, politicians showed increasing interest in the question of image and began to enlist public relations experts. The political demands of a society in the era of mass communication encouraged such practices as the use of ghostwriters for presidential speeches. Ghostwriters were first hired openly and full-time during the administration of Warren G. Harding. The overall relationship between politics and communications changed radically.[13] An electoral campaign assumed the characteristics of a promotional sale. A party convention became a spectacle oriented to the radio public. A presidential trip became a newsreel travelogue.

To cover the ever more complex area of interaction, the role of secretary to the President had to be modified. Herbert Hoover nominated three secretaries to replace the traditional one.[14] But nonetheless he was unable to use communication with the public to control the effects of the Depression. He avoided direct contact with journalists by supplying the press with statistics and optimistic predictions, and he asked that questions for his press conferences be presented beforehand in writing. The result of these tactics was that under Hoover the relationship between the President and the media reached the lowest point ever witnessed in modern America. In the wake of this failure, and at the bottom of the Depression, in 1932 Franklin D. Roosevelt entered the picture.

Roosevelt had demonstrated his mastery of the media since the radio broadcast of his speech to the Democratic National Convention of 1928. The speech had been conceived not for the delegates but for the public at home, listening to their radios.[15] Many of the traits of his later rhetoric style were formed as he developed his radio technique during his years as governor of the state of New York. He was an innovator of political communication. At the beginning of his political career, campaigning for the New York state senate, he toured rural districts in an automobile—a novelty at the time—and shook hands individually with as many farmers as possible. When he was nominated Democratic presidential candidate, he mailed a small phonograph disk with a recording of a short speech in his own voice to every Roosevelt-pledged delegate.[16]

"FDR" Is The "New Deal"

Cultural historians traditionally concentrate on the study of the producers of culture, and rarely on its consumers, probably in part because this aspect is usually more richly documented and uses a more standardized methodology of investigation. In the 1930s, Franklin Roosevelt occupied the center of the stage, but because of his management of communication, studying the production of political culture in this period also gives us precious insights into its consumers too. The history of the relationship between communications and politics in the New Deal period is almost completely identified with Roosevelt.[17] Many authors have observed that he was the most efficient symbol produced by the New Deal. In making this point Arnold writes, "In this highly organized age, attitudes toward the function of government must be redefined, and until that process is complete a personality will take the place of a philosophy."[18]

In the 1936 electoral campaign Roosevelt said, "There's one issue in this campaign. It's myself, and people must be either for me or against me."[19] At times in his speeches, he "identified himself totally and personally with New Deal legislation."[20] His search for the approval of public opinion inextricably mixed the actions of his government, his politics, and his image with his trust in the American people. Confident in this ability to reach and mold public opinion, Roosevelt "monopolized" the mass media, "making the presidency . . . the new center of the American governmental system."[21]

Roosevelt and his staff's approach to communication was politically innovative, inducing a tension between the definitions of information and propaganda. Once the administration had singled out a problem, Roosevelt made it the focus of a fireside chat or a speech. Then, in a series of press conferences, he outlined the possible solutions proposed by the government. The reactions to these public utterances were carefully evaluated. Administration staff members monitored the press, analyzed the mail directed to the White House, and through opinion polls and other forms of verification, tried to keep close touch with the "pulse" of the people. At the end of the process, the President would send a message to Congress, recommending approval of a specific legislative project. The democratic cycle between institutions and citizens was in perpetual motion, and the interplay of the media was global. The letters written to Roosevelt by the people were read one by one by a special staff person and replied to individually, not as preprinted form letters.[22] The content of these letters was synthesized and transmitted to the President, who often used references to them to add little touches of human interest to his public speeches. Divided into favorable and unfavorable on specific issues, these letters functioned also as a sort of empirical opinion poll.

To a certain extent, Roosevelt's personality and his use of public relations strategies sidestepped the machinery of the Democratic party. His contact with the people was a personal fact, conducted through the radio, the reading of the letters addressed to the White House, the trips to cities and to rural villages, and the work of the reporters whom he elected as his special reporters because he trusted them to communicate honest information to and from the people.[23] At the same time however, the New Deal re-operated the party system, introducing a complex dialectic between the emphasis on the national structure and decentralization, reversing, for a period, the trend toward the decline of the American party system.

Through attempts to achieve the political and cultural integration of unionized members of the working class and minorities—above all Catholics and Jews—and the project to rediscover American culture, the New Deal worked to encourage the country to forge or recuperate a feeling of nationalism. But it also worked on a local level. The local impact was achieved by the figure of the social worker or federal official, through the trips that allowed Roosevelt to be in touch with local reality, through the attention given to organized social groups. The relationship between the collective and the individual, between national and local, between countryside and city implied a dialectic interdependence.

1930s Consumers of Political Culture

By the mid-1920s the cultural and political diversity of the U.S. population had narrowed significantly. Most ethnic groups had been drawn into the cultural mainstream; most radical groups had been reduced in number and their political ideas excluded from the mainstream of political discourse. Centralizing tendencies in economics, communications, and culture all contributed to a nationalization and homogenization of the American experience that continued into the 1930s. "The implementation in the nation's largest firms of a new system of industrial relations—often called Fordism or the American plan—based on high productivity, high wages, and enlightened schemes of scientific and personnel management,"[24] the growth of national corporations with standardized marketing techniques, chain stores with standard brands, national newspaper chains, national magazines, radio, and movies meant that most Americans were consuming the same leisure-time cultural products.[25]

The trend toward standardization and Americanization should be seen as a mediating tendency, a dialectical process that could never encompass all contradictions and sociocultural tensions. Workers in Chicago in the 1920s and 1930s, for example, as Lizabeth Cohen points out, though participating increasingly in mass consumption, did not deny their class and ethnic identities. Nor did they find themselves unconsciously absorbed by the middle class. The commonality of their shared experiences through exposure to mass culture helped them, late in the 1930s, to forge the first permanent industrial unions in American history under the auspices of the Congress of Industrial Workers (CIO). "Workers were well aware that the political impact of mass culture depended on who controlled distribution—locally-owned stores and theaters or corporate chains and studios. . . . Chicago workers struggled to keep their own consumption within 'working class consumption communities.'"[26]

The working class went "national" in a political sense—by re-elaborating its mix of political traditions based on immigrants' homeland experiences with unions and the class struggle, and by adopting a more centralized union structure that absorbed the variety of ethnic and political components—and became interdependent with the Democratic party, forcing the party to take it into account in elaborating its choices in economic politics. It became national also in a cultural sense, as Gerstle has emphasized, criticizing Warren Susman's interpretation of the rediscovery of Americanism in the New Deal years as conservative and arguing instead for a "working-class Americanism." Gerstle sees Americanism, not as an ideology, but "as a political language, as a set of words, phrases and concepts," emphasizing its contradictoriness. "Many Americans in the 1930s, especially those of the middle class, drew from Americanism a comforting sense of community and security that saw them through hard times. . . . But for every individual looking to Americanism for comfort and security, we can counterpose another who found in Americanist rhetoric an inspiration for political revolt, and for every self-professed radical conflating his or her Americanism with Fordism, we can find another using Americanist rhetoric to focus attention directly on the unequal distribution of power between capital and labor that prevailed in the workplace, community and nation." Gerstle insists on four "overlapping dimensions" of Americanism: nationalist, democratic, progressive, and traditionalist. He also elaborates a very dramatic and dynamic "struggle" within Americanism: "The battle for control of the language of Americanism . . . can only be understood as a part of a series of political struggles occurring simultaneously on different fronts," in factories, in ethnic communities, and "in the increasingly important administrative institutions of the American state, where contending social groups tangled with each other and with 'public servants' for political and ideological authority."[27]

The very pronounced dual focus of the New Deal on the national and the regional, with the federal prevailing, has a parallel in the dialectic between ethnic traditions and modern American working-class culture typical of 1930s unions. Politics and communications again interact as the two mediating factors in this process, with mass culture strongly influencing the process.

FDR's Popularity

Franklin Roosevelt has been variously described as "the first nationally advertised chief executive"; "one of the nation's best salesman"; "the best actor in talking pictures," leaving "Clark Gable gasping for breath"; "the greatest single attraction" in newsreels, and a radio personality of the caliber of Eddie Cantor and Ed Wynn.[28] His popularity depended on his personality and on the positive image portrayed by the media. Because of excellent promotional work through the media, FDR's fame resembled that of movie stardom. His speeches inspired letters like fan mail to the White House or to the radio stations. Many people kept a photograph of the President attached to the radio or hanging in the living room, reminiscent of the cultist rites of admiration by movie star fans.

The image and the voice of FDR were commodities in and of themselves, protected and carefully administered by his staff to maintain the President's "special qualities."[29] Rules were instituted prohibiting the use of images or of the voice of the President in any audiovisual message for commercial or promotional use. It was also forbidden to use them outside the context of one of his official appearances, for example, by appropriating excerpts of newsreels, photographs, or radio messages to insert them in a narrative or commercial film or in a program or in any media production considered inappropriate.[30]

Roosevelt's staff protected his image against saturation by limiting his appearances in the media, which were always in high demand, and by instituting an absolute ban on impersonations. Impersonations could create embarrassing as well as dangerous confusions. (Incidentally, one may recall that Orson Welles, in *War of the Worlds,* his famous radio broadcast that simulated a Martian invasion, introduced a voice that sounded like the president's for the character of the secretary of the interior.[31]

Roosevelt established a monopoly over the major electronic medium of his time, that caused a "profound shift in the public's perception of how government worked in America." His voice "achieved a personal power new in the political experience of the nation."[32]

Through the media he was able to "sell" himself and his political programs, taking the position of a superior authority, above all parts. He reached the people directly. By asking his listeners to back his programs and then turning their reactions into political action by using them to help force Congress to support his reforms, Roosevelt transformed his listeners into political supporters. He loved performing. At Harvard he had honed his natural gift as a performer in amateur theater productions. "With Roosevelt," according to a contemporary observer, "one has the feeling not only that he regards the living contact with public opinion as a political necessity, but that he enjoys it as an aesthetic treat."[33]

Roosevelt's fame, far from being a form of pure self-advertising, was directed to a noble use and substantiated by his popularity, deeply rooted in the American imagination.[34] His popularity depended on the image constructed by the chiaroscuro of his personality, referring back to his character, to ethical components such as the suffering he had overcome, the force with which he could impose himself, the authenticity of his sensibility in social matters, his pragmatic and effective attitude, and the importance he gave to the "human factor" in his relationship with the nation.

The President's rhetoric was rich in references to traditional American symbols and images. A typical strategy was to "invoke witnesses from the past," to refer to important figures in American history, in particular (Republican) President Abraham Lincoln. This was not an escape into the past; on the contrary, the past became a dynamic factor, the source of a legitimation rooted in myth, above all parties and outside of time. Roosevelt had, as Michael Kammen notes, he "an astute sense of the potential role of myth and tradition as formidable political weapons."[35]

Roosevelt's figure mediated between the modern image of a charismatic political leader, effectively represented by the media and skillful at manipulating public opinion, and the traditional figure of a political leader, with widely shared but also partisan values, endowed with undoubtable ethical standards, and sanctioned by the people. According to polls taken throughout his first two terms, Roosevelt was more popular than either his policies or his programs.[36] Richard Hofstader suggests that there was perhaps "a vast disproportion between Roosevelt's personal stature and the Roosevelt legend," for what made the legend "was the magic of a man, based as much on illusion as on reality."[37] It was in the space of this disproportion that the New Deal functioned.

The Periodization of FDR's Popularity

Roosevelt's popularity falls into three phases: 1933–37, the "honeymoon" with the media and the people; 1938–40, the crisis with the press and with the upper classes; and 1941–45, the domination of war issues.

The dismay and bewilderment provoked by the Crash had paralyzed the country; the people "wanted experiment, activity, trial and error, anything that would convey a sense of movement and novelty."[38] During the 1930s a paralysis syndrome characterized the country: immobilized between the push of the Roaring Twenties and the fear of discovering that, around the corner, there was not happiness at all; crushed by the economic, social, and emotional rubble caused by the Crash; blocked by contradictions that seemed unresolvable.[39] Paradoxically, the salvation, the movement, the miraculous recovery from the paralysis arrived in the form of a President in a wheelchair.

The energetic efforts to revitalize the economy in the initial phase of the New Deal represented "a real concert of interests," or, as Roosevelt described it, "something for everyone." The four-sided strategy of relief, recovery, reform, and reconstruction that dominated the first New Deal inspired a feeling of unity. Roosevelt's leadership achieved a wide consensus that allowed him to live off his enormous initial popularity.

It could be argued that the first New Deal, with its rhetoric of planning, appealed to the culture of progressive nationalism. "In this phase Roosevelt embodied the figures of the warrior, the prophet, the preacher, able to offer guidance and reassurance and to propound ethical ideals of justice and a sense of responsibility."[40] According to Raymond Moley, the first New Deal was animated by an agrarian spirit with Roosevelt the "gentleman farmer" dominating the scene, while the second phase was more middle class and urban.[41] In my opinion, Roosevelt's agrarian spirit is *always* driving the use of metaphors and and images referring to the earth in the fireside chats and the media productions of the administration. His sense of solidarity, however, is not populist, but a sign of his heritage as an aristocratic benefactor of the rural community. The ethical force of his ancestral patrimony allowed Roosevelt to be disassociated from the class where he belonged—the world of finance, with its nationalist-progressive values; that had carried America to economic and social collapse.

By 1937 the economic condition of the country had not improved much and demagogic antagonists Huey Long and Father Charles E. Coughlin were competing with the President for popularity. During the second phase of the New Deal, Roosevelt proposed economic measures with neopopulist and antimonopolistic themes, including the so-called tax on wealth, and encouraged the development of unions.

The conservative middle class interpreted Roosevelt's proposal to "pack" the Supreme Court in order to stop the reverses his programs, especially "his" NRA, had been suffering there, as a revolutionary attack on the country's institutions. Roosevelt's popularity fell to such a point that his fireside chat on April 14, 1938, provoked, according to the correspondence directed to the White House, the most negative reaction ever recorded for one of his speeches.[42] A large segment of the press was by then strongly hostile toward the New Deal programs. At the same time, Congress did not approve the legislation proposed by the administration. Roosevelt's popularity was not a personal affair but served a political function, the support for the government's actions: having lost his mass appeal, Roosevelt lost the ability to impose his reforms. He was nevertheless still popular with the people, especially the lower classes.[43]

The New Deal entered into a stalled phase. In 1938, Roosevelt's attempt to "steal the thunder" from the demagogic speech of his antagonists, through an antimonopolistic political line, failed, and his relations with the most conservative sectors of the financial and industrial world deteriorated. The middle class was "uneasy" over his attacks on the press and the Supreme Court—two key institutions in the American democratic mythology[44]—all at a moment when there was a general fascist threat from without.

At this "darkest point of the New Deal," Roosevelt began working with part of the business community to put together what became the "first successful capital-intensive-led political coalition in history."[45] This coalition included the unions and the more modern businesses and industries, and it produced a new concept of welfare state, moving toward the Keynesian tenet of increasing government spending.

The international crisis created the need for national unity and reconciled the country with its paternal and reassuring President. In 1940 Roosevelt won election for an unprecedented fourth term. The positive economic impact of World War II, with its blood-stirring slogan of the "four freedoms," resolved many of the problems the New Deal had left unsolved.

FDR's Staff

Roosevelt's competence and control of media strategies were in themselves notable, but much of his success is attributable to the strength of his staff, which carried out assignments with tremendous skill, efficiently organizing the activities of the New Deal in the field of communications. Roosevelt's relations with the media were coordinated by Stephen T. Early, the press secretary who served him throughout his twelve years in office. Early's work signaled "the beginning of a coherent policy to meet the public relations needs of the modern presidency."[46] He took responsibility for the entire communications policy of the administration, which meant not only maintaining contacts with the media but also determining and controlling the President's public image and the information strategies of the New Deal in all sectors.[47]

An expert journalist, newsreel editor, and director of public relations, Early possessed an articulate competence in the functioning of the media. Moreover, his professional experiences guaranteed him a vast network of contacts, which allowed him to operate directly, through his personal acquaintances, bypassing rules of protocol and party structures.[48]

Early was working as a United Press reporter when, in 1912, he was given the task of following the activity of FDR, then assistant secretary of the navy. The two of them developed such an excellent rapport that Early was asked to work for Roosevelt's vice presidential election campaign in 1920 (this was the same campaign in which Will Hays, as national chairman of the Republican party, represented the winning opposition). This candidacy was a lost cause from the beginning, but for Roosevelt it constituted an important political experience and gave him the opportunity to put together a loyal and competent staff, the so-called Cuff Links Gang, which included, in addition to Early, Louis McHenry Howe, Marvin Hunter McIntyre, and Marguerite LeHand.[49] After returning for a short time to Associated Press in Washington, Early moved on to Paramount, where he exploited his position in the newsreels and his contacts in the media to support Roosevelt's 1932 presidential candidacy.

The members of the Cuff Links Gang, through their professional activities covered the entire sector of communications, significantly demonstrating the complex operational, financial, and personal interdependence of the media and their relation to politics. Howe was the political correspondent for the *Herald Tribune* in Albany and first worked for Roosevelt in the 1912 New York state senate race. When the attack of polio isolated Roosevelt from active political life, Howe kept his public image alive, earning the title of "President-maker." McIntyre was a journalist working for the *Washington Times*. He met Roosevelt during the World War I, while working at naval affairs on the Creel Committee, that is, the propaganda office. He then moved on to newsreels as a representative, in Washington, for all of the newsreel companies; following this, he was employed by Pathé.

When Roosevelt was elected, he maintained the tripartition of the position of secretary to the President and nominated Early, Howe, and McIntyre as his secretaries. Howe was assigned the highest position, for his long years of service. McIntyre was made personal secretary to the President and Early was made press secretary.

Early instituted an open door policy toward information. Particularly sensitive to the needs of the media, he was at the same time skilled at making representatives of the press work according to the designs of the administration. He made the work of the White House correspondents more efficient by drawing up a calendar of biweekly press conferences and by supplying them with detailed information and copies of the speeches on the reform projects, together with technical explanations of complex economic or legislative issues. To encourage the immediacy of communication, he abolished the rule requiring press conference questions to be submitted beforehand. He substituted the impersonal press releases of the Hoover administration with informal gatherings with the political correspondents. His duties included programming the radio broadcasts of Roosevelt's speeches.[50]

Although Early used his personal contacts in the media, he avoided favoritism and partisanship. His efforts to mediate between the President (who developed an acrimonious and impulsive relationship with the press), the correspondents (hungry for political news), and the newspaper owners (who defended their own interests and opposed the New Deal) is spatially symbolized by his moving his office to be closer to the press room than to the Oval office. Early's opposition to government interference with the communications industry helps to explain the equilibrium that characterized the attitude of the Roosevelt administration toward the monopolistic structure of the business. The visceral dislike of propaganda Early shared with the President, his respect for the professional demands of those working in communications, his role in helping to decentralize public relations in various government agencies, together with his absolute loyalty to Roosevelt, made him a precious operative extension of the President in relation to the media.

FDR and the Press

Roosevelt has been described as the best newspaperman who was ever President of the United States and as "the newspapermen's president" because he facilitated the work of reporters and their access to the news.[51] His control over news gathering and the charm he exerted on the Washington correspondents were so effective that during most of his first term he was able to use the press as a channel for the transmission of his politics. From the beginning, however, Roosevelt did have a conflictual relationship with the directors and owners of the newspapers, and throughout his presidency he regularly reiterated his thesis that "the press opposed him; that its opposition was proprietor-based; and that he was confronted, as a result of such hostility, not merely with widespread editorial disapproval, but with tendentious and distorted news reports."[52]

During the early period of "honeymooning," Roosevelt delighted journalists with his informal ways and his frankness. At times, during press conferences, the President would make suggestions to the journalists about how to present the news or explain something off the record, thus creating a climate of confidence. This relaxed delivery, strengthened by careful preparation, was a radical departure from the printed news releases generated by the Hoover administration. The press conference was an arena where Roosevelt could exhibit his showmanship, throwing out witty remarks and impersonations, while nonchalantly avoiding embarrassing questions.[53] He was pleasant and sociable with the journalists, often calling them by their first names.[54] He socially promoted the entire category of journalists, by inviting some of the insiders or veteran White House correspondents to official lunches.

"He talked in headline phrases; . . . he was copy," noted Jack Bell, of Associated Press.[55] His direct contact with reporters, along with his ability to make news, kept him on the front page of the newspapers, allowing him to combat the general editorial opposition with a constant presence.

Roosevelt had always had a close association with the printed page. He worked on the editorial staff of his college newspaper; in the 1920s, struck by the success of the popular tabloids, he proposed to the Democratic party to publish something similar; toward the end of his political career he even considered becoming an editor.[56] His wife, Eleanor, wrote syndicated columns, and his daughter, Anna, worked at the *Seattle Post Intelligence.*

The complexity of the sociopolitical problems of the 1930s had caused American journalism to abandon its traditional adherence to facts and became more interpretative.[57] There was, in this evolution, a reciprocal influence: Roosevelt, the "benign master," supplied information and encouraged discussion about his programs, with the educational intent of explaining the reforms to the people, but also with the promotional desire to make his point of view known. The press, on its side, did not want to be reduced to publishing press releases, as it had been forced to do under Hoover, and found itself in a position where interpretation was not only allowed but encouraged. Things went well as long as the two sides were in accord, and the newspapers functioned as an "echo" of Roosevelt's reforms. But, when the press began to be critical of the administration, the honeymoon ended.

Roosevelt and Early had an optimal system of monitoring the media. Roosevelt alone read about eleven newspapers a day and received clippings from collaborators and special services. The Division of Presidential Intelligence, organized for this purpose, each week sent him an update on the relationship between the press and government's activities. Early personally monitored the press and kept a file significantly entitled "Below the Belt," in which he collected articles hostile to the administration. He tried to separate himself from Roosevelt's continuous attacks on the newspaper owners, intervening only when he felt an attack on the New Deal or on Roosevelt was particularly malevolent. He persuaded Hearst's press, for example, to quit referring to the New Deal as the "Raw Deal"[58] and defended the image of the President from any reference to his paralysis.

Resentful of the growing editorial opposition to the New Deal and impatient with the editors to the point of publicly stating that they were out of touch with public opinion, Roosevelt began to single out hostile newspapermen or openly attack newspaper owners. As the 1936 presidential campaign got underway, Roosevelt complained that "85 percent of the nation's press opposed the New Deal."[59] By this point the press conferences had lost their informative value and become little more than a ritual. The President became evasive and gave preference to the radio and the newsreels in his media strategy.

In general, Roosevelt's use of the press was more successful than the owners' and publishers' efforts to abuse him in editorials.[60] The conflict with the press did not impair Roosevelt's popularity. The public had repudiated the press in the 1930s because it felt the press was out of synchrony with American public opinion. Eighty percent of the press opposed Roosevelt in the 1936 campaign, but he won by the largest percentage of the popular vote ever recorded.[61]

FDR and the Radio

Radio allowed Roosevelt a greater control over his messages. Relying on its ability to "restore direct contact between the masses and their chosen leaders" and its supposed inability to "misrepresent [or] misquote," he was the first President to make "professional use of radio."[62]

As soon as Roosevelt entered the White House, NBC and CBS put their facilities at his disposal "any time he wanted them."[63] Early took full advantage of this offer. In the first phase of the New Deal, the networks "donated" a great number of hours to government programming, perhaps because they depended on the federal authority, which assigned frequencies and regulated licenses. The government in this period was "the greatest single user of radio."[64]

In 1934, Roosevelt confirmed the appointments of the majority of the commissioners of the Federal Communications Commission (FCC). But not until 1939, worried by the expansion of radio station ownership by newspapers and by growing opposition from the press, did he order the FCC to undertake any serious regulation of the radio. He began by nominating James Lawrence Fly to the FCC and urging the commission to adopt less conciliatory policies.[65] Fly, however, was less interested in the problem of joint radio and newspaper ownership than he was in monopoly and in 1940 ordered an investigation into the monopolistic activities of the networks, following which the FCC ordered RCA to sell one of its channels, NBC.[66]

Radio permitted a direct rapport between the speaker and the listener. It also had the advantage—indispensable during the turbulent early days of the New Deal—of being immediate. Roosevelt and various members of his administration spoke on the radio 150 times in the first ten months of the presidency.[67] Because at that time there were still no real news bulletins on the radio, apart from CBS's *The March of Time,* this political and informational presence of the administration on the radio appears massive. Roosevelt gave an average of seven radio speeches a year between 1933 and 1938. Only a small number of these speeches were fireside chats. The fireside chats were characterized by a wide range of themes and were addressed to the entire nation, constituting "the most successful adult education programs in the history of broadcasting."[68]

The preparation for these radio speeches, whether fireside chats or presidential messages, was scrupulously thorough.[69] The initial phase of the writing was entrusted to faithful collaborators, including Samuel Rosenman, who was with Roosevelt from the time of the governorship until his death in 1945; Raymond Moley, in the first phase of the New Deal; and Robert Sherwood, during the war years. Experts often assisted on specific questions. These writers worked on an outline prepared by the President that was accompanied by precise indications on fundamental points, such as the number of words and the type of listener he wanted to reach.[70] They collected information, statistics, and other data from the government agencies involved in the projects on which the President intended to speak and organized this material, simplifying it and underscoring the points he had indicated. They also incorporated personal observations and notes from the President and his collaborators to give the speeches touches of human interest.

The speeches lasted an average of twenty-five minutes and were carefully scheduled to avoid their interfering with important events or with particularly popular radio programs.[71] Usually FDR's speeches were broadcast between 9:00 and 11:00 in the evening or in noncommercial network hours, in order not to hurt the networks financially but still to reach the greatest possible number of people in different time zones. Network lookups allowed him to reach the entire nation simultaneously.

Besides inspiring the content of the speeches and taking care that the exposition was fluent, Roosevelt always read them aloud to practice radio diction. For the broadcast he used a special kind of paper that did not rustle and wore a fake tooth to correct the light whistle in his letter *S*. He read slowly, with thoughtful pauses and an easy, natural rhythm.[72] He often improvised. The spontaneous greeting, "My friends," with which he began the first fireside chat became the trademark opening of all his speeches.

After every speech, the Division of Presidential Intelligence collected the press reactions, analyzed the mail, and verified the radio ratings. The sale of advertising on American radio had elaborated systems of verification and evaluation of audience reaction through such measures as ratings and polls. Roosevelt was so curious about this type of research, in fact, that the inventor of one of the largest accredited ratings systems, C. E. Hooper, gave him a "large color chart illustrating his rising radio audience from 1936 to 1942."[73] This monitoring of public opinion functioned as a sort of "episodic plebiscite" to Roosevelt's reforms.[74] In this way his speeches established a continuous cycle of political communication: from the people and from their questions or observations, to the elaboration of reforms and legislation in response to their expressed needs, to the broadcast over the airwaves, to the mobilization of public opinion in relation to the legislative bodies. Thus radio played a key role in the homogenization process of American culture in the 1930s, contributing to the creation of a sense of collective participation.

An analysis of Roosevelt's rhetoric reveals that, while the content of the speeches was of an advanced federalist reformism, the mode of address, with its educational inspiration, showed many traces of populism. Roosevelt loved to see himself in the role of the "benign schoolmaster" who was "taking the nation to school."[75] To be as informative and concrete as possible, he cited statistics and data, but simplified them to facilitate their comprehension, and used anecdotes and touches of human interest to involve the audience. In a speech in 1933, he explained that he was addressing himself to the "average citizen."[76] Even though his main target was the "common man," that is, the middle class, FDR included in his audience new political subjects, social strata that had been, until then, marginalized—ethnic minorities, union members, women, farmers, and so on. Not by chance, this was the same public, according to Paul Lazarsfeld, that had elected radio as the preferred source of information.[77] The ideological recuperation of these social forces enlarged the base of consensus. In the second New Deal, in fact, FDR was more popular with the low-income social groups than with the middle class.[78] Having come out of the lowest points of the Depression, the middle class showed a growing preoccupation with the institutional changes introduced by Roosevelt. To reconcile himself with the middle class, and with the urban lower middle class, which was characterized by populist inclinations—that is, with the inhabitants of Middletown and the Mandrake Falls of Frank Capra's films—Roosevelt evoked symbols and myths typical of American culture.[79] He said, for example: "I believe that what we are doing today is a necessary fulfillment of what Americans have always been doing—a fulfillment of old and tested American ideals."[80]

He frequently returned to a symbolic apparatus derived from agrarian populism. A country gentleman, he maintained a profound contact with the idea of the earth, and with American ruralism. In 1936 he dedicated a whole fireside chat to the problem of the dust bowls.[81] Although Roosevelt seemed to be opposing the "old" culture and aligning himself with the "new," he recognized the necessity of a mediation between the two. During his 1928 campaign for governor of New York, he stated, "We have today side by side an old political order fashioned by a pastoral civilization and a new social order fashioned by a technological civilization. The two are maladjusted. Their creative inter-relation is one of the big tasks ahead of American leadership."[82] His rhetoric was aimed at stimulating this "creative inter-relation." He addressed himself to all sections of society, explaining to the city dwellers the problems of those who lived in the country, talking about Labor Day as a holiday for the entire nation, attacking individual egoism and the groups clinging to their privileges, condemning the "ruthless past"—the era of robber barons, and stigmatizing "the chiselling of a few unpatriotic individuals."[83] His message through the New Deal project was social interdependence under the protective shield of the government.

Roosevelt's oratory formed an expository style that presented problems in an individualized way, without reducing them to impersonal or generic situations, echoes of the practice common to Hollywood cinema of personalizing conflicts and problems by reducing them to individual stories or personal cases. His opening "My friends" automatically established a rapport of participation, a personal tie with the listener. The frequent use of "us" reinforced this impression, taking the people directly into the White House. His paternal image was an effect of his speech, of the tone of his voice, and of the peaceful rhythm of his diction. Many of the letters to the White House spoke of the reassuring power of his voice.[84] The endings of his speeches were intended to have an equally reassuring effect. Roosevelt specifically instructed writers to close each chat on a high note, and often he wrote the conclusions himself.[85] On one hand then, Roosevelt adopted a rhetoric and a mode of address considered by Will Stott exemplary of the culture of the 1930s—close to reality, documentary, participant—and on the other his final words, pragmatic and optimistic, constituted a Hollywood-like happy ending, meant to give the nation confidence.

The Image of FDR

Roosevelt was a good subject for photographic portraiture because of his expressiveness and his smile.

> There are two Roosevelt smiles. There is the almost automatic smile of the man who perhaps attracts attention to his vivid, mobile face, in order to detract attention from his stricken body. . . . that is the actor, who says, "Look at my face, my eyes, my smile. That is me. Not the rest." But there is also another Roosevelt smile, . . . quick, spontaneous, infinitely winning.[86]

Photography was the emerging form of information and expression in the thirties. The enormous success of the popular tabloids, the introduction of illustrated magazines like *Life*, and initiatives such as the federal Resettlement Administration project to document Depression-era rural poverty through the talents of the great photographers of the time all indicate the impact of photography on the American cultural system, including literature.[87]

Within this photographic culture, Roosevelt evoked the strong image of a vigorous and dynamic man, despite the effects of polio. There was in fact a specific prohibition—rarely violated—against shooting pictures that would reveal the extent of the President's disability.[88] Reporters respected this rule out of deference to the man and to the President, and because public opinion had reacted harshly to the publication of "realistic" photos, considered injurious to his dignity. (When FDR fell while walking up to the podium during the 1936 Democratic National Convention, nobody took pictures, despite the fact that many reporters were in a position to do so.)[89]

Photography created a dynamic portrait of FDR through different forms of compensation. If a photograph did not depict him while he was active—traveling or at work—then the caption underlined his almost miraculous recovery after the illness. It was not a matter of falsification but a concession to the collective imagination, which preferred not to see the infirmity of the President, and developed "the impression that he was more nearly recovered of his power to walk, than he actually was."[90] To enforce this rule and to encourage the most positive photographic coverage possible, Early strictly regulated photographic sessions.[91]

As in other areas of communications, Early encouraged the identification of the President with his public function, never granting "exclusives" and forbidding the association of Roosevelt's image with commercial products for promotional purposes.[92] But he compensated for these limitations by offering photojournalists plenty of opportunities to be in the right place at the right time. (Not by accident did many photographs of FDR win awards.)[93] At times the press secretary allowed photographers to shoot informal photos during voyages, or in domestic and less conventional situations. The President became an expert in photographic poses and was remarkably patient. Sometimes he collaborated with the photographers, even suggesting poses ("Let's make one of this, boys").[94]

Roosevelt was a good amateur photographer with some talent for drawing.[95] This gave him a sophisticated visual competence and an awareness of the associative power of certain objects and clothing. The most memorable example is the cigarette holder clamped between his smiling lips. But there was also the strange collection of objects that always appeared on his desk, and the gray business suit he wore at the 1943 Teheran Conference that stood out in contrast to the military uniforms of Winston Churchill and Joseph Stalin.

Roosevelt dominated the Sunday rotogravure section of the newspapers as well as the front pages.[96] The constant presence of his image in the newspapers, as well as images of his family, produced a positive counterbalance to his conflict with the publishers. Eleanor Roosevelt appeared frequently in newspapers represented in one of her many roles, including wife, mother and grandmother to a large family, and socially active and engaged First Lady. The maternal image of Eleanor Roosevelt with children and in charity situations complemented the paternal image of FDR. Frequent photographs in the press of the Roosevelt's five children and twelve grandchildren evoke the idea of a big family, albeit unconventional.[97]

Given Roosevelt's interest in the function and technology of communications, it is appropriate that he was the first President to appear on television, on the occasion of the opening of the 1939 World Fair in New York, when the new medium was officially launched.[98]

Hollywood and Washington

Within the vast and complex world where communications and politics interacted in the 1930s, the network of personal contacts between the Roosevelts, some members of the administration, and the film industry supply us with a detailed map of the relationship between the New Deal and Hollywood cinema.[1] In this relationship Franklin Delano Roosevelt occupies the central position in the flow of images and messages and in the system of interpersonal relations. He knew many people in the media and had many contacts in Hollywood. Filmmaking know-how played an important role in his contact with public opinion: two of his collaborators, Stephen T. Early and Marvin Hunter McIntyre, had worked in newsreels; his favorite ghostwriter in the war years wãs the screenwriter and playwright Robert E. Sherwood. Besides, the President loved movies, which he consumed voraciously. At his side, Eleanor Roosevelt filled the essential role of selecting the film programs for the White House, keeping in touch with "film folks," and writing magazine articles promoting the educational and entertainment valve of movies.

The Roosevelts as Spectators

When Franklin Roosevelt was governor of New York, he watched movies regularly at his mansion in Albany. As soon as he moved to the White House, Warner Theaters and the Motion Picture Producer Distributor Association (MPPDA) both officially offered to continue providing films, gratis, to the Roosevelt family. A motion picture operator, borrowed from the Navy Department, picked up movies from the exchanges at the President's request and screened them at the White House, usually three or four times a week.[2]

In an article published in the July 1938 edition of *Photoplay*—"Why We Roosevelts Are Movie Fans"—Eleanor Roosevelt notes that movies were "the one and only relaxation which my husband has. . . . "The President never has an evening of his own planning without at least one Mickey Mouse film."[3] She describes movies as mainly family entertainment, insisting that the presidential family, in its position of privileged film spectators, was really just a family like many others and as fond of movies as most other Americans in the thirties. The picture she presents of the family abounds with references to the grandchildren and to the communal ritual of watching movies. The article promotes the Roosevelts as a family, but it also promotes cinema as a legitimate medium.

Eleanor Roosevelt, in the article, endorses such movies as *The Life of Emile Zola*—"very well acted by Paul Muni, I thought"—*The Buccaneer, Tom Sawyer, Arsene Lupin Returns,* and *Hurricane:* "All of them, I think, were a pleasant evening's entertainment and well worth seeing."[4] Providing "pleasant" entertainment, she insists, is the primary function of movies. But she sees also a socioideological function. Cinema in the thirties had the potential to "become a strong education[al] and character-building force." Newsreels in particular, she says, have educational value. They "seem to bring the whole world before us."

> I contend that seeing things is almost a necessity in this visual-minded period of our development, and the newsreels are probably doing as much as the radio, newspapers and magazines to make people world-minded today. Sometimes I hope they will go a step further and do an educational job by stepping back into history and bringing the past before us so that we may better understand the happenings of the present. . . . Perhaps we are going to find ourselves learning history and becoming better world neighbors someday as a result of new uses to which movies may lend themselves.

Given Eleanor Roosevelt's strong interest in social reform and education, her ideas about the function of cinema echoed the concerns of some public groups that at the time were debating the role of the medium in society.[5] Her opinions were given added weight by her position as First Lady. In that role she had entertained film stars in their visits to the White House, and she had visited the Hollywood studios of Warner Bros., MGM, and Twentieth Century Fox. She took a position that would have pleased Will Hays, "author" of the movie industry's code of self-censorship. In her article she discusses the need to change the audience's demands in order to reform the medium. This was one of Hays's favorite platforms.[6]

> [Pictures glorifying] the gangster and criminal. . . made us more sympathetic with the rascal than with the righteous man. . . . [But] it is harmful

to make small boys want to be the head of a gang, and I am very glad we
have begun to show that it is possible to have qualities that evoke admiration, and still be a policeman or a "G" man, or even an every-day good citizen. . . . The public demands excitement and sometimes seems decidedly
sadistic, enjoying cruelty and horror on the stage or in a film which they
might not be able to stand in real life. . . . This is a curious trait of human
nature; but it is also true that producers must, to a certain extent, cater to
the demands of the public and that if we wish to change anything in the
movies, on the radio, on the stage, in the newspapers, we must change
public demand.

The movie producer, she says, has the responsibility, because his audience is
vast, of "creating good taste."

The highly cultured people of the world are those who have good taste.
There is, of course, a certain kind of robust fun, even vulgarity, which is
not contrary to good taste, but some things in literature and the arts have
always presaged decadence. Those things must be kept from the drama if
we are to promote good taste. Here is the great challenge to the movie
producer of the future—will movies be an instrument in the development
of good taste and are we growing up to be a nation with artistic knowledge
and appreciation?

The Roosevelt family, through Eleanor Roosevelt's article, legitimized cinema as the ultimate democratic, American art form. Cinema could transform
an audience into a public, rotating its axis from offering a consumer product to offering a service—a *public* service—going from entertainment into education.

It is interesting to note that this article was published in the same month,
July 1938, in which the Roosevelt administration filed the *Paramount* case, its
antitrust suit against the film industry. Even though the timing was coinci-
dental, this semi-official statement by Eleanor Roosevelt that seemed like a
public blessing of cinema actually looked like an attempt to compensate for
the government's attack on the industry.

Film producers tried to use this legitimation of cinema by the Roosevelts-
as-spectators to promote their films. They were anxious to show their films at
the White House and hoped to receive favorable reactions and to use the fact
of these very special screenings in their publicity. But Stephen Early had a
strict policy that specifically forbade such promotional uses of the Roosevelt's
film viewing. He regularly responded to film producers and their friends that
there would be no endorsement of any film or any film project by the White
House. Those who produced films of special sociopolitical significance often
offered them for previews at the White House, given Eleanor's well-known
interest in "educational" cinema. These screenings would keep the President

informed and prevent possible objections about the political content. In October 1934, for example, King Vidor wrote to Early, hoping to get Roosevelt's reaction to a screening of *Our Daily Bread:* "I have felt since I first planned to do this picture two years ago that the idea projected was in accord with the President's plan of subsistence homesteads. . . . But even entertainment can carry an amount of propaganda and educational element. I deeply feel the screen to be the greatest power of exploitation and I cannot wholly ignore a social consciousness in producing a picture."[7] But Early was inflexible. Only during the war did his policy undergo some modification and only when Roosevelt's comments were to acknowledge a patriotic message, not to promote a partisan political position. Before the war the only noteworthy departure from Early's policy involved *Gone with the Wind.* Eleanor Roosevelt was so impressed when it was presented in a special White House Christmas celebration in 1939 that she told Early, "Let them have publicity." This screening, like the premier of *A Midsummer Night's Dream* in Georgia on FDR's birthday in 1935, belongs to a series of special film events that helped to strengthen the link between Hollywood glamour and Roosevelt's very special popularity.

A Touch of Hollywood Glamour

Hollywood added glamour to the social life of the presidential family. "Film Folks," as Eleanor Roosevelt describes them in a second article for *Photoplay,* published in January 1939, were a common feature at Roosevelt family celebrations and formal White House events. She writes with a tone of awe and reverence about the stars who "were kind enough to come to Washington" for these events and describes asking "with some trepidation" if they would like to tour the White House. The list of visitors to the White House includes Ginger Rogers (who "stands out as a charming personality"), Robert Taylor, Marsha Hunt, Maria Gambarelli, Mitzi Green, Frederick Jagel, Jean Harlow, Janet Gaynor, Louise Fazenda, and Fredric March. She notes that "pretty Eleanor Powell made two of [her] daughters-in-law extremely jealous . . . because [her] boys were extremely anxious to act as guides through the White House." Playing up the image of the Roosevelts as a family, she emphatically includes child actors on the list (Ann Gillis, Tommy Kelly, and, above all, Shirley Temple) and goes on to describe the special pleasure her grandsons took in meeting their favorite stars. Eleanor Roosevelt was fascinated by "film folks" and wanted to be in personal contact with them, in order "to understand a little better all that goes into giving us this entertainment." Traditionally historiography has assigned to her a special role in the New Deal's "desire to know"; in this respect, she occupied an important position as go-between for the Roosevelts and the films and "film folks."

Sometimes movie stars like Clark Gable and Carol Lombard added a touch of Hollywood glamour to a political occasion by witnessing a fireside chat.[8] The media exposure benefited the President and the stars. Film stars, like political personalities, depend on the media to reach their public, and on such occasions two audiences were mixed—the public that follows political events and the film spectator.[9] But beyond the simple game of reflections, in which the presidential family was illuminated by film stars and the film stars received a social promotion by their association with important political figures, was the additional gain for the Roosevelts of having their image reach a wider audience than just the public for political matters.[10] The Roosevelts used this touch of Hollywood glamour more often and more efficiently than had previous political personalities. These contacts provided publicity in the simplest sense for both sides, but, strictly speaking, did not constitute political support.

The first instance of a major Hollywood event that was an unequivocal political promotion of Roosevelt as a presidential candidate was the Motion Picture Electrical Parade and Sports Pageant staged by Jack Warner at Los Angeles Olympic Stadium September 4, 1932.[11] It was a spectacle in the style of a gigantic Busby Berkeley film and contained a "thrilling display of studio genius." For the 1933 presidential inauguration, *42nd Street,* a Warner production supportive of the New Deal spirit, opened in Washington. Metro and Warner Bros. appeared on Pennsylvania Avenue in the inaugural parade with trucks full of starlets and the popular cowboy star Tom Mix riding a white pony.[12]

Hollywood Politics

The support Franklin Roosevelt received from the Hollywood community confirms Hollywood's politicization in the 1930s. At the time, Hollywood, like much of American culture, was politicized as a result of extensive labor unrest, the relocation of entertainment personalities from the New York theater to the West Coast after the introduction of sound (the "newcomers"), and the arrival of emigrées from Nazi Europe.

I am not discussing at length here the relationship between Hollywood radicals and the New Dealers, because this is the trait most often described in relation to the film community's politics in the thirties. Recently this topic has gained renewed interest after publication in the 1980s of such well-documented research as *Inquisition in Hollywood,* by Larry Ceplair and Steven Englund, and *Film on the Left,* by Will Alexander, and publication in 1992 of

Brian Neve's re-examination, *Films and Politics in America*.[13] Neve relates "the obvious suffering of the period, particularly in the early thirties" to "the rise in interest in radical political ideas." He notes that "particularly attracted to the [communist] party, either as members or as sympathisers, were the children of the first-generation immigrants, individuals who, as they came at age amid the traumas of the Depression, were often alienated both from the culture of their parents and from that of mainstream America."[14]

Foreign origins seem to have motivated many in Hollywood to enter politics, but not necessarily radical politics. Whereas many immigrants and first-generation Americans became communist, others, like the movie mogul Louis B. Mayer, whose family had emigrated from Russia when he was a small child, joined the Republican party. Mayer, a "natural conservative," believed strongly in "family, patriotism, . . . [and] small-town solidarity." Like other immigrants, he held American values "more unreservedly than almost any native," to the extent that, "claiming that he had lost his real birth records during immigration, [he] had appropriated the Fourth of July as his own birthday." Through his film production, he became a propagandist of Americana.[15]

In his search for acceptance and legitimation, Mayer became a militant Republican. He volunteered in Calvin Coolidge's 1924 presidential campaign and so impressed the party with his hard work that he rose eventually to the chairmanship of the California State Republican Committee. William Randolph Hearst, whose wealth, influence, and culture represented everything to which Mayer aspired, probably had a major role in drawing him into politics.[16] (When Hearst created Cosmopolitan Pictures in order to launch his mistress, actress Marion Davies, as a national star, Mayer hosted the company and produced her films, while, in exchange, the Hearst press "looked benevolently" at MGM pictures.) The two began a close association when Hearst returned to California in 1924 after disappointing experiences with national politics. Mayer's work for the Republicans in California gained him direct access to the White House during the administration of Herbert Hoover. The association gave him an edge. Hoover, for example, allowed Mayer and Hearst "to acquire 'a satisfactory wave length' for a radio station they wanted to operate," and he lent the assistance of American ambassadors in film making abroad.[17]

In 1931 Mayer did not abandon Hoover but devoted half of his time to campaigning for his re-election. This time, however, Hearst did not support Hoover, though Mayer tried hard to persuade him to. By now a vice president and general manager at MGM (Metro-Goldwyn-Mayer), Mayer donated funds, staged the convention, and gave radio speeches directly attacking FDR. In the mean time, Jack Warner pulled Hearst into FDR's camp.

Hearst and Mayer were reunited in 1934 against Upton Sinclair. Hollywood is said to have discovered its own political potential in this campaign for the governorship of California. The Republican candidate, Frank Merriam, ran against the writer Upton Sinclair, who proposed a utopian program of social reform. In what is probably the only instance of movie moguls interfering directly in politics—capitalizing on the efficacy of the medium itself as a propaganda tool—film producers fabricated "newsreels of appalling crudity and immense effectiveness" that were distributed gratis to theater owners. "Actors on studio payrolls, dressed in false whiskers and dirty clothes, and wearing sinister expressions" to impersonate "disreputable vagrants," were filmed crossing the California border, apparently "prepared to expropriate the God-fearing the moment Upton Sinclair was elected." The cameras were supplied by a major studio.[18]

Although no such direct use of the medium was ever undertaken in support of, or against, Roosevelt, he did appear frequently in the newsreel, that the majors distributed. This notwithstanding the fact that most of the film executives were Republican, though expediency may have determined party affiliation in some. Jack Warner, for example, "kept two sets of autographed portraits of leading politicians—one of Democrats, one of Republicans. Whichever was appropriate could be exhibited to visiting dignitaries."[19]

Radical Politics in Hollywood

The politicization of some members of the Hollywood community and their affiliation with the Communist party in the 1930s can be traced not only to the sociocultural climate created by the Depression but also to the peculiar isolation of Hollywood, where labor organizations were either domesticated or divided, and to the fragmented work experience of the studio system. Screenwriters in particular were attracted to politics. They were frustrated by their lack of control and overwhelmed by a feeling of waste as they saw their intellectual work end in formula pictures. Fewer than two hundred people in Hollywood actually enlisted in the Communist party, but, in the second half of the thirties, most of the liberals there participated in politics by organizing antifascist associations, such as the Anti-Nazi League.[20] This phase, the Popular Front, united communists and liberals in Europe and in the United States, in a common fight against fascism. Studio executives were as alarmed by this political organizing as they were by union organizing, in part because some of the same people were involved in both activities. The executives did not like actors and others who worked in the film industry to take a public stand on any controversial issue for fear that they might antagonize potential spectators who held contrary opinions. But antifascism spread easily in Hollywood at a time when the country was still mostly isolationist and there were many people in Hollywood who were Jewish or were in contact with those who had left Nazi Europe.

The activities of the actors Helen and Melvyn Douglas, considered "pillars of the film industry's liberal camp," the screenwriter Donald Ogden Stewart, who joined the Communist party, exemplify the pattern of political affiliation in Hollywood in the 1930s.[21] In 1936, Stewart was among the organizers of the antifascist Motion Picture Artist Committee to Aid Republican Spain, which included screenwriters Dorothy Parker, Dashiell Hammett, and Lester Cole (one of the 1947 Hollywood Ten), and actors Melvyn Douglas, Paul Muni, Fredric March, and John Garfield. The committee collected funds (since then, one of the main roles played by the Hollywood community in politics), sponsored rallies and meetings, produced a weekly radio program, and published a biweekly newspaper.[22]

From broad idealistic issues, politicized Hollywood moved decidedly into party politics. The Douglases and Philip Dunne, a screenwriter, organized a group in support of Democratic candidates. The group included Dashiell Hammett and actresses Gloria Stuart and Miriam Hopkins and aimed at "working within the Democratic party, to support and extend the New Deal nationally and, primarily, to bring a new deal to California."[23] In June 1938 the group formed the Motion Picture Democratic Committee (MPDC), "Hollywood's first explicitly vote-getting organization." This group eventually developed a close association with the Democratic party and New Dealers.

In 1939 the Douglases met the Roosevelts through Helen Douglas's involvement in the problems of migrant workers. A friendship developed between the two couples, and soon Helen Douglas was drawn into Democratic politics.[24] In a very short time, she was appointed California's Democratic national committeewoman and director of the party's women's division in the state.

Communist party members were also involved in these organizations. As one screenwriter explained: "We were increasingly pro-Roosevelt, pro–New Deal, and the revolutionary stuff was something in the books, but it wasn't something we were working on. . . . We were working on elections, we were working on reformist programs."[25] In the Popular Front atmosphere, communism seemed to be as much a form of "Twentieth-century Americanism" as did the work of first-generation Americans like Frank Capra and Louis B. Mayer, who had developed a form of hyper-Americanism and become the best propagandists for the system. In the second half of the thirties their agendas, decidedly bearing the stamp of the New Deal, seemed to coincide because of the centrality of the concept of Americanism in the cultural politics of the time.

The intervention of the House un-American Activities (Committee (HUAC;

see Chapter 4) and the Hitler-Stalin pact drastically altered the scene. Hollywood's politics, scrutinized by HUAC, easily reached the front pages. And in an atmosphere of growing political conservatism, the same political activities that had been seen as commendable now made Hollywood a national scapegoat. When the anti-Nazi alliance broke up, the Popular Front seemed to dissolve.

After conferring with administration representatives in Washington, Melvyn Douglas severed ties with the communist group in the MPDC. But in the end, given the control communists had over the organization, the only solution was for the liberals to resign from it en masse.

"Hollywood for Roosevelt"

By the end of the thirties, not only the Communist party but also the two traditional political parties had set foot in Hollywood. During that decade the idea of "systematically funneling Hollywood into the mainstream of national partisan politics [had taken] root." Hollywoodians had very special qualities in this respect, in a media-dominated society. As Brownstein observes, "They were not only creatures of mass communication—raised to their exalted status by the enormous attention the new communications technologies made possible—but also tools of mass communication, vehicles for projecting fashions, values, and political messages."[26]

All of the electoral campaigns for FDR, especially in the late thirties, included shows, radio programs, and special events, casting Hollywood personalities. In 1940, it was estimated that more than 85 percent of the industry supported Roosevelt.[27] After a secession from the then-Communist-controlled MPDC, a group of liberal actors founded the Hollywood for Roosevelt Committee. Headed by Melvyn Douglas, they included Douglas Fairbanks Jr., Edward G. Robinson, Joan Bennett, Alice Faye, Henry Fonda, Rosalind Russell, and others. This committee maintained a direct relationship with the Democratic party structure and contributed to the campaign by conducting "a remarkable radio campaign."[28] In the week before the election, the Democratic National Committee purchased airtime for two national radio broadcast featuring such stars as Douglas Fairbanks Jr., Humphrey Bogart, Melvyn Douglas, Henry Fonda, Groucho Marx, Lucille Ball, Joan Bennett, and John Garfield.

To thank Hollywood for its support, when the campaign was over, Roosevelt donated to the Motion Picture Relief Fund the hat he had superstitiously worn throughout the campaign.[29] Edward G. Robinson and Melvyn Douglas bid $3,200 for it,[30] and in 1944 Robinson sent the hat back to Roosevelt, as an auspicious gesture.

But Hollywood (at least, at management level) was still mostly Republican in 1944 and again drew on the talent of Cecil B. DeMille, who had coached Alf Landon in 1936. In 1944, in support of the Republican candidate, Thomas E. Dewey, the famous director staged an extravagant show with elephants, bands, cowboys, lights, and appearances by such Republic Hollywoodians as Ginger Rogers, Fred MacMurray, Walt Disney, and David O. Selznick.

The Democrats, mean time, through the Hollywood for FDR committee, organized a dinner at which Danny Kaye, Gene Kelly, Phil Silvers, and Judy Garland performed musical numbers and Groucho Marx and Robert Benchley presented sketches.[31] Liberals and radicals were re-united, in this period, in the Hollywood Democratic Committee (HDC), which counted more than one thousand members, mostly writers, cartoonists, and stars. This committee was as Ronald Brownstein describes it, "the most sophisticated partisan political organization Hollywood had ever seen: well funded, fluent in the latest campaign technology, and committed to hardball campaigning."[32] Because of his participation in these activities, Melvyn Douglas in 1940 was the first actor to be nominated as a delegate to the national convention. Helen Douglas more and more involved in the Democratic party's activities, had grown closer to Eleanor Roosevelt. She gave 168 speeches for Democratic candidates in that year. When war broke out, Melvyn Douglas moved to Washington to supervise the arts division of the Office of Civilian Defense, but he had to return to Hollywood to fulfill a contract obligation to Columbia and joined the army. With the supper of the IIDC, in 1944 Helen Douglas was elected into Congress, "from an innercity Los Angeles district with a large black population."[33]

Hollywood figured prominently in the 1944 Democratic campaign. Jack and Harry Warner, Darryl Zanuck, Spiros Skouras, and Samuel Goldwyn donated money. Frank Sinatra, the new inter-media (radio and film) star, was invited to the White House because of his commitment in the Democratic cause; he even changed the lyrics of one of his songs in order to mention "Franklin D." His bobbysoxer fans wore buttons announcing "Frankie's for FDR and so are we," a tangible sign of how a star could move blocs of votes.[34] Hollywood politics also had Orson Welles as a star. His strong personality, in addition to his unique radio voice, and his very special qualities as a performer and an intellectual had made him a star-director. As a progressive New Dealer on the Hollywood Democratic Committee, Welles spoke over the radio and toured the country, campaigning very passionately (and effectively) for FDR.[35] He and Henry Wallace addressed a spectacular rally at Madison Square Garden organized by the Independent Voters' Committee of the Arts and Sciences for Roosevelt. The committee included Hollywoodians Fredric March, Bette Davis, and Eddie Cantor, and such intellectuals as Albert Einstein, John Dewey, and VanWyck Brooks.

The voter-appeal of the stars was so great that the HDC was overwhelmed with requests: "The advertising men wanted Olivia de Havilland; the Democrats in Washington State wanted Orson Welles, de Havilland, or Edward G. Robinson; the Independent Voters' Committee wanted Bob Hope. . . . From the DNC came a request for Humphrey Bogart to narrate a five-minute radio special in the last week of October."[36]

In the last feverish days of the campaign, both parties used all "their" stars. Ginger Rogers, Gary Cooper, Walter Pidgeon, Barbara Stanwyck, and Lionel Barrymore spoke over the radio for the GOP. The Democrats had the voices of Humphrey Bogart, Paul Muni, John Garfield, Gloria Stuart, and Edward G. Robinson. Orson Welles and Frank Sinatra joined Roosevelt for his final appearance in the campaign, on November 4 at Fenway Park in Boston.[37]

The Democrats made a final appeal on all radio networks on the night before voting. Scripted by radio writer Norman Corwin, the show had Bogart narrating, Judy Garland singing, and James Cagney, Groucho Marx, and Keenan Wynn in satirical sketches, plus some ordinary voices: "a Tennessee farmer, a brakeman on the New York Central, a Michigan housewife casting her first ballot." In this show we see a perfect integration of FDR's mode of address, his friendly approach to ordinary people, and show business stars. In the broadcast Bogart, the "voice of uncomplicated common sense," said: "This is Humphrey Bogart. . . . Personally, I'm voting for Franklin D. Roosevelt because I believe he is one of the world's greatest humanitarians; because he's leading our fight against the enemies of a free world." The show ended with rapid-fire endorsement from Hollywood stars Tallulah Bankhead, Joan Bennett ("for the Champ"), Irving Berlin, Claudette Colbert, Joseph Cotten, John Garfield, Rita Hayworth, George Jessel ("Hello, Mama Jessel. This is Georgie. Vote for Roosevelt"), Danny Kaye, Gene Kelly, Groucho Marx, George Raft, Edward G. Robinson, Lana Turner, and Jane Wyman. Then it moved on to New York, where another dozen celebrities "crowded into a studio—Dorothy Parker, Charles Boyer, Milton Berle, Franchot Tone, Frank Sinatra, the names flashing like freight cars, stretching out endlessly, like Roosevelt himself, encompassing the nation."

In the relationship between Hollywood and Washington, this campaign represents a watershed. It stressed the role media people could play in national partisan politics, confirming the power of radio messages to move voters and the ability of celebrities to command public attention for a cause. The HDC proved how energetic Hollywood could be when carefully organized, and Goldwyn, Zanuck, and Jack Warner showed the movie industry's potential as a source of political money.[38] In a moment of crisis during the campaign, when Roosevelt looked particularly tired and aged and rumors were being heard that he was on his death bed, Stephen Early made use of another type of Hollywood knowledge by bringing Hollywood lighting experts and cameramen to the White House to make a good portrait he could use to stop the rumors.[39] The relationship between Roosevelt, the New Dealers, the Democratic party, and Hollywood at the end of the 1930s inaugurated a quasi-institutional practice of publicity exchange and collaboration between Hollywood and Washington that continues to the present.

The Roosevelts in Hollywood

The growing film industry attracted many ambitious young people. The Roosevelt family was no exception. Franklin D. Roosevelt, in his youth, had written a treatment for a film about John Paul Jones and submitted it to Adolph Zukor at Famous Players-Lasky, but it came to nothing.[40]

The president's eldest son, James, went to Hollywood in 1938.[41] Up to that moment he had been a collaborator of his father in political affairs and had appeared frequently at this side, to support him physically (but discreetly) during official ceremonies or to take newsreels and photographs.[42] Although some people assumed that he was interested in film's potential for public service, he seemed to have steered clear of message films, perhaps to avoid embarrassment to his family and accusations of political propaganda in his productions; possibly he was simply more interested in the business opportunities offered by the film industry. He went to work for Samuel Goldwyn, producing films such as *Pot o'Gold,* which was directed by George Marshall and starred James Stewart and Paulette Goddard. In September 1940 he ventured into the production of "soundies," "miniature movies which, for the price of 10 cents, will not only play tunes, but will show the singers, musicians and entertainers on a miniature screen"—that is, the predecessors of video clips.[43] (This commercial venture gives us the measure of the Roosevelts' predisposition in the field of media culture—one that allowed them to divine communicative possibilities in the market.)

Yet despite James Roosevelt's avoidance of "political subjects," his presence in the film industry still ended up embarrassing his father. As vice president of Goldwyn's Productions, he risked being named as a defendant in the Paramount suit. In fact, his entry into the film industry at the same time as the filing of this suit was criticized and raised some questions about Roosevelt's attitudes in the case.[44] Furthermore, the young Roosevelt had compounded the embarrassment to his father by intervening on behalf of Joseph Schenck, who had loaned him $50,000 and had been convicted for tax evasion in June 1940.[45]

In 1940, in the midst of the ideological mobilization of the film industry, James Roosevelt released a British anti-Nazi picture, *Pastor Hall.*[46] In doing so, he aligned himself with the anti-isolationist front of the film industry, thus preceding on the screens the President's official sanction to a policy of anti-Nazi mobilization.[47] (Oddly, in the same period, Mussolini's son was equally involved in the destiny of Italy's national cinema and even attempted a project of co-production with Hollywood.[48] Given the differences in the relationship between government and cinema in the two countries, this parallelism appears to have little more than anecdotal value.)

Another member of the Roosevelt family had a stronger connection to the film industry than James's. John Boettiger was a journalist for the *Chicago Tribune,* a paper owned by a publisher hostile to the administration. In love with Anna Roosevelt, the President's daughter, whom he married in 1935, Boettiger was given a way to leave this embarrassing position as a critic of the New Deal, by Will Hays, who hired him to work in the New York offices of the MPPDA, in December 1934.[49] This hiring indicates a peculiar role of the MPPDA in relation to the administration, in that there was no obvious connection between Boettiger's professional training as a journalist and working in "publicity and research" at the trade organization of the film industry. Most of all, there was no open political or party alliance to justify this gesture, given Hays's prominent role in the Republican party. In order to allay any suspicion about Boettiger's position in the MPPDA, Hays re-stated in writing what they had agreed would be his function.

> It is definitely understood that you shall not in your association with us
> have any concern whatever with those of our affairs which may have to do
> with Washington; particularly, your work shall in no way be connected
> with any legislative or other matter—either with any department of the
> Federal Government, with the Congress, or with any state legislature, or
> with any individual connected with those agencies. Such matters consti-
> tute, indeed, a very minor part of our work here and elsewhere, as you
> know."[50]

Despite the apparent contradiction between the last sentence and what we know above Hays's (and the MPPDA's) successful lobbying strategies within various civic and political institutions, Hays tried to avoid involving Boettiger in these activities. At least on paper.

Boettiger's brief stay at the MPPDA put him in touch with the "heart" of the organization—its public relations offices. With the people he met there he kept up a constant flow of correspondence, characterized by an affectionate cordiality. In 1936, together with his wife, Anna, he left to work as the editor of a Hearst paper, the *Seattle Post-Intelligencer.* In his new role, Boettiger published articles and editorials about the motion picture industry that usually supported Hays's policies. But he did not limit his support to his journalistic work. In a letter to Kenneth Clark of the MPPDA, for example, he offers to help get certain senators to "vote with us."[51] The "us" underlines the great interest with which Boettiger followed film matters and his identification with Hays's positions, about which he kept himself constantly informed.

There was a complex exchange of favors between Hays and Boettiger, which began with Hays's offering Boettiger the job at the MPPDA and culminated with his helping Boettiger and Anna Roosevelt obtain a license for a radio station in Seattle.[52]

The correspondence between Hays and Boettiger helps clarify William Randolph Hearst's contradictory attitudes toward Roosevelt, integrating the story of his relationship with Mayer and Jack Warner. Although Hearst had supported FDR's nomination in 1932—to avoid supporting his old enemy, Al Smith, or the internationalist Newton Baker—after Roosevelt's tax proposal in 1935, Hearst renamed the New Deal, the "Raw Deal." Yet he hired Boettiger as resident publisher of the *Seattle Post-Intelligencer* the next year, "partly out of perversity," but also because he thought that hiring these "spotlight people" might help generate advertising and circulation and intimidate the unions.[53] Hays probably had some role in Boettiger's appointment in Seattle, as his letter to Boettiger about a meeting with Hearst implies.

> We have missed you very much—far more than you have any idea. I made this observation to Mr. Hearst the other day, and he characteristically remarked, "Certainly." Then we had a long talk about you. . . .
> He made practically the same observation as he did in his letter with you—that is, that the appointment was solely because he believed you had the capacity for real performance in journalism and that it was being shown already. He then told me that the circulation "was as much as before the trouble" and was enthusiastic in his appreciation of the way you have taken hold of everything.[54]

Hays also notes that the meeting with Hearst happened after an (apparently casual) engagement that included Joseph Kennedy. The personal contacts between Kennedy, Hays, Hearst, Jack Warner, and other personalities of the financial, communication, and political worlds on the West Coast punctuate these chronicles, delineating connections in which it is difficult to distinguish between sincere friendships and opportunism. Although Hearst attacked FDR's reforms in his newspapers, he hired not only the Boettigers but also FDR's son Elliott, who managed four of his radio stations.[55] Behind the official positions taken by the Republican Hays and by the antagonistic Hearst, a different scenario can be seen. Publicly Boettiger was in an embarrassing position at the *Seattle Post*. (Given FDR's difficulties with "85% of the press," few publishers could give him a comfortable berth.) Boettiger discussed that matter with his friend Clark of the MPPDA, stating: "Confidentially, I have come to this decision: We will support the administration when its is not in direct conflict with the Hearst policy; we will be silent for the most part otherwise."[56] Actually Boettiger did support the administration regularly in his paper, especially after 1938. He even printed a regular column by Eleanor Roosevelt and dedicated the front page of the seventy-fifth-anniversary edition to a letter of congratulations by the President, without ever hiding his relationship to the Roosevelts from his readers.

There was nothing subtle about the role the Boettigers played as part of FDR's "personal correspondents." The *Saturday Evening Post* defined them as "the White House's most intimate source of information on the happenings beyond the Continental Divide."[57]

New Dealers in the Hays Office

The recurrence of the name Hays and of the MPPDA requires a more analytical examination of the relationship between the Roosevelt administration and the trade organization of the film industry. Boettiger's experience was not an isolated one; on the contrary, the Hays Office, in the course of time, gave hospitality to more than one supporter of the Democratic administration.

Charles Pettijohn is a key example. As the MPPDA's general counsel and head of the Protective Department, whose purpose was securing "freedom from unjust and unlawful legislation" for the motion picture industry,[58] in effect, Pettijohn was chief lobbyist. Closely monitoring the press and constantly traveling, he maintained personal contact with local exhibitors, civic associations, and pressure groups hostile to the film industry's products. Such groups existed on the border between politics and communications. They had their own lobbies and frequently turned to the White House or to their congressmen to protest against "socially dangerous" films or against trade practices they considered harmful to free trade or to the liberty of consumption in a community.[59]

Under Pettijohn, the MPPDA approached public relations and public opinion dealt in much the same way Roosevelt's staff dealt with pressure groups: they closely analyzed the criticisms and frequently co-opted the group's ideological motivations and their specific projects. In this way antagonists were transformed into allies and the resulting policy was deemed useful to the "general good." A similar co-option of the Catholic positions helped to enforce the system of self-censorship.

Pettijohn, the pivot of this decentralized system, kept an eye on the local situation and developed intricate networks. In describing personalities and functions of the Hays Office, Raymond Moley, in his authoritative study, writes:

> In maintaining contact with the many people in the county who would be
> essential to this work, Mr. Pettijohn's multitudinous list of acquaintances

was invaluable. Moreover, he was helped by the fact that since some of the companies had theatres and, in consequence, important property interests in many cities and states concerned, they employed local law firms. There was to grow up, at the same time, an enormous list of officers of civic and welfare organizations with whom some department of the Hays Office was to remain in contact. Finally there were hundreds of local theatre owners and managers known to Mr. Pettijohn."[60]

Moley knew well that Pettijohn had long been adept at networking. Writing about the creation of the Brain Trust and the first phase of the New Deal, he remarked on Pettijohn's role on the train of Roosevelt's 1932 electoral campaign.

And there were two cars for the more or less permanent members of the troupe. These included Jim Farley, who joined us at Salt Lake City and left at Los Angeles; Joe Kennedy; Charles C. Pettijohn, a veteran of the movie industry, who watched over newsreel relations and, at every stop, made contact with motion-picture distributors and exhibitors to win their good will for the candidate."[61]

This was no small contribution to Roosevelt's political career: free electoral propaganda through the presence in the newsreels and access to the American screens (both newsreels and theaters were owned or controlled by the majors at that time and therefore represented by the MPPDA). In fact the Democratic Party made good use of the obvious attraction of Roosevelt's position as President, and his personal charm, to receive good coverage from radio, press, and the newsreels, especially in electoral years. This "free time" of favorable and conspicuous exposure in the newsreels can be considered an indirect "donation" by the film industry—closely supervised by Pettijohn—to Roosevelt's electoral campaigns.

Throughout the 1936 campaign, Pettijohn traveled with Boettiger—at that time his colleague at the MPPDA—all the while evaluating and charting the response of theater audiences across the country to newsreels covering Roosevelt or his opponent, Alf Landon.[62] Although clearly this research entailed the cooperation of the film companies and of the exhibitors, there is too little documentation to show how the information was collected. Nonetheless, this initiative appears to be an early instance of the study of mass political reactions—a typical mid-1930s activity that was greatly encouraged by the New Dealers.

The development of the social sciences in the 1930s through their application to different aspects of life in the era of mass consumption, mass communications, and mass politics is another indicator of the inextricable relationship among these three aspects, as Susman indicates. It is interesting to note that in a letter to Hays, Boettiger thanked him for sending "three charts showing analysed press comments on motion pictures," which indicated "the effectiveness of the public relations work done by the Hays Office." Monitoring the press was thus one of the ways by which the film industry studied the reactions to its activities. It was the same system used by the New Deal administration to evaluate the people's reactions to its policies and to Roosevelt's performances.[63] Until the development of more "scientific" systems of public opinion pollings, the Hays Office was probably a privileged source of knowledge of the public and of audiences—and not only of American audiences, a trait the other media, press and radio, could not boast.

The network of foreign distribution controlled by the film companies constituted in itself a system of continuous reporting on the state of the economy and on the politics of a given country. A letter that Pettijohn sent to Boettiger in 1937 about a trip he made to Italy reveals how involved the MPPDA was in foreign political affairs. He describes meeting Vittorio Mussolini. "He is a fine, quiet, modest, young man and expressed a very sincere desire to meet the President before he goes back to Italy. The President's son [John Roosevelt] met his father [Benito Mussolini] in Rome and I just suspect that the President would permit this boy to return the call."[64]

Pettijohn had met Vittorio Mussolini on his way to the United States to visit the Hollywood studios and to start a co-production project with Hal Roach. Pettijohn had earlier expressed his admiration for the young Mussolini in an interview published in an Italian American newspaper,[65] and he had met Benito Mussolini in 1935 in an interview for a newsreel. On that occasion, Pettijohn had suggested making a documentary, through which "about 70 million Americans would have understood better Italy's position."[66] He could guarantee distribution of the Paramount newsreel in "about 14,500 American theatres." The interplay of international communication and politics was complex and is still hardly explored. John Roosevelt had met Mussolini while traveling through Italy to accompany his grandmother Sarah Delano Roosevelt, in July 1937. He had expressed "his wish not to be officially welcomed" and therefore had only an informal meeting with the "Duce." As a consequence of Pettijohn's pressures, Vittorio Mussolini was invited for tea at the White House in the course of which apparently "there were no political undertones."[67]

Pettijohn's letter also included a comment ("I would also like the President to know that I am back and that I was very successful in a certain matter with which he is familiar.") that points to Roosevelt's penchant for secrecy. Hays shared it, and his correspondence is rich in coded words. Whatever this "certain matter" was—a political mission or a film business matter—the comment confirms that the MPPDA activities abroad always had wider repercussions and involved Pettijohn in a key role.

Pettijohn was a tireless supporter of Hays Office interests and of the President; his travels, his "multitudinous list of acquaintances," his contacts with local exhibitors, his relationships with public groups, made him "invaluable" to both until this pragmatic approach to public relations and to the monitoring of public opinion became outdated. In 1942 Pettijohn "resigned" from his position at the MPPDA, officially because of two major operations he needed. Actually, from an exchange of letters between Boettiger and Clark, it appears that he was forced to resign.

> For some time the lawyers in Hollywood, who are assuming more and more influence, have been dissatisfied with the handling of legislative matters. For example, they felt that the industry did not come off as well as it should in the wage-hour act. They blamed Charlie [Pettijohn]. Then, certain Hollywood executive worked themselves into quite a state later on because they felt that our office did not respond vigorously and quickly enough to the Nye-Clark-Wheeler charges.[68] They did not want Charlie to handle our presentation at the hearings in Washington. . . . Some weeks ago the Hollywood Association appointed a committee of three lawyers to work with three lawyers here to survey and report on Hays Office activities. . . . It was evident from the start that the lawyers were determined to "get" Charlie. . . . The lawyers also want to strengthen "public relations." Under their promptings the New York advertising and publicity men are being integrated more closely into this work."[69]

It was a depressing (and unexpected) ending for a long career in defense of the film industry's interests. It was also a turnover—a definite change in public relations policies, which seems to indicate on the part of the industry the decision to move toward a more scientific, less pragmatic and intuitive, approach to public opinion. The entry of advertising people into this field was thus particularly significant.

After Pettijohn left the MPPDA and recovered from the operations, he wrote to Boettiger, offering his services to the President: "I believe I can be useful to the President somewhere. . . . I will appreciate it if you or Anna will drop the President a note telling him that I am available, without compensation, and will be glad to serve him or my country anywhere he may see fit to use me."[70] The documents do not indicate whether Pettijohn's offer was accepted.

When Democratic party members with close connections to Roosevelt came to work at the MPPDA, it was with Hays's blessing. Certainly hiring personnel from the Democratic party to work in an office that was under constant threat of government regulation was an effective and reasonable strategy. But there were reciprocal advantages that made this relationship more complicated and less unilateral: access to the screens for the administration, "image counseling," the help of professionals who were then learning how to analyze audiences' reactions—in a word, access to public opinion, in both material and abstract terms.

Edward Roddam was an obvious choice for Washington representative to the MPPDA.[71] A reporter who had conquered Early's confidence to the point that, during the 1936 campaign, he was given special information and instructions by the President's press secretary, Roddam had left Universal to work for the Democratic National Committee. He worked with Early to bring public pressure on Congress in favor of revision of the Neutrality Act and played an instrumental role in enlisting Hollywood support for preparedness and anti-isolationism, before the war.

Kenneth Clark was a strong Roosevelt supporter who had been hired at Boettiger's suggestion and appointed head of the Public Information Department of the MPPDA.[72] When he was offered a job in 1942 at the Office of Civil Defense, he refused, because he felt that he would be better able to serve Roosevelt and his country from within the trade organization of the film industry.

The presence of this personnel from the Democratic party in what has usually been considered the lodge of Republican Hollywood, the Hays Office, and their specialization and connection with Roosevelt's campaigns is further evidence of the value the Democrats put on Hollywood knowledge of how to construct images and myths.[73]

The Hays Office was the site of a doubly successful contact with the public. Its public relations policy had stabilized and reformed the public image of Hollywood and its product, and cinema had proven to be a very popular form of entertainment—together with the radio—a "depression-proof" industry. Roosevelt's positive relationship with both radio and cinema had obviously to do also with the pragmatic consideration of their success as media in that period (where the press was out of step with the masses), and perhaps with their success as public opinion testers and public relations administrators.

Hays and FDR

Will Hays's personal relation to Roosevelt was quite friendly and close—unexpectedly so, given Hays's prominent role in the Republican party and in particular in the 1920 campaign for Warren G. Harding, in which Roosevelt, nominated for the vice presidency on the ticket with James Cox, was defeated. In his autobiography Hays distinguished between the professional differences he had with the President about politics and about some of the industry problems and the personal side, which he characterized as "contacts . . . on a plane of extreme cordiality and friendliness."[74] The tone of the correspondence between Hays and Roosevelt confirms this statement. Beyond the differences, there was reciprocal esteem, favored by the interaction through the Boettigers, a particular "vehicle" of communication through which Hays was able to communicate directly with the President and vice versa—a means of communication not exempt from a trace of affection. After Boettiger moved to Seattle, Hays wrote to him: "We saw the President and Mrs. Roosevelt a week ago last Saturday. . . We had a quick talk with them then and all four agreed that we now have another mutual interest and that is in missing Anna and you. I talked to him at length the next day and we planned something together—all good."[75]

But when Hays discusses the New Deal in his autobiography, he is absolutely antagonistic.

> As I try to get a bird's-eye view of these trends it is hard to see why an alien philosophy of statism, which in other countries had already proved harmful both to creative art and financial success, should have gained credence here. The country experienced a series of new invasions into fields of private initiative such as the film industry. We witnessed a growing conception that a politically appointed commission or bureau, by some strange infusion of official wisdom, could show creators how to create and executives how to execute. The words "regulation" and "control" were increasingly used to express a new relation of government to business.[76]

Hays even saw the government as a "competitor" because of its documentary film production, which he magnified with the typical Hollywood penchant for gigantism. When he was in agreement with Roosevelt's actions, however, he was quick to acknowledge the positive aspects.[77] He was particularly close to the President in the war-related issues—although probably with no disinterested motive, given the importance of the foreign market to the film industry. It was indeed during the war and on international issues that Hays and Roosevelt were in firm agreement. The administration, in fact, protected the film industry's interests abroad throughout the thirties.[78] In a letter to Boettiger Hays indicated that "the State Department was utterly invaluable to us" regarding matters in Italy and England and that "the President's trip to South America was of transcendent consequence."[79] On the foreign scene, political and economic considerations in relation to cinema were indeed inextricable. Of great importance in this sense was a trip Hays made to Rome in 1936 in which he encountered both Mussolini and the Pope, defending the interests of American film business and affirming the universal ideological power of American movies, after their "reformation" through the Hays Code and because of their support of basic moral values.[80] (The "sequel" to this trip, Pettijohn being its protagonist, as we have already seen, strengthened the interconnection between Roosevelt, Italy, and the MPPDA.) Roosevelt and Hays shared some fundamental beliefs about exporting the image of American democracy abroad. They also shared some crucial personality traits: enormous political craftsmanship, ability in mediating opposing interests, and knowledge of public opinion. They also shared a common belief against censorship and propaganda, which was the sound basis of their mutual respect. Not unexpectedly, Roosevelt supported Hays's guidance of the MPPDA, encouraging him to continue his work in 1941 by stating: "You are the kind of Czar that nobody could call 'a Dictator' because you are fairminded and do not use a whip but still get things done for the general good."[81] Interestingly enough, Hays's intention to retire and leave his position to Eric Johnston was perceived as "handing over the greatest propaganda machine in the country to the Republican party,"[82] almost as if Hays had been a Democrat.

The Insiders

Within the Democratic party and the Administration a number of people had business connections with the film industry. Among them were Frank Walker, Raymond Moley, Joseph Kennedy, and Col. William J. Donovan. Each was protective of the industry's interests, but their influence is not easily traced.

Frank Walker was chairman of the Democratic National Committee and postmaster general (the same roles played by Hays in the Republican administration). In 1933 Roosevelt appointed him director of the Emergency Council, an agency composed of the heads of the various emergency agencies and executive departments, and responsible for collecting data and transmitting information about the progress of the New Deal programs. Walker thus played a crucial role in the New Deal's system of communication, as the head of the closest program the administration had to a propaganda machine. Although he was one of the President's closest collaborators and advisers, Walker was not as prominent in the press or in the public image of the New Dealers as, for example, Hopkins.[83] Because of his official role at the National Emergency Council (NEC), Walker was indeed the main "reporter" to the President on the New Deal's effects. He traveled around the country to assess the Civil Work Administration (CWA). He told the president:

> I'd pay little attention to those who criticize the creation of the CWA or its
> administration. Hopkins and his associates are doing their work very well. . . .
> It is amazing when you consider that within the short time since the CWA
> was established, four million idle have been put to work. . . . This has averted
> one of the most serious crises in our history. Revolution is an ugly word to
> use, but I think we were dangerously close at least to the threat of it.[84]

In this capacity and in that of chairman of the Democratic National Committee he was entrusted with the complex duty of the administration's public relations, showing a sensibility and competence FDR particularly appreciated.

The film business was the source of Walker's personal fortunes. In 1925, he moved to New York to help his uncle, M. R. Comerford, manage a string of movie theaters, which they eventually sold to Paramount, leaving Walker with a small fortune in profit. But the theaters "bounced back" to Comerford in 1932 when Paramount "went bust."[85] His personal connections with film business went even further, because his father-in-law was the first vice president of an association of film exhibitors, of which Walker was general counsel for a period of time.[86] It is not surprising then that, at the administration turnover in 1933, it was suggested to appoint Frank Walker at the helm of the MPPDA, to replace Hays.[87] In the secretive correspondence between Hays and the White House, in reference to the *Paramount* case, in the crucial period of the elaboration of the consent decree, the head of the MPPDA reiterated: "We remember, of course, that Frank Walker can be of great help any place along the line. No one has more knowledge of the business and no one is more dependable."[88] Walker was with no doubt the "gray eminence" in the relationship between the New Deal and cinema. Although because of his involvement in the "Comerford affair" he risked being among the defendants in the *Paramount* case, he had an important role in the signing of the consent decree, which eased the antimonopolistic pressure on the majors. Walker's interests transcended mere "lobbying" and personal interests; he was a New Dealer more inclined toward industry self-government under government supervision than toward antimonopoly. Being himself a "keen businessmen,"[89] he represented that section of the New Deal that was not aggressively antibusiness. Yet he also believed in a real reformation of business methods, based on his Catholic faith, one that emphasized the community rather than the individual. Walker, then, was important both as an individual and as a Catholic, representing the Democratic party and the New Deal wider political participation of minorities or ethnic groups previously ignored by WASP politics—but a new morality as well. (This changing role of Catholics in American cultural and political life was mirrored somewhat in the elaboration of the Hays Code of self-censorship, where Catholics exerted practical and political leverage [see Chapter 4] and inspired the ideological and moral content of the Code.)

In the first period of the New Deal, Raymond Moley was FDR's closest adviser, responsible for having "invented" and selected the Brain Trust. Like Walker, he was not considered an antagonist of business; on the contrary, he believed in self-regulation.[90] His study of the film industry's system of self-regulation through the Hays Office is one of the most authoritative accounts of the functions of the MPPDA.[91] Actually Moley had started working on this study in 1936, after a "troubled evening" in which he had a violent discussion with FDR and became gradually estranged from the administration.[92] (The Hays Office worked also in that instance as a sort of "shelter" for Democrats who wanted to detach themselves from the administration, without severing their connections, as if politics and film business were two sides of the same coin.)

In the Forward to the first edition of his book, Moley identifies the Hays Office as a prototype of self-regulation.

> In these days of heated debate over the relations of government and business, such a story is not without general significance. There are those who believe that government regulation of business has gone too far. There are others who hold that it has not gone far enough. All, however, agree that it is highly desirable that business learn as much as possible about governing itself. This book describes an effort to do just that. It was Will Hays who once said that this country needs "more business in government and less government in business," although that expression was subsequently used by a President of the United States.

In this book Moley analyzes the structure and the operational methods of the film industry's trade association, studying its two interrelated functions, that of trade self-regulation and that of self-censorship. According to Moley, both activities were positive and to be preferred to federal regulation. In his view, self-regulation had to accompany the cooperation among government, industry, business, and social forces, with the purpose of solving the economic crisis and of "reforming" outdated or aggressive industrial trade practices. It was the spirit of the NRA and of its codes of fair competition. In this first phase of the relationship between the New Deal and the film industry, the administration maintained a positive attitude toward Hays Office activities. After 1937, with the adoption of an antimonopoly policy, the New Deal began denouncing the monopolistic implications of the film industry's system of self-government in the *Paramount* case. On this occasion, the Antitrust Division of the Justice Department went as far as identifying the MPPDA as the site of the monopolistic practices of the film industry.

On the issue of self-censorship, however, Moley and the New Deal were always in agreement. Moley, founder of *Newsweek,* was always curious about information processes and recreation media; and he was personally involved in the fight against what he defined as "political censorship." On its part, the goverment never wanted or tried to control or censor film production, with the possible exception of the war period.[93] Moley was therefore another New Dealer with a strong interest in communication processes who concentrated his attention on the film industry, and, in a way, protected its interests by legitimizing its institutions through his authoritative study of the Hays Office.

One would have expected that Joseph Kennedy—financer, prominent figure in the Democratic party, film producer, "film historian," and, as such, great legitimizer of film as sound business and worthwhile cultural enterprise in the 1920s—would have played an important role in the interaction between the New Deal and the film industry.[94] On the contrary, the documents seem to indicate quite an unimportant one. Kennedy was present at some key moments such as the Warner brother's decision to support Roosevelt in 1932, but his role does not appear, all in all, determinant. According to Hays, Kennedy helped the film industry in the 1940 crisis when he was the American ambassador to Great Britain.[95] But Kennedy was probably too directly associated with film business to be administration "consultant" above suspicion. Besides, the documents reveal a very cold relationship between Kennedy and Roosevelt, both politically and personally.

A less-well known figure who moved mysteriously but actively between the administration (although he was a Republican, and a friend of Theodore Roosevelt's sons) and the legal and financial film world was Col. William J. Donovan. "Wild Bill" Donovan was a veteran of World War I and a Wall Street lawyer who served as a high-ranking official in the Antitrust Division during the Coolidge administration.[96] In the *Paramount* case, however, he defended the majors. In a memorandum for the files, dated December 4, 1939, in the *Paramount* case papers, Donovan is mentioned as "representing RKO." Another source in fact stated that he "played an important role in the RKO reorganization proceedings."

In view of the war effort, Donovan proposed a project for the unification of government information, propaganda, and espionage within a single agency, capable of moving with agility and determination to counter the Axis propaganda. To carry out this proposal he founded the Office of Strategic Services (OSS), from which the CIA later grew. His moves in this field were mysterious: "Cryptically he undertook to collect strategic intelligence materials throughout the world. To accomplish that task he engaged in espionage and subversion through secret agents behind battle lines, and in other locations affected by the war."[97] During the war, Donovan took on John Ford and Gregg Toland, allowing them to make *The Battle of Midway*. The OSS, because of its "strategic" position, was able to make some of the most spectacular documentaries of World War II.[98] At the end of the war, Donovan regained contacts in the film industry, becoming part of the Argosy, John Ford's independent production company.

Walker, Moley, Kennedy, and Donovan were all related to the business aspects of the film industry, and not to its creative or production side. Their important political roles allow us to think of them as particularly well-informed traits d'union between the film industry and government, having direct access to Roosevelt, and granting the President direct access to the film industry. To think of them as "lobbyists" would be reductive and simplistic. Like other representatives of industry and business who enjoyed a close relationship with Roosevelt, they were likely to support the film industry interests with the administration. But when—as in the antitrust suit—other forces in the administration took a different or opposing stand on an issue, and Roosevelt believed that these groups had a superior ideological or political position, he would not stop them. Thus, even these powerful figures could not guarantee the film industry absolute protection. It is clear though that, as with the members of the Roosevelt family connected with film business, the closeness of these people to the President was such that most of their communications about film matters would not be in writing and therefore not documented. This does not mean that it was hidden or secret—only that it should be inferred.

Taking the *Paramount* case as a significant test, we can say that these people defended the economic interests of the industry: Moley, indirectly with his studious "defense," Walker discreetly, Kennedy deductively, Donovan directly and officially. In this sense, they constituted the advanced nucleus of the film lobby within the White House itself. But it cannot be said that in exchange they put the cinema at the service of the administration—nor would Roosevelt have wanted or expected them to. Donovan, with his move from the *Paramount* case to the OSS is the exception. He embodies the radical change that came about in the relationship between the Roosevelt and administration and the film industry, from the legal battles on the monopoly front to the mobility of Hollywood in uniform.

The Film "Know-How"

In contrast to the administration insiders who were connected to the business aspects of the film industry, others who developed close ties with the White House offered specific competences connected to film production. Screenwriter Robert Sherwood served as the ghostwriter for Roosevelt's speeches in the war period, and the Warner brothers offered a more generic political support.

Warner Bros. contributed to Roosevelt's political career with financial help and promotional activities of various forms. Out of all the film industry, Warner Bros. can be said to be the only company that consistently produced films supporting the New Deal message and the administration's political interests, including foreign relations, between 1933 and 1942. Warner Bros.'s production of the thirties has been so closely identified with the New Deal that a book about its history in those years has been entitled *A New Deal in Entertainment*.[99]

In 1932, Harry Warner (described by James W. Gerard as one of the "64 men who governed America"),[100] became one of Roosevelt's Great Electors. His association with that section of the business community, including the financial firm Goldman, Sachs, which was leaving the Republican party to support FDR, might have influenced his choice. He immediately drew in his youngest brother, Jack, calling him to New York to discuss with the leading National Democratic Committee executives how the California campaign should be conducted. "Harry and I had always been faithful Republicans," Jack Warner explains in his autobiography, but in 1932 Harry proposed a "political switch." "The country is in chaos," he said. "There is revolution in the air, and we need a change." The Warner brothers' involvement in Roosevelt's cause seems to have arisen therefore more from fear than true political belief. Jack did not hesitate to state that he accepted the task with "some misgivings,"[101] but he plunged in nonetheless and organized spectacular political events in California to support Roosevelt's candidacy. When he mobilized "all the greatest Hollywood stars" for the grandiose parade, he was surprised to find "how many hidden Democrats crawled out of the woodwork." To re-enforce the impact of the event, the Warners made use of radio publicity through their own radio station in Los Angeles, KFWB. This is another internal connection within the system of the media, justified by the fact that Warner Bros., with the introduction of sound, had developed close links with radio technology and financial groups, representing a very advanced model of a multi-media organization. Thus Warner Bros. support to FDR implied the mobilization of a vast sector of entertainment.

When Jack Warner met Roosevelt during the 1932 campaign they began a friendship that "endured to the day of [Roosevelt's] death." It was a relationship that implied reciprocal benefits but also was characterized by cordiality. "In exchange" for electoral support, FDR appointed Jack Warner as Los Angeles chairman of NRA (National Recovery Administration) and invited him to go fishing on his yacht, hoping to "pick his brain for information about the film industry" and "getting the pulse of the people." Later, according to Jack Warner's autobiography Roosevelt offered him "a diplomatic post overseas." He refused, stating, "I can do better for your foreign relations with a good film about America now and then."[102] And indeed Warner Bros. films of the late thirties were important in presenting the themes of international politics.

In the 1930s, the Warner brothers—Harry, the true boss of the studio, and Jack, who controlled film production in Hollywood—were often guests at the White House, operating as a link between Hollywood and Washington. Their letters addressed directly to the President seeking "favors" for the film industry suggest that they were also the leaders of an interest group within the White House. Harry Warner, because he made all the political and business decisions for the company, had the most complex relationship with the President. The correspondence at the Roosevelt Library shows clearly that the more delicate questions were in his hands.[103]

The relationship between the Warners and Roosevelt, however, was not as idyllic as Jack's autobiography and Hollywood legends might lead us to believe. In the mid-thirties, the government began an antimonopoly civil suit against Warner Bros., accusing the studio of having restrained exhibition in the St. Louis area. A temporary cooling occurred in the relationship between the studio and the President. Later, however, either because of similar views on foreign policy or because of reciprocal interest, the relationship took on a new footing, to the extent that the Warner's mediation facilitated the signing of the consent decree that closed the first phase of the *Paramount* case.[104]

Robert Sherwood, a successful author, screenwriter, and playwright, was a New Dealer and a fervent interventionist. His book *Roosevelt and Hopkins: An Intimate History* is our most authoritative source on the final phase of FDR's presidency and on American foreign policy from 1940 to 1944.[105] He worked for years as Roosevelt's ghostwriter. The pages he devoted in *Roosevelt and Hopkins* to a detailed description of this activity constitute precise testimony to the way FDR worked with the media. He highlights the personality of the President in a vivid portrait, veined with affectionate admiration. He pulls himself back from the scene, but in reality, he contributed to some of the most important of FDR's speeches in the forties.[106] In addition to his ideological consonance to the New Deal, his assets to the administration included his particular ability with words, images, narrative structures, and identification strategies. That is, he made available to the administration the expressive and rhetorical "know-how" of the cinema and the theater of the thirties. At the same time, his "ghost" function gave him the opportunity to express a personal interpretation of the New Deal and of foreign policy, through his collaboration within the process of delivering messages. It must have been an interpretation completely in line with that of the White House, given the fact that he was appointed head of the overseas branch of the Office of War Information (OWI), the government agency that controlled information and propaganda during World War II. His trustworthiness in political matters and his ability in drawing up messages were therefore channeled in this activity, which involved the presentation of the American image abroad, the export of the American dream—exactly what American cinema was doing at that time. Sherwood was particularly suited for this purpose because his cinema and theater work was involved in the reformulation of Americanism and in the analysis of social reality. This synthesis of realism, participation, and revitalization of American values, born in the thirties, can be well seen in *The Best Years of Our Lives,* the film he was working on when he started writing the Hopkins biography.

Sherwood embodied an ideal of propaganda very different from what Donovan was proposing at the time, "propaganda as a weapon of war."[107] Sherwood believed in information "based on the truth," not manipulated, to promote the image of a democratic America. "All US information to the world," he said, "should be considered as though it were a continuous speech by the President."[108] For Roosevelt, he was more than a "consultant on messages." His constant presence at the President's side in the early forties and his participation to important decisions indicate that he was gifted with remarkable political qualities.[109] Sherwood represents a particularly complex example of the interaction between politics and cinema. His work "cinematizes" the New Deal message, indicating how much the administration recognized the political value of cinema.

In the diachronic display of these political-institutional events, the relationship between the administration and cinema implies the development of an integrated know-how. The interaction of communications and politics in the 1930s, caused a reciprocal and definitive modification that resulted in the stealing of a magic that transformed Roosevelt into a screen star, in competition with Clark Gable.[110] Cinema also offered and stimulated other "knowledges": the development of instruments of analysis of public opinion; the development of new techniques in nationwide public relations, simultaneously widespread and local in their penetration; and the elaboration of economic-legal theories able to examine the development of advanced capitalism and to define monopoly.

Cinema was "inside" the way in which the New Deal and Roosevelt communicated with the masses. The personalizing of a conflict, the simplification of reality, the emotional identification with the characters, and even the happy ending were ingredients both of Hollywood classical cinema and of Roosevelt's oratory. It was not by chance that FDR had a screenwriter among his more direct collaborators.

One should also underline that, while the economic-institutional reforms of the New Deal were only partially effective, it was how they were articulated and publicized—cinemalike—that lent stability to the American sociopolitical system. "FDR's most effective palliative" for the Depression, according to Peter Roffman and Jim Purdy, was "psychological rather than real, and the New Deal 'a triumph of appearances over reality.'"[111]

The events and individuals singled out in this chapter demonstrate the importance of studying media as interactive systems. The influential men discussed here were involved in several forms of communication: Boettiger concerned himself with journalism, radio, and cinema; several members of the Roosevelt family had, over the course of time, contacts with different media contexts; Hays nourished a real passion for communication technology, Hearst was at the head of a newspaper, newsreel, and film empire; in the twenties, Mayer and Hearst together acquired a radio license; the Warners had film, radio, entertainment, and music publishing connections; the film industry itself, with the transition to sound, both technologically and financially, related in a complex manner to radio. The creative interaction between radio and film is perfectly embodied in Orson Welles, who was also a key example of their political interaction.[112] This system of the media is always characterized by both an internal articulation of the role of the individual medium and by a hierarchy, within which, in the period examined, the cinema held the dominant position.

In her first article on cinema, Eleanor Roosevelt emphasizes the important function of cinema apart from entertainment: "Here is something which may be used to shape public opinion, to bring before a tremendously wide audience a great variety of facts and thoughts which can be a powerful imaginative stimulus."[113]

The Roosevelt administration decided never to use Hollywood cinema "to shape public opinion," but if we consider the government documentary and newsreel production in general, we must recognize the considerable presence of a New Deal filmic discourse. The American documentary filmmakers of the 1930s professed aesthetic values and had a professional training that was anti-Hollywoodian. Thus one might conclude that the government film production was anti-Hollywoodian in style and approach. But the New Deal also used the documentary image created by the newsreels that were distributed by the Hollywood studios. Therefore it is hard to draw a precise map of the New Deal film practices and establish its orientation in reference to Hollywood. And yet, such was Hollywood's domination of the geography of the world of imagination that it reached Washington, D.C., when Mr. Smith's going to Washington infused the postcard of the capital's monuments with ethical and symbolic values.

3

Cinema and
the New Deal

American cinema of the 1930s (traditionally defined as classical Hollywood cinema) played an important ideological and emotional role during the Depression and shared critical functions with the New Deal.[1] That is, both worked toward stabilizing the society and articulating a new Americanism. Through the elaboration of the Hays Code and the consequent adaptation of cinema's narrative and expressive system to its rules, Hollywood publicly assumed its ideological responsibility, proposing a "universal" vision of the world.

A Cross-Class Audience and Its Geography

According to a widely accredited hypothesis, elaborated by Margaret Thorp, 1930s cinema elected the middle class as its preferred audience because in those years people who were unemployed or penniless could not buy a movie ticket.[2] In fact, everyone went to the movies during the Depression. Cinema was recognized as a necessity by the Hoover administration, which, in the midst of the crisis, distributed food, clothing, and tickets to the movies.[3] These tickets kept the people off the streets and offered them refuge and comfort; the administration was offering, in a sense, *panem et circenses*. Owners of small theaters realized that the movies were the answer to the depression of the American housewife (before Woody Allen did, with *The Purple Rose of Cairo*); they gave away china sets or connected lotteries to the purchase of a ticket, aiming at the impoverished middle class, which needed material incentives to quiet its puritan sense of guilt over such "superfluous" consumption as the movies. The invention of the double feature, "two films for the price of one," during the crisis—an innovation that radically transformed the production and marketing structure of cinema—corresponded to this idea of "movies for everyone." The enormous number of tickets sold this way at a low cost did not generate the kind of profit the industry was most interested in; it drew its main profits from the first-run theaters. Nonetheless the industry took on the burden of this market, despite its modest income, probably because it considered it a social responsibility.[4] On the other side, movie patronage grew despite the hardship of depression. "Instead of exhibiting a psychology based on scarcity and necessity," Lary May suggests, "audiences approached popular culture with wishes for abundance."[5]

Like Franklin Roosevelt, the movies aimed at a large public, identified as "people" rather than "masses."[6] And, like Roosevelt, the movies in the 1930s enjoyed their greatest popularity with the less well-to-do classes. This is documented in a local analysis of 1935 moviegoers that reveals that the largest section belonged to the lower ranks.[7] In a new profile of the film consumer in the New Deal period, May confirms that, according to Gallup polls in the late thirties, audiences were centered in the urban bourgoisie but "now also included a large group with less income." But, he notes, "movie going increased among the 'new' ethnics from Southern and Eastern Europe between the age of 12 and 33, exactly the age when a new American identity was being formed for youths of immigrant background. . . . Blacks, Indians, and Mexicans were absent or segregated."[8] It is evident (as well as significant, and, in my argument, expected) that the transformations we have identified in the political constituency of the New Deal parallel the formation of film audiences in the 1930s.

The "lower classes," and especially the working class, had changed some of their traits between the 1920s and the 1930s. They were more Americanized, more fluent in English. They bought standardized products from the same chain stores. And they were all "listening to the same national commercial network radio like the *Jack Benny Program* and Major Bowes' *Original Amateur Hour* in place of the local programming that they were used to in the twenties and watching the same movies in theaters that were now owned by the Hollywood studio chains rather than frequenting the more intimate neighborhood theaters that they had previously preferred."[9]

The 1930s re-elaborated the relation between the lower strata and the movies, standardizing the film experience in many ways. The popular entertainment industry perfected its strategies toward both working-class and ethnic communities, which had always been an important section of its audience, and toward middle-class communities which it had already conquered in the 1920s. "The quest for a middle-class market," Richard Butsch notes, had "resulted in the absorption rather than the abandonment of the working-class audience."[10] The institution of a cross-class audience implied both a widening of the ideological spectrum and a more individualized attention toward social and ethnic groups. In this respect, the points of resemblance with the working of New Deal ideology and political practice are particularly marked.

In the 1930s American cinema broadened its audience to the maximum extent in an effort to appeal "to many classes and groups at the same time." Like other industries whose marketing approach was to encourage "consumers' identification with the upper class and its luxury in an effort to promote consumption as a value," the "entertainment industries in particular appealed to middle-class aspirations to upward mobility." The result was "not a class-neutral product or marketing approach but one 'with class'."[11]

The cross-class address involved two interacting cultural elements, Americanism and universalism. Nineteen-thirties Americanism is a key homogenizing factor. It was an attempt to reconcile in a comforting whole—one that could also boast mythical roots and powerful cultural traditions—many different projects, a plurality of Americanisms. Americanism is in fact the ideological jargon that holds together conservative and progressive ideas, democratic and nationalistic tendencies. In filmic terms it equates to Frank Capra and Louis B. Mayer, but also Orson Welles (the title of *Citizen Kane* was indeed American) and radical filmmakers, America First and the Communist party's "Twentieth-Century Americanism."

The same versatility is present in universalism, the trait of Hollywood classical cinema that conceals class and national cultural relations in the name of a cross-class message. Paradoxically, the simultaneous concealing of class and national traits ends up obscuring Americanism through its perfect assimilation in the Hollywood product, so American and so "classical" as to become a geographical abstraction—the nowhere land of dominant ideology.

In the 1930s Hollywood cinema selected as its preferred audience the middle-class—a bourgeoisie that was not completely conservative or exclusively WASP (given the important role of Catholics in the elaboration of the Hays Code). It was the provincial middle class. The versatility and the consequent ideological extensibility of American cinema arose from the dialectic between the bourgeois aspirations and lower-class inclinations. Hollywood films did not so much project a seamless band of dominant ideology as explore contradictions. Even after the Hays Code was written, the gangster was punished at the end of a picture that glorified his gestures and sexually transgressive behavior was chastised—but only after it was described in the most minute and seductive detail.

The audience for mass culture (and mass politics) in the 1930s was not homogeneous. It was fragmented. Socioeconomic instability "proletarized" large sectors of the middle class and amalgamated within mass culture the younger elements of the working class. Blacks in the South were physically segregated in film theaters, while marginal minorities with linguistic differences were culturally segregated by sound films. Even the localized tension between the majors and the small independent exhibitor does not allow us to think in terms of a smoothly operating homogeneous filmgoing experience. And there is still the little-studied phenomenon of the persistence of live entertainment within the urban movie palaces and rural areas where the film theater became the community meeting space.[12]

The profile of 1930s film audiences is too complex to project on the notion of the spectator of Hollywood classical cinema, as a mechanical textual implication of the studio system.[13] We should cast the spectator of Hollywood classical cinema, not only within the straightforward statistic data of film attendance, which reflects in impressive numbers the cinema's popularity in the 1930s, but also on a diversified map that charts fragmentations and differences.

The Modern Theater and National Distribution

In at least two ways Hollywood cinema performed a special national role in the 1930s: It re-elaborated the concept of Americanism as a mass culture, and as an industry, it moved toward a national organization. The two are interdependent, however, not only in economic terms: Americanism was the ideological justification of a new national organization of the socioeconomic structure. The rise of the modern theater was at "the forefront of a major expansion into new markets—a process," according to May, "that has to be seen as a powerful force of nationalization. When coupled with the fact that viewers often divided by class, region, or ethnicity now saw the same talking films, in similar moderne theatres across the country, the standardized moderne became the symbol of new common ties being forged across the country."[14] Changes in the site where movies were consumed in fact represents another key transformation of American cinema in the 1930s. The decadence of the exotic, extravagant, and luxurious movie palace gave way to comfortable, "democratic" modern theaters of small dimensions (and therefore lower operating costs) and better acoustics. The ornate and pretentious style of the extravagant movie palace was abandoned; balconies and boxes of "foreign taste" were eliminated. A modern look was adopted, incorporating materials like cement, formica, and steel. It recuperated the spirit of the American school of architecture in the construction of space, generating "an overall effect of coordination and dynamism." The theorist of this transformation, the architect Ben Schlanger, describes the change as simplification.

> In opposition to the vertical pilasters, towering ceilings, and soaring, ornamented columns characteristic of the lavish movie houses, the new struc-

ture should have a gradual simplification and omission of forms as they re-
cede to the rear of the auditorium: the forms used should have a strong
horizontal direction, instead of vertical emphasis, fastening the eye on the
screen, the focal point.[15]

This "horizontal direction" implied the elimination of class divisions in the
theater. In the modern film theater, "the division between art and life re-
ceded: the fan too was part of an integrated whole." Schlanger's modern
theater was functional to the project that characterized Hollywood classical cinema, tending to heighten the absorption of the viewer into the
screen.

This new type of theater sprang up everywhere, in the suburbs and in tiny
rural towns, adapting itself to the locality through the use of materials typical of the buildings in the area. The new theater even changed its name. Exotic names like Alhambra, Rialto, and Tivoli gave way to The Roosevelt, The
Lincoln, The Liberty—names that proclaimed Americanism. The nationalism expressed by this transformation was a movement at once backward and
forward; it was a reach back for historical roots and traditions, both local and
national, and it was a reach forward for a new identification between linear
and efficient design and American industrial products.

In the late 1920s some neighborhood theaters closed because they could
not afford the costly technology of sound and they could not adapt to changing demographics, to the middle-class movement to the suburbs and the new
dynamism cars created within the neighborhoods. Most neighborhood theaters, however, entered a chain management. Thus neighborhood movie going did not disappear in the 1930s, but it changed radically. The small independent theater became rarer and rarer: neighborhood theaters were taken
over by chain operations whose owners, both majors or big theater chains,
had the necessary capital to install sound to compete in the increasingly concentrated market. Therefore, as Cohen argues, "workers would still find theaters in their neighborhoods during the 1930s, but their ambience had become as standardized as the films on the screen." But the conditions of this
cultural consumption had changed.

> Even if local communities did not control the production of motion pic-
> tures during the 1920s, they still managed for a good part of the decade to
> influence how residents received them. The independent, neighborhood
> theater in that way resembled the neighborhood store, harmonizing stan-
> dardized products with local, particularly ethnic, culture. Both buffered
> the potential disorientation of mass culture by allowing patrons to con-
> sume within the intimacy of the community. Rather than disrupting the
> existing peer culture, the peer culture accommodated new products. In
> both cases, too, aggressive expansion by competing chain enterprises, not

community's abandonment of these local alternatives, undermined their viability in the years shortly before the depression.[16]

The configuration of the urban theater in the 1930s includes therefore at least three different aspects: the residual movie palace, either declining or becoming more of an inter-media outlet, with live performances, often by radio stars and orchestras; the neighborhood theater, and the new modern theater.

The sanitation and legitimation of the places of popular entertainment is a result of this reorganization of film exhibition in the 1930s. As Richard Butsch notes: "Working-class women first and then more affluent middle-class women and men had to be persuaded that certain public amusements were 'respectable.' . . . Movie exhibition [had] followed a . . . trajectory from male arcades to working-class family nickelodeon to middle-class movie palaces."[17] In this respect, reformism is not an exclusive of the middle class.

In addition to proposing the film theater as national/modern/urban, financial considerations motivated the film exhibition strategies as adopted in the 1930s. In a discussion of Warner Bros.' male stars of the 1930s, in *City Boys,* Sklar analyzes the sociocultural characters of the urban audiences, which expressed the "city boys," stressing the economic motivation for the productive and creative casting choice embodied by James Cagney and Humphrey Bogart: the studio wished "to maintain its special relation with the New York crowds, not only for sentimental and cultural reasons, but for the important revenues produced at the Strand and other New York theaters."[18] This socioeconomic geography of film exhibition was analyzed in the preparation of the *Paramount* case, because the majors held a monopolistic control of the market in specific areas and cities. In the case of Warner Bros., there is an evident relation between the geographic dislocation of its theaters, their socioethnic characteristics, and its film production. The Strand is the perfect example of a first-run theater catering to a working-class audience, which was both a key source of profits and a sensitive promotional outlet for the culturally diversified Warner Bros. genres.

Hollywood cinema translated the tension between "local" and "national" in its own workings by reorganizing the system of distribution, according to a national tendency of centralization.[19] By the end of the 1920s distribution was rationalized. The large production companies instituted thirty-two centers, called exchanges, which circulated prints of the films. The small production companies distributed their product (which was usually mediocre) through agencies, called States Rights, that worked mostly with small theaters, had modest investments in publicity, and were limited to local service. Because these two systems were mutually exclusive, the independent and local element gradually became identified with a low-quality product, while the majors were identified with "national" production and distribution.

Beginning in the second half of the 1930s the New York offices of the production companies organized the launch of a film, centralizing the publicity practices according to "scientific" criteria of entrepreneurship. Old "localized"—and, at times, gross—types of film exploitation were replaced with press campaigns and radio (i.e., national) promotion.[20] This erosion of the small exhibitor's role in film exploitation was clearly written into the booking contracts offered by the majors. As the block booking hearings revealed, these contracts, around 1935, began recording only the number of films in distribution, grouped in sections, somewhat, but not necessarily, related to their budgets (six A films, eight B films, etc.). These contracts discontinued the traditional practice of describing a film still in production by referring to stars or film genres. This new form of blind selling,[21] the climax of the studio system, brandished only the studio's name as a guarantee of success. Small exhibitors protested vehemently against this manifestation of distribution control by the majors; as expressed in the block booking hearings, their protests became part of a more general populist reaction or localized resistance to the gradual "nationalization" of the cultural and institutional life of the country.

During the same period the majors began promoting films with premieres in locales other than Broadway or Los Angeles; for example, the link to local history launched *Gone with the Wind* in Atlanta and *Knute Rockne, All American* in South Bend, Indiana. The movement toward national film promotion had both a centrifugal and a centripetal direction. In this it was similar to the dynamic process of cultural decentralization and federalization activated by the New Deal.

Ideological Functioning of Hollywood Classical Cinema

Aware of its social function, the cinema transformed the audience into a public, proposing itself not only as a product but also as a service. The modern film theater became "a vital part of community and civic live."[22] Hollywood cinema offered fun and education, deeply influencing the attitudes of the audience. By supplying spectators with models and suggestions, it promoted global images of society, the relations that took place in it, desirable ways of life, and a range of acceptable political choices.[23] Faced with the Depression and, later, the administration's experimental reformism, Hollywood films described "reality" in their own way, promoting adaptation to the new social demands of the citizen at a loss. They elaborated explanations and reassuring interpretations rooted in common sense, rather than explicit ideology. Films turned the real into narrative, simplifying it through the personaliza-

71

tion of social and ethical conflicts, filtering it through the rules of plot construction and the system of film genres. This choice corresponded to the American tendency, of puritan origin, to internalize social guilt, causing it to fall within the sphere of individual responsibility—a tendency that imputed dysfunctions not to the system but to the individual or to outside agents. If the causes of problems belonged to the realm of individual responsibility, then they were controllable, easier to cure, by returning to traditional virtues such as courage, faith, or personal initiative.[24]

Public and industry negotiated this public service of the movies through the elaboration of the Hays Code (see Chapter 4). It was a mediation between the paternalistic tendency of the reformers and an appropriation of a peculiar "public sphere" by the audience.[25]

Given its cross-class target audience and its technological changes, American cinema of this period was engaged in a dialectic of innovation and tradition that shaped its ideological contents, narrative plots, and expressive modes. Movies proposed new behaviors as well as new ways of "seeing" and "hearing" while they plunged into tradition. Literary traditions, for example, influenced narrative construction and inspired many literary adaptations.

With the adoption of sound and color, cinema performed an authentic sensory revolution. The decade of the thirties, as Warren Susman describes it, "was a most dramatic era of sound and sight. . . . It is impossible to recall the period without recourse to special sounds: the 'talkies,' the machine-gun precision of the dancing feet in Busby Berkeley's musical extravaganzas, the 'Big Bands,' the voices of Amos and Andy, to say nothing of the magic of Franklin Roosevelt's Fireside Addresses."[26] We could add to this list, the speed of Cagney's delivery of lines, the tempo of screwball comedy dialogue, the incredible rhythm of the Marx Brothers.

The visual dynamism and verbal hyperactivity of the films of the 1930s—excessive stimuli—can be interpreted as an expression of the restlessness and social confusion of the moment. With its camera movements, rapid editing, impressive images of transportation and communication, and focus on social mobility, this cinema proposed the idea of movement in every sense. Reacting with its own images and narrative modes to the paralysis that had blocked the country, it created, as Roosevelt had, an illusory movement, an expressive and narrative construction, that served, however, as shock therapy for the pathological stagnation of the system.

In this respect, musicals had an important ideological function. As a genre, they emphasized singing and dancing together, in synchronized movements. Their dynamism acted as an antidote to the Depression. They mobilized a physical response to the social paralysis, valorizing the chorus—"the people"—and productive organization.

Nineteen thirties Hollywood cinema also worked on an emotional level.

Frank Capra, a highly successful director of the period, understood the need for this, stating that his films tried "to elevate the individual, restoring the contact with his fears and emotions."[27] There is no doubt that the ritual of the Hollywood happy ending had a reassuring function. Even in the most problematic situations, this guaranteed happy ending arrived, but only after having run every route, every curve, and every conflict of the plot. If, on one hand, the predictability of the happy ending reassured viewers in advance, the unravelling of the plot kept their attention alive to the obstacles that had to be overcome and guaranteed the constant affirmation of individual activity and responsibility. (Roosevelt, too, understood the effectiveness of the happy ending; he always closed his speeches on a "high note," adding an optimistic message he usually wrote himself.)[28]

The sensuality associated with classical Hollywood cinema satisfied the spectator's erotic compulsions on several levels: overall, through the contemplation of the star and voyeurism, and in genre-specific ways such as the physicality of the musical, the allusiveness of sophisticated comedy, the sadism of gangster films, and the homosexual tension in adventure films. This sensuality assumes a particularly significant role in the thirties, if it is considered in the light of Theodore W. Adorno and Max Horkheimer's view that the "ability to take pleasure out of the emotional and sensual aspects of life" is an anti-authoritarian personality factor.[29]

The heterosexual young couple, protagonist of Hollywood classical cinema, does not encompass, however, all sentimental relations that figure prominently (or disappear) in the 1930s. The family is absent in the musicals: obviously golddiggers have no relatives, but even Shirley Temple is an orphan, or is living apart from one or both parents. The family is depicted with very negative connotations in the kept-women cycle, as significantly expressed by *Baby Face*–Barbara Stanwyck. The Depression creates a tension on the representation of the patriarchal family as a key element of socio-ideological order that either explodes in rapist violence (*The Story of Temple Drake*) or acquires incestuous tones, as in *Scarface*.

Strangely enough, the cultural type that elaborates a different male-female relationship is the city boy. "Here was a figure," writes Sklar, "strikingly different from the main masculine types in popular entertainment. The cowboy of the movies and the pulps generally kept his distance from women, even when he was not overtly antagonistic toward them. Then there were the charming and clever young heroes of the genteel middle-class background (juveniles or romantic leads, in stage lingo) who wooed and wed, and held their women in romantic thrall. The roughneck sissy neither escaped from women nor conquered them. His most important relation to women was not as lover but as son. . . . The formation of the city boy as a cultural type was fully interwoven with the broader social discourse about overprotective mothers and overdependent sons."[30] Urban environment, social unrest, and the Depression redefined family relations and psychological, emotional attachments, creating the roots for the solitary world of film noir.

In the 1930s, the "antagonist" of the city boy, and of his complex sentimental rapports, was the small-town boy, as embodied by Andy Hardy in the saccharine series produced by Louis B. Mayer—an all-American teenager, living in an all-American small town, within an idealized patriarchal family.

Hollywood cinema reconciled viewers with social reality *ideologically*, by confirming the nucleus of the American dream, *rationally*, by adapting behavior to social rules, and *emotionally*, by gratifying viewers in the erotic-affective sphere and supplying them with a mythical screen on which to project and rediscover themselves.

In those years the need for this type of ethical, ideological, and affective synthesis was brilliantly and effectively performed by Rooseveltian rhetoric as well as Hollywood cinema.[31]

Cinema and National Image

The promotion of the American way of life did not entail problem-free acceptance of mass consumption; it was instead an internalization of an ideal through the diffusion of gestures and the stars, through the propagation of living style and decor. People around the world came into contact with this way of life through the movie-going experience; in the United States the experience occurred in the new theaters of the 1930s—modern, comfortable, and "democratic." Hollywood cinema elaborated a new profile of Americanism by confirming individualism, pragmatism, and free enterprise initiative—the ideological pillars of the American system. (Most narrative studies of Hollywood classical cinema, though, connect the structure of the plot and the presence of these specific recurring elements not to an American idological system but to narratological abstractions.) Sound technology became another vehicle for Americanization. At the end of the 1920s, writers from the avant-garde New York theater and other literati from the East Coast, European political exiles, and journalists and popular authors all went to Hollywood, where the "talkies" needed agile pens for dialogues and plot construction. Joining the professional screenwriters, they formed a rank of "word workers" who created the language of sound movies. They produced a linguistic naturalism that standardized geographic and social gradations to make them comprehensible. This fundamental work on language undertaken by Hollywood cinema, alongside that of the radio, constructed the American way of speaking in the 1930s—a lingua franca that had infinite translations.[32]

Sound standardized movie culture and changed the atmosphere in the theater.

> No longer did the audience provide the spoken words, mediating between the film and the community as it commented and jeered. Now, movie actors talked directly to individuals in the audience, whose group affiliation received little reinforcement from the crowd, since with sound, audiences hushed all interjections. As one film historian has aptly phrased it, "The talking audience for silent pictures became a silent audience for talking pictures." Sound also helped chains banish the live entertainment that had previously framed feature films. Taped shorts distributed nationally replaced ethnic troupes and amateur talent shows in neighborhood theaters and even eliminated stage shows at all but the largest picture palaces.[33]

The wide diffusion of the literary adaptations constituted another element in the process of cultural homogenization. This cinema in search of legitimation and universality began translating great (and minor) literary works from every place and time, thus constructing the "library of the average American" and, through international distribution, constructing a kind of global library.

More narrowly, Hollywood cinema endeavored to reveal the workings of powerful institutions. Capra dedicated a series of films to the hero-citizen Smith-Deeds-Longfellow, and numerous films dramatized the work of the FBI; Warner Bros'. social films attributed miracle-working powers to federal authorities, and the newspaper pictures typically uncovered and uprooted corruption in the big city.[34] Also contributing to civic-historical acculturation were the biographical films dedicated to larger-than-life Americans from Abraham Lincoln to *Citizen Kane*, or historical films such as *Gone with the Wind*, which dramatized the deep wounds inflicted by civil war on American society in a great spectacle; or Capra's pictures, where heroes in moments of crisis visited historical monuments. This didactic form and hagiography reduced American history to simplistic lessons aimed at recent immigrants or established Americans searching for a return to a mythicized past innocence.[35]

The 1930s had seen an epocal mythological turnover: "The gangster for the first time surpassed the cowboy as a subject for Hollywood moviemakers." Sklar notes how cowboy and city boy, the 1930s urban male hero, "both embody a traditional dilemma for the American male—independence and isolation, on the one hand, attachement and responsibility on the other. The cowboy, however, was and remained fixed in the past. For the movie audiences of the 1930s, however, the city boy was a contemporary, one recognizable both in daily headlines and in daily life." But he was also "the product of genre and convention. . . . The formation and definition of the city boy came not only from dominant practice—both in ideology and commercial exploitation—but also from oppositional culture."[36]

The renewal of the star system advanced a new definition of American identity. The thirties saw the rise of stars and actors who evoked new ethnic and racial stereotypes, like Edward G. Robinson and Paul Muni, or new cultural types, like James Cagney, "the American hero, whom ordinary men and boys recognize as themselves" and "the first definitely metropolitan figure to become national." "Representing not a minority in action, but the action of the American majority,"[37] the semi-literate, lower-middle-class city boy Cagney had rural counterparts in James Stewart and Will Rogers. This trend to some degree was a rejection of the exotic and aristocratic foreign stars who had dominated the screen in the 1920s.

Although Brian Neve identifies Hollywood stars of the 1930s as prevalently WASP, he insists on the nationalistic function of the 1930s star system: "By presenting the primary WASP Hollywood stars as role models and generally down-playing ethnicity in the social rituals and practices portrayed on the screen, the cinema arguably played a key role in promoting and even defining a new national culture, at a time, in the late thirties, when more young 'ethnics,' low income and rural Americans were joining the urban middle classes in the cinemas."[38]

The rankings of the most popular stars of the 1930s point to the contradictions of the period. In the Depression era and during the first New Deal the most popular stars were Marie Dressler and Will Rogers,[39] two middle-aged, folksy figures who expressed a common-sense populism. Between 1935 and 1938 Shirley Temple and Clark Gable reigned, disconcerting the stereotypical heterosexual couple as the focal point of classical Hollywood cinema. Shirley Temple, all innocence, optimism, and vitality, had a bit of cunning and an adorable way of tap dancing out of the Depression, hand in hand with a benevolent parent figure. Gable embodied the American masculine stereotype, virile, but at the same time more in his element in lively action than with a woman in his arms. The family portrait of the Depression, embodied in two middle-aged actors, a little girl, a man of powerful build (the mythical image of Gable in *It Happened One Night*), and a President in a wheelchair was not truly reassuring.

The adult female stars of the 1930s, Bette Davis or Joan Crawford, were women who wore tailleurs and were not out of place in an office or in a middle-class home. "Earthy" alternatives to the vamps in languid satin, the suffragettes, and the flappers of the twenties, they were able to take care of themselves, both as stars and as film characters.[40]

According to Lary May, in 1932 exhibitors had complained about exotic productions geared to "arty and aristocratic critics" and stars who spoke

"Broadway English," because "international picture stars as known during the silent days" turned fans away.[41]

Thus, the American cinema of the 1930s represented an America of individual, regional, and class differences, but it also participated in a complex process of cultural, linguistic, and ideological homogenization.

The Newsreels

According to Roosevelt's press secretary, Stephen Early, former editor of Paramount newsreels, "The newsreel brings to a modern world a truer picture of itself, and of its people, than any other agency heretofore known to mankind." Roosevelt himself admitted being "a constant and interested observer of them" and pointed out that "their function had become more and more important."[42] For FDR and his staff the newsreels represented a privileged vehicle of information, especially with the expanded expressive and informative power acquired through the addition of sound.

Five newsreels, all controlled by the majors, ran regularly.[43] *Fox Movietone News,* the largest, had at its disposal numerous foreign posts and was able to record sound directly; Hearst's *Metrotone News* (later *News of the Day*) was distributed by MGM beginning in 1927; *Paramount News* was famous for its "scoops"; the operations of *Universal News* were "penny-pinching" but imaginative, *Pathé News* served the independent market until it was absorbed by RKO.

In the thirties the newsreels were an autonomous communication format, popular to the point that some theaters screened nothing else. Political figures were a big draw. Roosevelt, in particular was "the greatest single attraction."

> Announcement of his fireside chats, which were always filmed, brought hundreds of patrons to the theater. Anti–New Dealers came to hiss. The vigorous years of the New Deal under FDR and the rise of Mussolini, Hitler, Stalin and Chang Kai-shek aroused great interest in the newsreels. Each had his adherents in the city, who flocked to the Embassy Theater when their favorite was on the screen.[44]

The majors distributed pre-packaged programs of newsreels, films, and "shorts" to theater owners in blocks, excluding the independents from the market.

As a spectacularized, popular, highly visual form of journalism, newsreels transformed political personalities into celebrities. They carefully avoided politics, social issues, and other controversial topics that could call for commentary or interpretation. They transformed news into curiosities, concentrating on spectacular achievements or catastrophes, sensational crime stories (the capture of gangsters was a popular story), exotic locales, and mildly titillating fashion parades—that is, the visually dynamic. The documentary movement of the left tried to use the newsreel to provide counter-information and sometimes "borrowed" from "regular" newsreelmen footage shot at strikes or protest marches, which the newsreels almost never used.[45] The most famous of the 1930s newsreels, *The March of Time*, adopted a different stance. By being informative and taking a position, it bordered on being partisan and expressed its point of view mostly in the voice-over narration. But a good part of *The March of Time* was made of re-enacted scenes, shot in a studio, with actors and impersonators. It thus maintained a fairly indirect relationship to reality, to the point that its status as information would appear dubious to a contemporary eye.[46]

The newsreels eagerly offered themselves to Roosevelt throughout his presidency. In March 1933 Carl Laemmle of Universal assured the President that "the Universal Newsreel is at your disposal at any and all times to give the public by way of the motion picture screen any message you may care to deliver. While ordinarily our newsreel is devoted strictly to news events, I am ready to follow your precedent by breaking any precedents which stand in the way of action toward national recovery. While the printed word is effective the talking motion picture is more so and our newsreel is ever and always at your command."[47]

On the occasion of the first fireside chat, Early wired the newsreels requesting that the event be "released in full at earliest possible moment," because "any delay in release nullifies purpose of statement."[48]

The newsreels covered the inauguration with a colossal mobilization. They prepared a special one-reel edition (the length of the entire issue), accompanied, in the distribution phase, by illustrated material useful to publicize the event in the theaters. The occasion was doubly memorable: the country had high hopes for new leadership and these were the first sound newsreels to document a presidential inauguration.[49] But from the point of view of operations, the same conventional journalistic rules applied to newsreels cameramen as to photographers: no exclusives, and they all shot together and when the President was ready.

As in other media, Early was careful not to saturate the screen with the newsreel image of Roosevelt: he appeared in them roughly every two weeks. The press secretary's specific competence in the area allowed him to use this medium to the maximum of its potential. He took a somewhat directorial role. He understood the needs of the cameramen, assisted their activities, and was able to suggest how to shoot a scene.[50] His work at *Paramount News* had given him a network of personal contacts, which might be the reason that Early's well-known impartiality was less rigid in this area. In certain cases, the press secretary favored the newsreel for which he had worked, considering its cameramen "the President's personal crew," and supplying them with precious information on the President's movements. "In exchange," *Paramount News* donated to the President a copy of every issue in which he appeared.[51]

From an analysis of the *Universal News* issued during the first two terms of Roosevelt's presidency, the representation of the President's more "personal and multicolored" aspects dominated: he was shown mostly on trips (34 percent), or in nonpolitical ceremonies (30 percent); following these, were his official speeches (24 percent). The representation of FDR in his role as a politician and social reformer was almost absent. "The newsreel presented Roosevelt as a vigorous and active president," but rarely did they include his statements in the sound track, preferring instead to emphasize, in the voice-off commentary, "geography, personality and human interest."[52]

Close analysis of the "Roosevelt effect"[53] in *Universal Newsreel* coverage of FDR confirms that it depended on the vitality of his gestures and the expressivity of his face in oratory situations. With the exception of his acceptance speech for the candidacy in 1932, in which he was forced to shout, he generally maintained a strong and clear but not "thundering" voice. He underlined the key word with particular modulation, using dramatic crescendos in the moments of major impact and accompanying his speech with head and arm movements, which came across as forceful but never discomposed, as little shudders of controlled energy. In the first years of the presidency, when standing, he usually moved his left arm, because he used the other hand to hold onto the podium. He used voice and body to interpret the message: force, reassurance, and faith came across in the words and in the performance.

The nonpolitical Roosevelt was also carefully presented. Next to the convincing political orator was the lovable and jocular FDR, who knew how to tell jokes with consummate style. In one of the newsreels, for example, he accused the Republicans of having attacked not only him but his family—his wife and children and even his dog, Fala, which, he admonished, was a scotty and therefore hot-blooded. In another, he said to the students at Chapel Hill College: "They told you that for breakfast I have a dish of grilled millionaire—pause for laughter—Instead I am a mild person, a firm believer in the capitalistic system and in scrambled eggs for breakfast." He adopted an Irish accent for a speech at a Democratic banquet and playfully asked, "Which one should I break?" as he stared into the camera before throwing the first baseball of the season. Another highly effective communicative element was his frank, hearty laugh. He would throw back his head in complete abandon, whether in response to a joke by Will Rogers at Olympic Stadium in 1932 or in a delayed reaction to his own humor in an exchange of quips with Vice President Garner in the 1940 electoral campaign.

In public appearances, FDR's ambulatory problems were masked in a variety of ways. In the early days of the presidency he was shown walking for short stretches, but usually he appeared, *in medias res,* on the arm of his son James or discreetly leaning on a support with a hand often out of frame. Grouping and composition were organized to distract attention from his support.[54]

In the film presentation of the fireside chats, he was seen sitting at his famous desk or in another strongly evocative setting, such as literally at fireside, with his wife beside him knitting and his mother listening attentively, or in a close-up with a model ship in the background. This image was rich in subliminal information, reminding viewers of Roosevelt's passion for the sea and for boats and of his experience as assistant secretary of the navy, and suggesting movement in the sense of adventure and liberty evoked by the sea. This movement by association enhanced the mobility of the President's face and upper body.

In numerous newsreels Roosevelt appeared in a car, sometimes at the wheel, more frequently in the back seat of a convertible. The car was surrounded by people or tightly framed, with some privileged listeners to represent the onlookers in the shot, and with the President's elbow and his entire upper body protruding from the window, projected toward the listeners. The car connoted movement and comfort, transforming the implicit wheelchair into an instrument that allowed for contact with the people and with the surroundings. When Roosevelt the candidate gave an extemporaneous political speech to a huge crowd from the back platform of a train the imagery evoked by this brief stop on a journey was of movement across the country and among the people.

Roosevelt's clothing was carefully selected to eliminate the risk of typecasting and avoid fixing his image in a single social group or class. His hats varied from sailor berets to silk toppers. He wore four-in-hands and bow ties. He might wear a dark suit and a white carnation in his lapel, or even appear in shirt sleeves.

FDR's image ended up amidst the spectacular events, humorous scenes, and various "actualities" typical of the American newsreels of the period. In 1933, for example, he appeared in newsreel stories about the earthquake in California, the Senate Committee interrogation of J. P. Morgan, the transoceanic flight by the Italian pilot Italo Balbo, and the repeal of the 18th Amendment. The newsreels' tendency to avoid polemics and political factiousness worked positively for him, placing him above all parts and emphasizing his presidential leadership, without questioning the merits of his policies and programs. They contributed enormously to the creation of the "Roosevelt effect," that sense of reassurance and consequent social control exercised by the President mostly through his image and voice.

Because the newsreels were structurally contiguous to the narrative films that followed them in the program, and because they too provided entertainment, dynamism, adventure, and an emphasis on personality and performance, in the end they rendered FDR analogous to a movie star.

During the hearings on block booking, Charles Pettijohn upheld the value of the newsreels and reinforced the idea of the President as celebrity.

> They picture the news. The President bathing in a pool—I remember that picture. I do not know that you could call that politics, but the people are interested in what their President is doing. . . . In pictures there are certain men that just happen to click. . . . As to politics—the newsreels will reach approximately 65 to 70 million people, and that would represent an enormous circulation for any newspaper. . . . The newsreels have not taken sides in politics.[55]

Other than newsreels or compilations such as *The Man of the Hour* and *The Fighting President* (which was produced by Universal in 1933 and later donated to the White House), Roosevelt's filmic image is fragmented, because the use of his image was prohibited in narrative or promotional films. In October 1936, *The March of Time* shot a clip of FDR, "which gave close descriptive detail of the Presidency."[56]

In support of the 1936 Republican Presidential campaign, the Sentinels of the Republic produced a series of satirical animated cartoons portraying the President "as a boy-like figure astride the Democratic Donkey," and as "the driver of a broken-down fire engine."[57] One cartoon "shows what happens when a fire starts in Uncle Sam's farmhouse. The New Deal Fire Company, headed by President Roosevelt and composed of 'brain trusters,' answers the alarm" and does "everything imaginable" except put the fire out. Another short represents the New Deal debt as "a chain of dollar bills [extending] seven times to the moon and back." These controversial shorts received wide publicity in the anti–New Deal press and even logistical support from the film industry (the sound was recorded in the Fox Movietone studios),[58] but when the "Sentinels of the Republic tried to distribute them in the theaters, they encountered resistance from the film industry and local censors. The state of Ohio banned the cartoon *Amateur Fire Brigade* because it "encouraged disrespect for the President of the United States," and film industry representatives said they believed "that the screen should not be used for personal attacks," and that they intended to make sure that "both sides would be given their say."

American newsreels never became a privileged channel of rhetoric for the New Deal as they did for the government in fascist Italy. But they did perform a crucial role in the construction of FDR's popularity and celebrity. At the end of the 1930s, the international crisis strengthened the political and communicative function of newsreels enlarging the range of their content to document the European situation and open a breach in isolationist American public opinion.

The New Deal's Film Production

In 1908 some federal departments began producing educational documentaries and audiovisual materials.[59] When the crisis in White House–press relations developed in the mid-thirties, the administration decided to use the film medium in a more direct and "aggressive" way. First to move in this direction were the Works Progress Administration (WPA) and the Resettlement Administration (RA), two of the more innovative New Deal agencies, led by two major, dynamic New Deal personalities, Harry Hopkins and Rexford Tugwell.[60]

Harry Hopkins was FDR's right-hand man, always on the front line. He moved from directing the WPA to acting as the President's personal representative on the international scene during the war. The WPA administered public funds to fight unemployment. Together with the National Recovery Administration (NRA), it was the most experimental (and, as a consequence, the most criticized) federal agency; it included cultural programs such as the "Writers Project," the "Federal Theater," and the "Federal Art Project," which hired unemployed writers, painters, actors, and artists to paint murals in public buildings, write tourist-historical guides for each state, produce shows such as the *Living Newspaper,* and so forth.[61]

Rexford Tugwell, a professor of economics at Columbia University and an expert in agriculture, was a key member of the Brain Trust and the theorist of "government planning," that is, of the economic policy of the first New Deal.

Hopkins and Tugwell chose two different informative strategies, but both surpassed Early in the access and use of the media. In 1934 the WPA produced *Hands,* a documentary by Ralph Steiner and Willard Van Dyke that "concentrated on hands: idle hands, hands at work, and finally hands putting earnings (from government relief projects) back into circulation."[62] Made by radical filmmakers of the Film and Photo League, the film was thus associated with their expression of an anti-Hollywood culture and affinity for European (including Soviet) avant-garde cinema as well as with the world of New York photography and theater.[63] This relationship between New Dealers and radicals grew out of an authentic ideological compatibility and a similar understanding of film's instrumentality. But the relationship unleashed criticism, especially from those who resented the use of federal funds, allocated as subsidies, to cover the full cost of film production; and, worse yet, "artistic" films directed by "leftists."

Hopkins also promoted his reform programs through other film projects. For example, he contracted with Pathé "for a series of New Deal newsreels designed to feature the successes and triumphs of the Roosevelt administration," another initiative that stirred up criticism as "propaganda . . . paid for out of relief funds."[64] Reflecting the film industry's resentment of government intrusion, the *Motion Picture Herald* carried the headline "WPA Setting Out to Buy Way to Theater Public" over a story about the Pathé contract providing for the distribution of a monthly issue of this WPA newsreel.[65] Indeed, government films were hindered by limited circulation, but the hostility provoked by the New Deal's employment of a great many intellectuals and artists hampered the WPA's efforts to gain greater public access. Criticism was so harsh in an election year that the Pathé-WPA newsreels were not distributed.[66]

Tugwell, having gradually lost his power in the Brain Trust, was appointed head of the RA, a federal office that dealt with the resettlement of farmers and sharecroppers forced to abandon the Dust Bowl area. The RA's sphere of action was limited: it operated on the margins of big agriculture, and it represented, not large organized groups, but poor farming families deprived of their populist rebel spirit by the ecological disaster that had undermined the sense of community. The RA's function was simultaneously ideological and economic, in that it provided for the reorganization of small agriculture, transferring entire families to more productive zones, modifying cultivation and culture in the process. "So long as hundreds of farm families live in ignorance and destitution," Tugwell argued, "they will continue to act as a drag upon the rural communities in which they live, just as city slums exert a downward pull upon the culture and moral standards of metropolitan centers."[67] The RA had to explain the land and its problems to the people in the cities,[68] and Tugwell was perfectly suited to the job. He embodied the New Dealist mediation between city and countryside. His economic and ideological experiments involved modern agricultural methods that respected the ecological system and efforts to integrate a neopopulist spirit of solidarity, typical of the small town, with the entrepreneurship of the city and of the modern market system.

From its institution, the RA showed an interest in documentary, activating a "photo unit" that included Walker Evans, Dorothea Lange, Ben Shahn and others. These photographers traveled around the country documenting natural as well as economic and social disaster. Their pictures of the damage caused by sandstorms in the Dust Bowl and of the dry and suffering faces of impoverished sharecroppers appeared in photographic exhibits and books like *You Have Seen Their Faces* or *Let Us Now Praise Famous Men*.

Roosevelt returned repeatedly to the theme of the land. In 1933 he created the Civilian Conservation Corps (CCC), a kind of guardian of the ecology. In a famous fireside chat in 1936 he described the desertification of the prairies he had seen on a visit to the Great Plains. In the speech, FDR equated the Dust Bowl with the Depression, thus transforming the New Deal into the saving agent of the "American land."[69] With the image of the violated earth and the myth of the garden that (re)flowers in the desert Roosevelt conjured an ideological background for the RA's activities.

The Plow That Broke the Plains and The River

The RA-produced documentaries, *The Plow That Broke the Plains* and *The River*, received both public and critical acclaim but also incurred criticism as federal propaganda. Tugwell did not initiate these pictures, but he responded to a proposal from Pare Lorentz, journalist, film critic, and New Dealer, who fervently believed that a documentary should be "good enough technically to bear comparison with commercial films and entertaining enough to draw an audience."[70] Lorentz wanted to make a film on the Dust Bowl. After collecting materials and attempting unsuccessfully to convince Hollywood to finance the project, he presented his idea to the RA.[71] Tugwell shared Lorentz's interest in well-made documentaries and in the problems of soil conservation, and in June 1935 the RA took on the project. Lorentz went straight to work, with radical filmmakers Paul Strand, Leo Hurwitz, and Ralph Steiner from the Film and Photo League. Despite ideological differences, the lack of a final script, and trouble during the on-location shooting from Texas to Montana, the filming was completed.[72] But then Lorentz encountered considerable resistance from Hollywood when he tried to find stock footage for the historical section. Director King Vidor succeeded in breaching the opposing front of the studios and obtained these materials for Lorentz. Hollywood unwillingly collaborated perhaps because the government aired the threat of considering this behavior of the industry as a manifestation of its monopolistic tendencies, which were at that very moment under the strict surveillance of the Justice Department.

The strength of *Plow that Broke the Plains* is in its soundtrack, composed by Virgil Thompson, its poetic and informative commentary (written by Lorentz himself), and its dry images, in the style of RA photography. The arrival of the Oakies at a federal camp in California comes across as a "tacked on" ending, in marked contrast to the gloomy sense of collective guilt expressed by this "melodrama of nature."[73]

The Plow that Broke the Plains was an unusually interesting product for being a government documentary, but this did not help Lorentz find distribution for it. The majors declined with the excuses that the film was too long for a short, too short for a feature film, and too easy a target for criticism as government propaganda. *The Plow* was distributed by the RA to the traditional circuit of socioeducational centers and federal agencies, to rented theaters, and to small theater chains in the midwest that offered their facilities at no charge.[74] The film enjoyed notable success, to the point that FDR would have sent it to Congress as a "presidential message" if the Capitol had had adequate screening facilities.[75]

Despite the specific political criticism and the absorption of the RA into the Department of Agriculture, Tugwell supported Lorentz's proposal for a film on the Mississippi, to be titled *The River.* Lorentz gathered facts about the problems of deforestation and flooding from a WPA report on the Mississippi valley and transformed the dry bureaucratic-political language of the report—"We cannot plan for water unless we also consider the relevant problem of the land. We cannot plan for water and land unless we plan for the whole people"—into poetry—:"But you cannot plan for water unless you plan for land. . . . But you cannot plan for water and land unless you plan for people." This phrase becomes a leit motif in the film's commentary. Like its theme, *The River*'s rhetorical structure is typical of New Deal cultural praxis for the manner in which it tapped information and drew inspiration from various discursive strategies. Virgil Thompson's musical score fused popular and folk themes. Lorentz's script drew from an article on floods he had written for *McCall's,* from the WPA report, and from FDR's fireside chat on the Dust Bowl. Its Whitmanesque lists of trees, cities, and rivers created an intermittent and majestic movement, like a river flowing.[76]

The film was shot by the Woodward brothers, Willard Van Dyke, and Floyd Crosby (the cameraman of Murnau-Flaherty's *Tabu*) and edited by Lloyd Nosler, a Hollywood professional who had worked for King Vidor. Visually interesting, *The River* could be seen as an American appropriation of Soviet intellectual montage and frame composition. Actually the expressive choices of this film likened it to the British documentary school of Grierson and to Soviet cinema, more than to the style of *The March of Time,* the American documentary format par excellence in the 1930s. This production established a contact between the more politically committed segment of Hollywood and the radical filmmakers, a contact mediated by the New Dealers.

The sound brought together a multiplicity of voices and variety of usages. The music integrated the redundant poetic rhythm of the off-screen narration. The fusion of the poetic phrasing with the ostentatious narrational tone (the bureaucratic terminology, the radio announcements, etc.) was more than "informative": it called attention to itself. As with the text for photography books, the commentary imposed itself on the harsh images, authoritatively interpreting them for the spectator. A similarly manipulative editing strategy oscillated between rhythmic and intellectual montage. This mediation of a reality so in conflict with the public's nostalgic desires could not be done except by melodramatic emphasis, a work of persuasion. But, given its depressing tone, the film did not come across as an obvious act of government propaganda. Yet, its formal operations implicitly figure the off-screen presence of an authorial agency, which, while "mediating" the reality represented, indicated the need for an exterior (i.e., federal) intervention.

When Roosevelt saw the film, he said, "Magnificent! What can I do to help?" When Lorentz had explained the problems this type of cinema encountered in distribution and proposed that the government set up a documentary production program,[77] the President turned to Tom Corcoran, a young neo-populist and an important figure in the second New Deal, who immediately put pressure on Hollywood. He threatened antimonopolistic action if the industry continued to hinder the production of federal films. Paramount, one of the majors being investigated for monopolistic trade practices and the producer, at the same time, of the newsreel closest to the White House, reluctantly agreed to distribute *The River.*

The U.S. Film Service

In September 1938 the Roosevelt administration set up the U.S. Film Service, headed by Pare Lorentz, to coordinate the various cinematic projects of the federal agencies. Among the projects which the service intended to produce were two documentaries by Lorentz himself. The first, *Ecce Homo,* about unemployment, was never finished, despite later efforts by RKO. The second, *The Fight for Life,* is about medical assistance during pregnancy. In this film Lorentz broke away from the earlier forms by using professional actors and adopting the aesthetics of reenactment typical of *The March of Time.* The tone, like that of *The Plow* and *The River,* is gloomy. *The Fight for Life* presents a struggle against death rather than the affirmation of life implicit in the title.

The U.S. Film Service entrusted two major documentary filmmakers, Robert Flaherty and Joris Ivens, with the task of making films with rural themes. Flaherty's film was originally an Agricultural Adjustment Administration (AAA) project, intended to dramatize the need for conservation of national resources and stabilization of agricultural prices. Where Lorentz's editing often calls attention to itself, *The Land* depends on a slower rhythm and a less "intellectual" organization. The photography does not approach the land as primitive or exotic nature (as in Flaherty's previous films, *Nanook* and *Man of Aran*); it instead continues the realist photographic tradition of Evans and Lange. In its lean images, *The Land* dramatically portrays soil erosion, the social and ecological disaster of the Dust Bowl, and the hard life of the rural worker. At the center of the film's narrative is the figure of the migrant worker, the synthesis of the unemployed, the hobo, and the farmer betrayed by his land, the synthesis of rural depression. But history passed it by; *The Land* was finished at the start of the war and was not distributed.

Ivens's *The Power and the Land* is remarkably less poetic than the other New Deal rural films. From the outset, it constituted itself as a much more direct propaganda project in support of the Rural Electrification Administration. The film shows how a family that decided to participate in the federal electrification project ("kilowatts that never get tired") improved its standard of living, but the happy ending seems out of synch with the lean reportage on living conditions in the initial sequences. This documentary's more detached tone, less bitter or elegiac than the others, perhaps owes to the fact that Ivens was Dutch (and more distant from the reality he was describing), and that the film promoted a specific federal agency; still, it is far from being a straight promotional message.

The U.S. Film Service had a relatively brief life span. In 1939, caught up in political backlash and mounting international tension, it was dismantled, along with the RA. The official justification was waste and unauthorized use of public funds. Actually, neither agency could withstand the political controversy in which it was immersed, one for its "propagandistic" function, the other for its attempt to modify marginal agriculture.

We could associate another interesting text to these U.S. Film Service documentaries: *The City,* derived from one of Pare Lorentz's projects about Rexford Tugwell's plan for the Greenbelt Towns. It was directed by Van Dyke and Steiner for the American Institute of City Planners and the Carnegie Foundation, with the addition of a written commentary by Lewis Mumford. In this film, human decay and the standardization and unhealthiness of metropolitan life are shown in opposition to the serene life of a small suburban town, the Greenbelt Town. As in other documentaries by Lorentz, the most powerful impact resides in the polemic metropolitan section, which depicts the horrors of mass production—assembly lines that include even meals at robotic cafeterias—and the dangers of chaotic traffic, with dry, ironic images and Soviet reminiscences in the editing. The final series of idyllic scenes of healthy, happy children playing in Greenbelt Town seems too brightly optimistic compared with earlier sequences.

The discord between harsh representation of reality and optimistic happy ending that recurs in these films may be imputed to Lorentz's personality: his strength was in polemics and description, not in propaganda. The discord was also connected to the ideological tension between radical filmmakers and New Dealers, to their divergent analysis of what was wrong with society, and consequently, their very generic agreement on the possible explanations and "cures."

Washington's Film Production and Hollywood Cinema

The New Deal venture into the terrain of film production was a critical and aesthetic success but provoked great resistance from the film industry and the political establishment. The idea that the "most powerful weapon," the cinema—though, in the documentary, in a minor version—could be at the service of the administration disturbed too many opposing forces. The analysis of the films created by Pare Lorentz or produced by the U.S. Film Service reveals that they were anything but "publicity," given their desperate tone and the catastrophic anxiety that pervaded them. These documentaries strangely resemble the commercial production by great interpreters of the American reality of the 1930s, Frank Capra and Warner Bros., with its social films: a progression toward catastrophe followed by an optimistic ending, tacked on in a notably implausible way. I find it ironic that the government documentary production program failed because of the presence of these happy endings, which cast the administration in the role of deus ex machina. Compared to the negative emotions evoked by the documentary representation of problems, the final promotional message in the happy endings was indeed ineffective.

The New Deal screen representation of the land was neither idyllic nor romantic. It figured the fatigue and desperation produced by an imperialist fencing-in of the frontier myth. The documentaries "reported" that the American dream of transforming the forest into a garden had become a perverse fable, a nightmare where man did not live in harmony with his surroundings. They did not differentiate the New Deal countryside from the city as a place of healthy and beauty. Instead these documentaries presented the land as desolate as, if not more so than, the metropolis. It had been reduced to misery by a selfish financial system that had deprived it of its resources. This was not a land to return to. It was a land to save.

A neopopulist mentality could perhaps tolerate the image of a city in ruins, for that equated with its being a place of corruption and standardization, but images of an extremely depressed rural America were much more unsettling. Something had to be done to save the land because the land was America itself. Most of all, it was necessary to recognize the interdependence of the city and the countryside. In the fireside chat on the Dust Bowl FDR spoke eloquently of the dire consequences of large numbers of farmers migrating the cities.

> If, for example, in some local area the water table continues to drop and the top soil to blow away, the land value will disappear with the water and the soil. People on the farms will drift into the nearby cities; the cities will have no farm trade and the workers in the city factories and stores will have no jobs. Property values in the city will decline. . . .
>
> The very existence of the men and women working in the clothing factories of New York, making clothes worn by farmers and their families; of the workers in the steel mills in Pittsburg, in the automobile factories of Detroit, in the harvester factories of Illinois, depend upon the farmers' ability to purchase the commodities they produce. In the same way it is the purchasing power of the workers in the factories in the cities that enables

them and their wives and children to eat more beef, more pork, more wheat, more corn, more fruit and more dairy products, and to buy more clothing made from cotton, wool and leather. In a physical and a property sense, as well as in a spiritual sense, we are members one of another.[78]

In *Bottlenecks of Business*, Thurman Arnold also considered the unbalanced relationship between agricultural economy and consumption, emphasizing the need to reorganize distribution in order to avoid destroying harvests to maintain market prices, while in the city and in the countryside people were starving.[79] Social interdependence and rationalization of the productive system formed the ideological nucleus of these films. Like the New Deal, the films denounced liberalist economy, blaming it for the ecological disaster, but their weak conviction "translated" the inconclusiveness of the New Deal agricultural reforms that only succeeded in attenuating rather than ending the crisis.

Lorentz's films and those of the U.S. Film Service chose as their protagonist the forgotten man, symbolized by the suffering and authentic face of the sleeping boy, who, in *The Land*, continues to move his hands as if hulling the cotton, even in his sleep. Wrinkled faces and torn clothing fix themselves on the film and in the memory, like archetypes of that "one-third of a Nation, ill-nourished, ill-clad, [and] ill-housed" FDR described in his famous fireside chat on March 9, 1937. These documentaries restored to the land, at the same time, myth and history. On one side they supplied socioeconomic explanations for a disaster of biblical proportions, like the Dust Bowl; on the other, they represented the landscape of the prairie—*the* mythical American space—in its real, eroded, deserted image, with the evidence of an implacable photography.

The New Deal rural films contain different ideological stratifications, as they were neither simple government propaganda nor a purely populist nostalgic call for a return to the values of Jeffersonian democracy. Rather, they proposed an impossible synthesis between populism and federalism, and between populism and the frontier. They expressed this particular form of populism through the grievances against the system, the choice of an underdog social strata as protagonist, the extension of the spirit of good neighbors to collaboration with the government, love of the land, trust in the farmer, and above all, through the ideological assumption of the operation itself, that is, a diffused, uncentralized democratic process of education and information through film. The "federalist" elements reside in their production, in their being government-financed and offering active promotion of federal projects (even if cannot be said that the government proposed its candidacy for the role of protagonist in the action). From the frontier spirit, they recover the myth of a perennial beginning, the need to begin all over again, to discard useless traditions and embrace new solutions, in order to bring back the garden in the desolate land of the Dust Bowl.

The story of the New Deal film production is inscribed in the space where the documentary spirit and Americanism meet, because of the reciprocal desire to inform and to know, conjugating realism and social commitment, instituting a collective enunciation and a circular communicative process in which America is simultaneously the source and the destination of the message. It is a story that brings together for the first time in American cultural history, populism and patriotism, as messages and activities of the New Deal.

The New Deal documentary juxtaposed itself to Hollywood in its manifest social commitment, assuming the responsibility of showing Depression America to Americans. In this role it substituted for Hollywood cinema, which reacted only indirectly to this reality, not so much because the film industry decided to hide the destabilized social situation, but because it considered it depressing, hardly reconcilable with the optimism necessary for recovery.[80]

At least in principle, these documentaries presented themselves as anti-Hollywood also on the expressive level, even if the presence of a dramatic structure was more prominent than in other national documentary experiences. They tried to blend the lesson of the avant-garde, that is, the attention for composition and framing and the inclination toward associative montage, with Soviet aesthetics, with the frequenting of contiguous traditions of American culture of the 1930s, that is, photography and realist literature.

The federal film production of the thirties proposed a new productive model. Radical filmmakers had long been interested in developing alternative and independent forms of film production, structurally and aesthetically different from Hollywood's. With rare exceptions, they did not succeed in making this aspiration concrete because of the difficulties encountered by noncommercial production before the availability of more agile and economic formats, such as sixteen-millimeter film. Government film production functioned therefore as an alternative to Hollywood, allowing these filmmakers to mature in the field. At a more immediate level, the Roosevelt administration, with its patronage, guaranteed the survival of these groups of filmmakers.

Hollywood considered the government's intrusion in film production a dangerous form of competition. This accusation seems ridiculous today, but it was even argued by Will Hays in his autobiography.[81]

In the background one can always discern Hollywood, the great antagonist, reversed model on the basis of which the New Deal documentaries were produced; a materially obstructive presence that hindered the production of these films. Yet Hollywood in the 1930s is not a fortress, castled in defense. On the contrary, it appears as a half-open door, manifesting a timid availability toward both political and aesthetic experiments—an availability evidenced, among other things, by Sergej Eisenstein's offer to make a film at Paramount and by King Vidor's collaboration with Lorentz and by the fervent labor and political activity of directors, actors, and screenwriters.

In those years, Hollywood cinema assumed a different mission, a different form of social responsibility, which prevalently excluded the automatic reflection of reality and paternalistic educational projects. It proposed instead a cathartic evasion, an itinerary that moved away from the difficult life in the streets into the comfortable space of the studios—an itinerary emblematically scoured by Preston Sturges in *Sullivan's Travels.*

Hollywood's New Deal

A New Deal message has been identified in many sociological readings of the American cinema of the thirties. As much as I agree with Andrew Bergman's interpretations of the film genres of the Depression, and with Nick Roddick's description of Warner Bros. film production in the 1930s, my object here is not to produce another social and historical analysis of American films but to investigate through historical documentation the presence of FDR and the New Deal in Hollywood productions.

Hollywood reacted negatively to the administration's documentary adventure, perhaps because since 1933, it had at times proposed to put its own screens at the service of the New Deal and had repeatedly asked to use the image of FDR in its fiction films. In both cases it had received negative responses from Early. The press secretary's stand on the subject was firm: the administration could not officially back film messages or projects or permit the use of the image of the President in a narrative context or in a commercially sponsored film.

Soon after Roosevelt's inauguration, messages began to arrive at the White House that caused the administration to worry about the formation of antagonistic forces in Hollywood. Given the well-known Republican affiliation of most film executives, it was a valid concern. For example, Democratic senator Joseph Robinson warned the President's close adviser Louis Howe:

> I am advised that a subtle campaign is being started through the media of
> moving pictures designed to render the Administration unpopular. Lines
> and pictures are to be shown relating to the "Forgotten Man" on the
> screens throughout the Country in connection with the reduction of al-
> lowances to service men. No doubt some of the framed up cases will be
> given further publicity. . . .

You will recall that Mr. Will Hayes [*sic*], Former Chairman of the Republican National Committee, has been occupying for some years the position sometimes called the Dictator of the moving picture industry.

It would be just about within his calibre to inaugurate a movement of this nature. If it is not counteracted, injustice may result.[82]

Notes penciled on the letter suggest that Howe sent copies to Early (because he had been "a moving picture man"), and to Frank Walker, Jesse Jones, and the Warner brothers, that is, to the trusted friends of the administration with contacts in the film industry—a sign that Robinson's warning was taken seriously.[83] Yet the participation of the Warner brothers in the electoral campaign, the grand celebrations for Roosevelt's official visit to Los Angeles as a presidential candidate, and some instances of collaboration between the MPPDA and the administration had already led Roosevelt's staff to believe that the film industry would be cooperative.

Correspondence from March 1933, for example, about *Gabriel over the White House,* a political thriller with disturbing connotations (a benign presidential dictatorship, characterized by an expert use of the radio) suggests that the White House and the film industry were both testing the water. The White House followed the project quite closely and read the screenplay, which had already been modified to exclude references to the present. Will Hays, for his part, "expressed his fear that the hostility generated in Congress by *Gabriel over the White House* might provoke punitive tax or censorship legislation." He insisted on further modifications of the editing, to attenuate the risk of antagonizing the new administration. At this stage, the film's producer, Nicholas Schenk, offered to "eliminate all the objectionable material," and even proposed to show the final cut at the White House before releasing it. Early personally thanked Hays in the name of the President for the interest he had shown in the case, and for the spirit of collaboration demonstrated by the film industry.[84]

In the first months of 1933 a system of self-censorship initiated by the Hays Office was still in its experimental phase, and yet the industry was able to prove its adequacy in a very short time. The election of a Democratic administration probably triggered this promptness.[85]

Hays also earned the gratitude of the White House for his intervention in the production of *The Beer Is Here,* a fiction film that disregarded Early's rules about the use of the President's image.[86] This infraction convinced Early to clarify his position.

It is the President's policy not to permit pictures made of him by newsreels to be used in other productions. This applies to all productions where professional talent is employed. . . . Newsreel producers have been requested not to permit the distribution of the President's pictures to companies desiring their use for feature purposes.[87]

Reluctantly Hollywood went along with this policy but continued to request the President's appearances in its films, using different arguments. During the Hundred Days, even MGM, the stronghold of conservatism, sent Early a telegram signed by (Republican) Louis B. Mayer, asking for an opening address by the President that they might insert in the film *Looking Forward,* so titled in homage to the book published by FDR in 1933. According to Mayer, this film had been praised by William Randolph Hearst, who was still in his pro-Roosevelt phase.[88] (*Looking Forward* was a minor production, set in England, a sign that, while Warner proposed inserting New Deal messages in its key films, MGM confined them to B movies.) The film came out with the following dedication:

FADE IN
Gratefully we employ President Roosevelt's own splendid phrase, "Looking Forward," as the title of this picture.
"We need enthusiasm, imagination, and ability to face facts. . . . We need the courage of the young . . ."
Franklin Delano Roosevelt
FADE OUT

All of the studios asked to use FDR's image at one point or the other, almost as if his image taken from a newsreel or his voice stolen from the radio, purified of its partisan connotations, constituted a very special narrative ingredient, an additional attraction at the box office.

Warner Bros., which probably believed it had acquired enough credit with the administration to be allowed a certain amount of discretion in this respect, tried to insert a shot of FDR engaged in the ritual first pitch of the baseball season in the film *Elmer the Great.* But this breach of Early's rules provoked the alarmed intervention of Hays. To clear itself the studio argued that it was not a scene taken from a newsreel (an action that would have made one of the newsreel companies an accomplice) but a shot by a special crew of its own. Under Hays's pressure, however, Warner Bros. did conform to the rules and eliminate the scene.[89]

Early was more likely to give his consent, however, to the use of FDR's photos in narrative films because they did not generate the illusion that FDR in person had entered the fiction. Universal asked McIntyre for permission to use a photo of Roosevelt for a musical number in *Moonlight and Pretzels,* stressing the film's New Deal message: "When you see this picture you will better appreciate the fine boost we have given to the new 'job drive.' It ties in perfectly at this time. We tested this picture at a preview and the optimistic note struck by this part of the picture drew sustained applause from the audience."[90] The letter was signed by Joe Weil, director of Exploitation, that is, the sector that took care of film promotion. Universal's proposal to use FDR's image as a publicity stunt indicates the industry's will to demonstrate its adherence to New Deal politics and its faith in FDR as a box office attraction. But the letter also supplied an indirect service of public opinion monitoring, through the report of audiences' reactions to the presentation of FDR or of New Deal programs on the screen. Producer Louis Lewyn of Paramount sent FDR a print of *Hollywood on Parade* to demonstrate his pro-NRA publicity idea: "In this particular release I have presented a new significance to the NRA insignia—a significance which has been given an especial forcefulness by superimposing your likeliness over that of the Blue Eagle."[91]

The rule against showing the President in fiction films was absorbed into the practice of Hollywood self-censorship and gave rise, as with other censorial absences and cuts, to a system that implied his presence through metaphor.[92] There are no notable exceptions to the rule until the war, when Hollywood was allowed to use FDR's radio speeches or analogous narrative solutions, because the patriotic context made this appearance of the President nonpartisan. One of the responses to many of Early's revised rules is the insertion of a radio speech by FDR in the film *The Story of Dr. Wassel*.[93]

The cinema, in search of a definitive legitimation and an opportunity to make amends for the bawdy and violent films it had produced during the early part of the Depression, offered its screens to FDR and the New Deal message. Careful examination reveals, however, that this offer applied to only a minute fraction of its products, and often to the marginal ones, such as shorts and B-films. Fox, for example, paid its tribute to the New Deal by dedicating the film *The Man Who Dared* (1933) to Anton Cermak, the Democratic mayor of Chicago who was killed during an assassination attempt on FDR. Fox also made *Stand Up and Cheer* (1934), a musical with Shirley Temple, in which the Secretary of Fun, played by Warren Baxter, spread good cheer as an antidote to the Depression.[94]

The movie industry dramatized the federal activities that lent themselves to that purpose, like those of the FBI, or presented the beneficial effects of the New Deal on society, or exploited FDR's charisma; but it carefully avoided presenting controversial reforms. For example, when the Housing Administration tried to reach the screens to present its programs, it encountered the industry's resistance. In this instance, Early and McIntyre refused to intercede for the federal agency, because "if we did do it, it would place us under real obligations to the Hays organization and motion picture producers. We would have to pay them too much for the favor—many times more than we would get."[95] The administration was afraid that its relationship with the Hays organization could become a continuous trade-off, because the film industry was always engaged in lobbying activities against unfavorable legislation on trade practices and censorship.

Companies other than Warner Bros. demonstrated their interest, however, in making New Deal propaganda films, as evidenced, for example, in a letter by J. McDermott of Paramount, in which he proposes using the screen as a sort of "resonance box" for Roosevelt's message during a time, following the elections of 1936, when the relationship between the administration and public opinion was particularly strained.

> By this means President Roosevelt could preach more subtle sermons that would get across. I am just itching to make such a story, especially since the last election. The villains we could use are so clear cut, the forces that are trying so hard to undermine everything that Mr. Roosevelt is trying to do. What a delight it would be, to show them up for what they are. Also if the picture were produced now, it could draw to great advantage upon the Federal Project and utilize this organization in a manner that would really count.

Early's response was, as always, negative: "I regret to advise you that I cannot hold any hope that this proposal can be given favorable consideration at this time."[96] McDermott's letter does demonstrate, however, that Hollywood was not entirely averse to presenting contemporary issues and wanted to emphasize its potential as a medium of communication. It was aware too of the political and experimental work conducted in the theater, as evidenced by the contracts offered to many representatives of this world, after the introduction of sound.

Despite the administration's continual rebuffs of overtures from the film industry and its articulation instead of an autonomous film discourse through documentary production, Early continued to receive requests from Hollywood for approval of (or comment on) politically relevant film initiatives. The administration was approached about the film adaptation of *It Can't Happen Here,* in production of MGM. The details of the complex relationship between Hollywood and Upton Sinclair, and between Sinclair and FDR are not important here. It is enough to record Early's dry response: "Never in the past six years have we approved or disapproved any proposed motion picture."[97]

Fervent New Dealers from Hollywood, like Melvyn Douglas, proposed "to secure the production of some films, through the regular commercial channels, which would have a bearing point to the objectives of the New Deal."[98] But representatives of the production branch of the film industry were not the only ones to offer their collaboration to the administration. In March 1933 Abram Myers of Allied States Association, an independent exhibitors' organization, suggested a role for movie theaters.

The most inspiring thing has been the cheerfulness and optimism of the people themselves. This must continue until the President's ends are achieved. The motion picture theaters can render a great service in this connection. I suggest the use of slides, trailers, or lobby displays containing a message along these lines:

STAND BY YOUR PRESIDENT
President Roosevelt is doing a great job. He is restoring order out of banking chaos. He is preparing for the resumption of business. He is paving the way for prosperity. All this can not be done in a day. In the meantime, all he needs is a continuance of the same cheerfulness and patience that the American people have displayed thus far. Our lot may be tough, but his is tougher, so let us all help him as best we can.[99]

The White House acknowledged the proposal "with satisfaction." Other independent theater owners made available "the facilities of the screens as a medium for the dissemination of any propaganda the Administration desires to pass along to the public." But, without hiding their opportunism, they asked in return to be "given consideration in any development that concerns the motion picture industry."[100]

Only toward the end of the 1930s in the wake of war, when the issues at stake could no longer be seen as partisan propaganda, and the need to sensitize the public about foreign policy was widely recognized, did the government begin a tight collaboration with the exhibitors (and in general with the film world). In January 1939, the same Myers from Allied (which, in the meantime, collaborated with the administration on the *Paramount* case) proposed to Early to show "patriotic trailers" in his organization's theaters. The press secretary accepted the offer and sent along some photos of FDR, accompanied by a presidential message.[101] The next year, Myers offered "the cooperation of the independent exhibitors to the government in the dissemination of authorized information or otherwise in times of national emergency": the war mobilization and the tension between the government and the film industry induced by the *Paramount* case were inextricably linked.

Warner Bros. Presents the New Deal

The studio that most explicitly upheld the New Deal in its production was Warner Bros. The documents of the Warner Special Collection at the USC Library offer us useful information about the production process of these films.[102] In 1933, Warner Bros. produced a curious musical short starring Dick Powell, *The Road Is Open Again,* directly supporting the NRA. In this film, the spirits of Presidents Washington, Lincoln, and Wilson are hanging about in the room where the composer Powell is looking at the piano for inspiration. Here is an excerpt from the script:

> WASHINGTON: Poor kid. He's been writing a song for the NRA and has fallen asleep.
>
> WILSON: There's nothing like a good song to inspire a nation.
>
> LINCOLN: (*reading newspaper*) Things are getting better every day.
>
> INSERT NEWSPAPER HEADLINES: More Than One Million Jobs Created by NRA
>
> THREE SHOT WASHINGTON LINCOLN WILSON
>
> WASHINGTON: Well, Abe, it looks as though we can stop worrying about our country. Roosevelt has it headed right again.
>
> LINCOLN: All it needed was a plan of action . . . and a man with the courage to carry it through.
>
> WILSON: There isn't a person in America who won't benefit by the NRA, if every man, woman and child does his part.
>
> WASHINGTON: You can always depend on Americans.

When the composer wakes up, the three Presidents explain to him the significance of the NRA in a typical Hollywood popularizing style. The political message is fairly advanced even for a company like Warner Bros. Lincoln, for example, says: "I lived to see the freedom of the slaves, but this is the first step toward freeing the slaves of the sweatshops—eliminating child labor—and giving the toilers a chance to enjoy the beauties of life." At the end, the composer, inspired by the Presidents, has written the notes for *The Road Is Open Again*. Then:

> During the song and before the chorus, Powell gets up from the piano and sings to the audience, asking it to join him in a second chorus, the words of which appear on the screen, over the photographic action, one line at a time. During the singing of the song, we cut in newsreels shots of men going back to work, factories humming with activity, big close-up of President Roosevelt, the NRA banner and the American flag.

The short used ingredients, besides propagandistic naiveté, typical of Warner Bros. production at that moment: music, the ever-popular Dick Powell, and references to contemporary life.[103] It was a brief but not minor version of a Warner Bros. musical—a genre that in its major and more successful versions, such as the trilogy *Gold Diggers of 1933*, *Footlight Parade*, and *42nd Street*, expressed a New Dealist tension.

In 1933 Warner Bros. inserted explicit New Deal messages in *Footlight Parade*, directed by Lloyd Bacon, and in *Heroes for Sale*, directed by William Wellman.

In *Footlight Parade,* the number "Shanghai Lil" ended with sailors dancing and marching and, by firing their rifles in formation, composing alternately the image of the NRA eagle and FDR's face. The preproduction documents show that this number was shot and added after the film was finished.[104] It was announced in the publicity materials, but its contents were not made explicit and there were no accompanying illustrative photos. There was just a reference to its spectacularity ("Shanghai Lil Scene Smashing Climax"). The production plan provided for a musical number on the theme of prosperity, which was later substituted by "Ah, the Moon Is Here." Subsequently Warner Bros. decided to launch a clear patriotic and pro–New Deal message by adding this finale to the dance. The film's promotional intentions were evident from the press book, in which the plot synopsis describes the producer choreographer James Cagney–Chester Kent as "a New Dealer," and the dialogue includes the line, "We're giving you a new deal." The critical literature on the film recognizes this intention, superimposing the choreographer Kent on FDR: "Chester Kent can be seen as a surrogate of FDR, a strong director leading the 'little people' in the chorus into the order and success of the completed show."[105]

There is a peculiar visual analogy between "Shanghai Lil" and the images of the Electrical Parade Jack Warner organized at the Olympic Stadium in honor of candidate Roosevelt in September 1932. "Aglow with lights, and trimmed in tinsel and gold, sixteen floats, bearing the cream of studio talent and the most beautiful women of Hollywood . . . were the center of the thrilling display of studio genius in the Electrical Parade."[106] The photos of the parade show a remarkable resemblance between these floats and some of Busby Berkeley's musical numbers, using a complicated electrical apparatus and human geometrics of bodies reminiscent of the mass choreography typical of Nazism. "Shanghai Lil" represents a peculiar interaction between spectacle and politics, within which style and message, occasion and context are so cleanly superimposed that one cannot determine to what extent the dance inspired the parade or vice versa.

In *Heroes for Sale,* the New Dealist propaganda comes out in a speech by FDR printed in a newspaper, which the hero—a typical "forgotten man" from Warner Bros.' social films of the 1930s—reads to a friend to cheer him up. The documents reveal that Darryl Zanuck, not the front office, decided to quote FDR. His main motivation was drama. He in fact wrote to the director, William Wellman, and to the producer, Hal Wallis, suggesting that the dialogue be modified to make it more "contemporary." Thus the protagonist's final lines were: "It's no optimism—just common horse sense—did you read President Roosevelt's Inaugural Address? I cut it out of the newspaper yesterday and the more I think about it, the more I realize that I am right when

I say that it takes more than one sock in the jaw to lick a hundred million people." Zanuck further explained:

> The reason I use the Inaugural Speech at the finish is because everyone throughout the world is talking about Roosevelt's speech. It was a bombshell and is being compared to great speeches like Lincoln's Gettysburg Address and it seems to me much more reasonable and constructive for Tom, as his character, to talk about something somebody else said than to be talking about what he himself thinks, after all, we can believe that the President could be a prophet but it is hard for us to believe that a down and out bum could be a prophet.[107]

Within a few days, Warner Bros. tried to make Roosevelt even more present in the film, asking in an exchange of telegrams to "borrow" his voice and image. Jack Warner himself wrote to Howe about the project, which, at that time, had the significant working title of *Breadline*.

> The moral of the picture depicts happiness and a better understanding for the people of the United States with an improved outlook on conditions and life. I am asking if it would be possible to secure the President's permission to use his photograph and voice at the close of this production. We desire to use a portion of one of the President's banking speeches wherein he concludes as follows: "Confidence and courage are the essentials of success in carrying out our plan. You people must have faith. You must not be stampeded by rumors or guesses. Let us unite in vanishing fear. It is your problem my friends no less than it is mine. Together we cannot fail."

The studio also indicated its willingness to eliminate the scene later if, at the viewing of the film, this solution seemed inappropriate. Early, however, was inflexible and asked that the request be withdrawn "on the grounds that if such permission once is given it opens door to certain future embarrassment."[108]

These two instances are interesting because they coincide with the beginning of Roosevelt's presidency and therefore provide immediate support, but they demonstrate also that the studio was acting out of its spontaneous will. Whereas the "Shanghai Lil" number was probably added on an order from the front office, the closing scene proposed for *Heroes for Sale* was definitely a (creative) suggestion originating with Zanuck.

Throughout the thirties Warner Bros. dealt with the New Deal in "social films," presenting the administration "usually in the guise of federal judges, G-Men, or benevolent civil servants—as the solution to all social problems."[109] A good example is Wellman's sullen *Wild Boys of the Road* (1933). "Designed for a Warner Brothers working-class audience, [it] neither attempts to ignore the concerns of the day, nor [does it rely] on the usual technique of appealing directly to conventional values, but rather risks arousing the audience's latent hostility to authority and rebellious feelings in order to demonstrate their supposed inadequacy: only once this has been done, these feelings purged, can assent be gained for the film's final solution: a renewal of trust in the workings of capitalism and the state."[110]

In the ending, in fact, a judge resembling Roosevelt stands under the NRA eagle, benignly haranguing the boys from the street and sending them back to their homes: "I'm going to do my part if you do your part. Things are going to get better, not merely here, but all over the country." It was a paternalist response to the instances of social denunciation the film had depicted to that point. Thus, the alternative community, embodied in the film by youths, is shown to be a failure. Better, for the "wild boys" an (improbable) return to the system—to society, miraculously healed by Roosevelt charisma. This happy ending that in no way could blend itself with a desperate film was a tacked-on narrative solution.

In the film *Massacre*, directed by Alan Crosland in 1934, Warner Bros. directly supported the legislative projects on Indian rights. At the center of the story is a pugnacious hero, a rebel Indian, who, "having passed through an initial stage of irrational aimless violence, now embraces practical politics, the policies of the New Deal government" and proposes to his people a "square deal."[111] The Breen Office, which administrated the Hollywood self-censorship system, insisted that the project had a negative political impact and referred the studio to the commissioner for Indian affairs in Washington, because an analysis of the script suggested that the edifying ending, supportive of the federal government, was not enough to dampen the film's polemical tones.[112] Warner Bros. succeeded in obtaining the commissioner's authorization to proceed with the film, which remains, however, a peculiar text. The film presents a sour indictment of the conditions in which American Indians were living and proposes an explicit connection between the Indian problem to the racial issue.[113]

The rotation on its axis Warner Bros. production made between 1934 and 1935, transforming the gangster James Cagney into an FBI agent, has been seen as a manifestation of the ideological support given by this company to the New Deal. The representation of FBI activities, in addition to being good material for action films, was a response to the criticism by public opinion of the glorification of the gangster, implicit in the genre. And so the gangster was again the villain, and the federal agent the hero. An examination of a specific example of this transformation, *Public Enemy Number One*, reveals that this thematic turn, like others, was not dictated by the front office. The screenwriter for the project, Manuel Seff, in a letter to the producer, Hal Wallis, proposed following the administration's lead in making the criminal the villain.

100

The election of President Roosevelt and Repeal started the whole thing, followed by the amazing and thrilling pronouncement: The Government is going after criminals!

President Roosevelt himself has outlined the best screen treatment in his speech to the Attorney General's crime conference in Washington. Some of the things he said were:

Relentlessly and without compromise the Department of Justice has moved forward in its major offensive against these criminal forces.

In many instances, we may as well frankly admit, bandits have been better equipped and better organized that have the officials who are supposed to keep them in check.

IT IS OUR POSITIVE DUTY TO KEEP BEFORE THE COUNTRY THE FACTS IN RE-GARD TO CRIME AS A WHOLE—TO BUILD UP A BODY OF PUBLIC OPINION WHICH, I REGRET TO BE COMPELLED TO SAY, IS NOT IN THIS DAY AND AGE SUFFICIENTLY ACTIVE OR ALIVE TO THE SITUATION IN WHICH WE FIND OUR-SELVES.[114]

Like Zanuck, Seff and Wallis drew inspiration from the newspapers, the privileged source of Warner Bros.' "realist" cinema. Because of the productive and ideological choices it was making, this studio drew people, both New Dealers and radicals, who were particularly interested in dealing with contemporary reality and reform.

The attorney general, Homer Cummings, welcomed this Hollywoodian enthusiasm for federal agents up to a point. Worried about the swelling wave of films about FBI agents that were being distributed by the studios, he reminded Hays that the Department of Justice had not approved any film about the FBI. To ensure that only a "dignified and technically accurate picture" would be produced, he suggested that the Justice Department have "an opportunity to consider the matter."[115] Hays hurried to inform Harry Warner: "As indicated by the Department during the Crime Conference, they would like to cooperate with the industry in the production of a picture in which the Intelligence Bureau is a factor in a way similar to the cooperation by the Army and the Navy." That Hays went to Harry rather than Jack means that the question appeared to him of political weight. Hays suggested that particular care be taken in the making of *Farrell Case*. "We are advised," he said, "that the government men are represented as thoroughly intelligent, courageous, honorable, etc.," but he insisted that the studio get in touch with the FBI as soon as possible, in order to obtain its official collaboration.[116]

Warner Bros. was not the only studio dealing with the FBI. In the same period Universal produced special newsreels to help the Justice Department capture criminals.[117] But beginning in January 1937, the film industry had very different contacts with the FBI. The Justice Department had begun the investigation for the *Paramount* case; and collecting information and evidence in an antitrust case is the work of the FBI. From then on, the majors and the MPPDA received frequent visits from federal agents, cast in a less romantic and less entertaining role than the G-Men image Hollywood had helped to construct.

The New Deal did not use Hollywood cinema to promote its message, but it did use the film medium, directly, to produce its documentaries. This choice made the administration aware of the problem of access to the screens, stubbornly hindered by the industry. Through its documentary production the Roosevelt administration, like any independent producer, confronted the limited access to the film market and the excessive power of the majors. The government's attack on the industry's structure in the *Paramount* case thus derived from a direct knowledge of how this industry operated.

FDR and the New Dealers always worked within the documentary format and guaranteed their control of the productive operations. In this respect, the administration excluded Hollywood by hiring liberal filmmakers like Lorentz and radicals like Leo Hurwitz, both advocates of anti-Hollywood aesthetics. Furthermore, Early and McIntyre's experience in this format might have accentuated their anti-Hollywood snobbery.

The relationship between the New Deal and Hollywood appears to be ambivalent. The musical number "Shanghai Lil" sanctioned the image of the NRA eagle—the same eagle that presided over "the codes of fair competition" signed by government and industry in 1933. The relationship became strained with the antimonopolistic action of the *Paramount* case; but it was later recuperated through collaboration in the war effort. In this phase, the government delegated great authority to Hollywood, using film professionals to produce government information and propaganda documentaries (like the series *Why We Fight,* directed by Frank Capra), and showing Hollywood films on the front throughout the world, and on the homefront.

The Roosevelt administration did not control the screen as much as did the Nazi-fascist regimes. The American screen elaborated the images of Roosevelt and the New Deal autonomously, through the newsreels, which dedicated ample space to the President, promoting his charismatic popularity and authority, and through Hollywood films, which publicized some aspects of the New Deal because of the industry's spontaneous initiative. A curious document, however, evokes other possibilities: Florence K. Amos, an American tourist, wrote to the President from Italy, stimulated by a screening of *Camicia nera* (by Gioacchino Forzano, 1933), and suggested that he see this film, in order to draw inspiration from it, in that "it coordinated visually, a national program, and would give impetus to our American one. The basic things which need to be done in our country are the same, however much the details differ."[118] These "details" were, indeed, anything but insignificant. The administration did not entrust narrative cinema with any New Deal propaganda project.

At the end of the thirties, the relationship between politics and cinema changed because of the interventionist mobilization. Because the administration's foreign policy was not linear, one can not mechanically connect the "premature" anti-isolationism of certain Hollywood films to a specific order issued by the White House. Some studios, given also the origins of the producers, voluntarily mobilized themselves on this front, as indicated by a Warner Bros. telegram: "Personally we would like to do all in our power within the motion picture industry and by use of its talking screen to show the American people the worthiness of the cause for which the free peoples of Europe are making such tremendous sacrifices."[119]

In the same period Hays and the MPPDA worked closely with the administration to confront, with its influential support, the difficulties created by the international crisis for the distribution of American cinema abroad. The support, always guaranteed by the government, for the export of Hollywood films was motivated by economic interests—the pulling power of cinema with respect to foreign commerce—and by political and ideological considerations. Significant in this respect is the exchange of notes between the White House and the State Department, in May 1940, about the Warner Bros. film *Juarez*. Warner Bros. proposed to exploit the release of the picture (which dealt with the deposing of Napoleon III by the Mexicans) so that FDR could send a presidential message to the people of that country, "calling attention to property of U.S. citizens seized by the Mexican government." After a consultation with the State Department, the President responded negatively to the idea. In his answer, he underlined that, even if it "was a fine thing that some of our producers are beginning to turn to the history of the other American republics for their dramatic material," it was better not to "link the film to the petroleum and agrarian issues," because the oil controversy had been the subject of direct negotiations with Mexican president Lázaro Cárdenas.[120] The complex relation of U.S. cinema and Central-Latin America cannot be discussed here. It is sufficient to point out that, when film export to Europe was stalled by the international crisis, U.S. film moved to South America and, for a time, might have been influenced by the Catholic faith of the majority of those countries.[121]

Even if it was not declaredly interventionist, the Roosevelt administration was manifestly anti-fascist. The ideological consonance with Hollywood on this matter produced an almost automatic alliance, useful to both but necessary to the administration, given the isolationist orientation of American public opinion. In this respect, it has been argued that the administration succeeded in "deviating" the screen in an anti-isolationist direction, by exercising political pressure on Hollywood and through an "exchange of favors," that is, with the offer of a consent decree, which drew the majors out of their antitrust problems.[122] Actually, it is unclear why the administration would have tried to gain such control over the screen, on foreign policy objectives that were not yet defined within the government itself. Hollywood was penalized, however, for its "premature antifascism" by the Nye-Wheeler congressional committee.

At the outbreak of World War II, the American film industry lined up on the patriotic front, working closely with the government and zealously agreeing to become carrier of propaganda messages. These messages went beyond partisan politics, even if they did promote values that had been revitalized by the New Deal. What Hollywood cinema propagandized then was simply "America."

4

The Film Industry
in the Thirties

The history of the New Deal and the film industry in this period consists of myriad contacts or encounters with the government, from the National Recovery Administration (NRA) codes to the Temporary National Emergency Committee (TNEC), and concluding with the *Paramount* case.[1]

Beginning in 1922, the nucleus of the film industry's institutional activities was the Motion Picture Producer Distributor Association (MPPDA), or Hays Office. This trade association dealt with all the problems concerning the industry: the administration of the self-censorship system (the function for which it was most famous), the rapport between producers and exhibitors, or among the companies, relations with labor and guilds, Hollywood's foreign policy (which, with Hays, became more systematic), legislative activity, and, above all, public relations.[2]

When Hays had accepted, along with a lavish fee, the job as head of the MPPDA, after his successful direction of the Republican National Committee, he took on its multiple image problems.[3] Hollywood personalities had been involved in headline scandals, shady affairs of sex and drugs, even homicide. Civic groups protested the spiritual poverty and the licentiousness of the films, insistently asking for the institution of censorship.[4] The film industry needed more than good public relations in order to gain a more solid and legitimate position on the industrial scene, if it wanted to attract the attention of Wall Street, whose help was indispensable in this decisive phase of expansion. Toward this goal, Hays propagated the image of cinema as a business with enormous investments, especially in real estate. It had its movie palaces located in commercially strategic positions, often very central, and the vast areas of the studio lots in Los Angeles. This real estate empire was accompanied by a large accessory business, and by a flourishing foreign commerce.

According to David Bordwell, Janet Staiger, and Kristin Thompson, "Under the strong leadership of Will H. Hays, the MPPDA took steps to solidify the industry. Besides controlling subject matter through self-censorship regulations, the MPPDA was credited with the 'encouragement of better business practice, such as standardized budgets, uniform cost accounting, uniform contracts, and the arbitration of disputes.'"[5] This project was in line with the reformist effort, begun in the 1920s by Republican progressives, to moralize the business world, encouraging the formation of trade associations that would undertake the self-regulation of trade practices and of the production system. (It was a form of self-regulation notably different though from that proposed later by the New Dealers).[6]

The MPPDA formulated choices concerning the entire industry, on such matters as the introduction of sound, the lighting of the set, and union contracts. This coordinating role, in the end, favored and was favored by the monopolistic concentration of the structure and encouraged the ideological standardization performed by self-censorship.

According to a legend that Hays helped to create, the MPPDA arose from the need to mediate the ferocious competition within the industry, typical of the phase of the struggle between the Patent Trust and the independent producers, in order to move toward an efficient oligopoly.[7] This capitalistic rationalization by the industry meant that the pioneers' unscrupulous methods were replaced by the more "refined" but no less ruthless methods of the financers and lawyers who assumed managerial control of the industry. By the end of the 1920s, the studio system was in place. In these years, the studios carried out a rapid vertical integration, known as "the battle for the theaters," in which some production companies acquired large theater circuits to guarantee themselves an optimal outlet in the market.[8] Through this expansion into exhibition they also received the "cream of the profits," derived from first run theaters. Thus the majors, Paramount, Warner Bros., Loew-MGM, and Fox (RKO was formed in 1928), could depend on a national distribution network and theater circuits, while the minor companies, Columbia and Universal, and the distributor United Artists, were not vertically integrated and occupied a marginal but stable role in the market.

This transformation encouraged (and implied) a stronger concentration of power, situated in the trade organization, which constantly bordered on monopoly. Therefore the MPPDA had to "cover up" some of its functions, fragmenting its activities, giving them semi-autonomous structures between one coast and the other, but, above all, emphasizing the individuality of the studios—with the concept of the "studio styles"—and developing mythologies around the movie moguls, characterized by strong personal profiles.

The MPPDA's position with respect to the industry's interests was clearly indicated by the geography of its offices: the central offices were in New York, near the financial center, and were transferred to Washington only in 1945, while in Los Angeles operated the departments closest to production, among them the Production Code Administration (self-censorship code), headed for a long time by Joe Breen (and sometimes called Breen Office).[9]

The Elaboration of the Hays Code

In 1930 the American film industry adopted a system of self-censorship constituted by a written code, that is, a series of drawn-up and annotated principles, of true commandments, called the Hays Code.[10] The industry opted for this solution also because cinema did not fall under the First Amendment protection of freedom of expression, having been excluded by the Supreme Court in the case *Mutual Film Corp.* of 1915, in which it was held that cinema was "a business, pure and simple, originated and conducted for profit, . . . not to be regarded . . . as part of the press of the country, or as organ of public opinion."[11] It should be remarked that this decision, very relevant to the discussion of censorship, was made in the context of an antimonopolistic action. It was overturned later by the decision in the *Paramount* antitrust case, which tangentially conceded this delayed protection to the cinema, favoring the corrosion of the old institution of self-censorship.[12] In the 1930s and 1940s, monopoly and censorship were therefore two closely interconnected elements, and the MPPDA was the site of this conjunction.

The absence of constitutional protection rendered American cinema vulnerable to the threat of federal censorship—a threat aggravated by the proliferation of state and local censorship boards. This form of local censorship implied continuous financial risks for Hollywood, because the applied standards could vary by region, making the commercial run of a film unpredictable, or requiring the out-take of scenes that had already been shot. Such financial considerations, coupled with the medium's ideological precariousness, encouraged the adoption of a self-censorship system and the hiring of Hays, at a time when there was a mounting wave of legislative projects proposing state or local censorship. Given the pressures on this front, Hays went to work to formulate principles and strategies able to produce a socially and culturally acceptable cinema for the mass public. In an effort to bypass the Supreme Court decision, he declared cinema a service "not unlike the press, the newspaper and public education," thus including it among the media of mass communication and among institutions of immediate social utility. But this move could have been dangerous, in that the concept of "public interest" opened the way to federal regulatory intervention. It was not by accident that Hays's public statements usually contained two apparently contradictory concepts: the ideological-social function of cinema, and its being above all "entertainment." Balancing the two, by articulating the code and applying it required a masterful acrobat. Defending the cinema as "service," Hays brandished the issue of censorship, fighting reformers on their own grounds and requiring them to come out in the open, well knowing that Americans generally abhor censorship. He claimed his first victory when he blocked a censorship bill in the state of Massachusetts; mobilizing the massive human and financial resources of his office and supported by a strong consensus, Hays was reassured of a near-permanent public opposition to censorship.

In the second half of the 1920s, Hays's work on self-censorship produced its first fruits. To supplement the Thirteen Points elaborated in 1921, he put out a list of Don'ts and Be Carefuls, defining the forbidden zones and those at risk, in the map of the possible Hollywood narrative itineraries.[13] This list was published purposely to coincide with the Federal Trade Commission hearings to look into the film industry's trade practices. Deflecting the issue of self-regulation from the area of economics the area of censorship was a typical Hays maneuvre. Reforms affecting films rather than the economic structure would be less burdensome for the industry. This first attempt at a self-censorship code operated on two levels: on one level suppressing or repressing certain themes and situations; on the other, encouraging the adoption of "good taste," within a system of self-censorship that also had didactic functions. The Don'ts and Be Carefuls embodied the same principles later found in the Hays Code and were based on the same attempt at ideological standardization aimed at guaranteeing the widest consensus. The abundance of terms like "good taste" and "good sense" suggests a goal of "universality" that sinks (and conceals) its class roots in a middle-class mentality. The list was the expression of a bourgeoisie in a phase of hegemonic expansion and redefinition during the 1920s.

But, even if everyone—producers and exhibitors, independents and majors—affirmed the need for this policy and their willingness to practice it, the list remained one of a number of Hays's aspirations, without real and efficient applications. The observance of its principles depended on the good will of the producers, who seemed to remember it only in their official statements or while facing the protests of pressure groups, but who did not take note of it in their daily practice. Nonetheless, Hays's commitment did produce some results, because through the list Hollywood trained itself to target different cultural models. It tried to integrate a plurality of cultural groups, from that section of society defined by Warren Susman as "Puritan-republican, producer-capitalist" and composed of the "discontented of antiquated mentality" who invoked censorship, to the popular classes or those less conventional segments of the public who appreciated films with a pinch of sex or violence and without ethical nuances. Cinema was torn between two images or projections: it could be educative or it could remain a popular form of entertainment. If it became educative, it would have responded to the ideology of the middle class—which included the conservative WASP bourgeoise—and the reformers inclined toward paternalistic behavior, who were worried by the possible harmful effects of a means of communication that operated according to commercial principles.

In the 1920s at a moment of social unrest and accelerated modernization, members of the dominant class faced these threats to the social order by trying to construct consensual cultural values and imposing a hegemonic order, a project of Americanization that did not exclude repressive interventions, for example, on the immigrant working class. From an ideological point of view, Hays was part of the same progressive community from which civic groups developed, representing in a whole, those "authorized interpretative communities" that circulated their vision of culture through an institution of cultural control, such as the MPPDA, that was close to the seat of economic and political power.[14] And yet their enlightened vision did not succeed right away, because of resistance by the more conservative sections of the middle class, and because of the characteristics of the movies as popular entertainment in the silent period. The movies were then still a melting pot of popular culture, a synthesis of spectatorial experiences (magic lanterns, variety shows, circuses, fairs, etc.), participation in collective viewing rites. Cinema evoked a fantastic world that attracted the lower classes, but it also exercised its "appeals to the assimilationist and upward mobile tendencies of the workers and immigrants."[15]

The battle between these two possible models of cinema was a key phase in the great ideological struggle identified by Susman as typical of the 1920s and 1930s, that is, between the "culture of abundance" and of communications, and that of Puritan conservatism. Clearly it was not a struggle that could end with the unconditional surrender of one of the contenders. The Hays Code was in fact the result of a compromise between different tensions; and a big step toward the "culture of abundance."

The masses were not deceitfully seduced by the system into the rites of the new consumer religion, as some radical scholars would have us believe.[16] They just pursued happiness—a right guaranteed by the American Constitution but liable, in this phase, to economic quantification. It was the Depression, if anything, that brought into question the direction and meaning of this movement toward happiness.

One can observe, in this context, that the movie moguls—who boasted of an intuitive understanding of the public derived from their experience in the field of exhibition—shared the culture of their customers. Through the discussions about the Hays Code, they negotiated their Americanization and adaptation to the standards of "good taste" too.[17]

In the mid-1920s, Hollywood silent pictures had reached an expressive, narrative, and ideological maturity that allowed them to deal with almost every theme, even subtle spiritual conflicts. Sound introduced a phase of experimentation in film language, modifying both productive methods and expressive forms. Cinema presented itself therefore as a new medium—"plastic art in movement" integrated by the word, which until then had been the asset of theater and radio. As with all innovations in the area of communication, sound attracted the attention not only of those who saw every invention as a step toward the utopia of universal communication but also of those who always interpreted technological innovations as seeds for obscure social and cultural catastrophe.

Sound films experimented with new methods of storytelling. Professionals in the use of words were hired in great numbers (journalists, writers, playwrights) to construct the new linguistic competence of the medium of various levels. The linguistic homogenization performed by the "talkies," mostly through dialogue, played an important role in the process of Americanization, but one that has not yet received sufficient attention. And the cultural efficacy of this process is perfectly aligned on the ideological project of the Hays Code.

The script thus changed from a blueprint for direction into an autonomous, creative discourse that took on artistic and professional dignity. At the same time, it became the key text on which (self-)censorship could be exercised, because synchronous sound made cuts on the film very impractical and costly.[18]

Stylistic experimentalism and, more visibly, thematic boldness were pushed to new extremes by the arrival in Hollywood of East Coast intellectuals (later followed by European émigrées), in the stage of refoundation through which cinema was then passing. Pre-code talkies give the impression that everything was allowed, both in expressive and narrative terms. The historical context of their production, that is, the period following the Crash, which had eroded the social bases of some fundamental ideological nuclei such as work, family, and social mobility, is usually considered an explanation for these characteristics. This phase of commercial, technological, and expressive experimentation expanded the "sayable" in films, to the point of including controversial and scandalous aspects of social reality:[19] the provocative lines of an explicitly sexual Mae West, the anarchic and wild satire of the Marx Brothers, the violence of the "city boys," the prominence of gold diggers and "kept women." It was at times an unselfconscious, pessimistic, amoral representation, with that realistic quality the middle class charged to the literature that documented the ills of society without indulging in edifying sermons.

A new wave of protests rose against Hollywood cinema. It was accused of being socially irresponsible, either because of its evasiveness (as in musicals or Cinderella comedies about social mobility), or because of an excessive realism (urban pictures, gangster or sexually explicit films). In 1930 the MPPDA elaborated a code of self-censorship, inspired by the Roman Catholic clergy but "forged in the fires of experience, hammered out on the anvils of long debate." According to Hays, it articulated "a production ethic, capable of uniform interpretation and based not on arbitrary do's and don'ts, but on principles. Mere rules, however adequate for the moment, are pragmatic; the time will come when they will not be observed unless rooted in immutable laws."[20]

Even though the code was ready, and everyone—the producers, who had long been fighting with public opinion, which was certainly not fond of them, and the exhibitors, who were tired of combating local pressure groups that wanted censorship—expressed support for the document, its application was not immediate. As Hays observed, "Trying to preach morality in a cataclysm of that sort was like a voice sounding off in the desert":[21] the ideological-social climate of the period rendered a complex commercial and cultural operation, such as the adoption of the self-censorship system, impracticable.

The code was enforced three years later, in 1933, two days after Roosevelt's election,[22] thus indicating that the industry was afraid that an administration that championed federal intervention like the New Deal would interfere with film affairs. In 1933, exhibitors and distributors reached an agreement on their conflictual relations, through the offices of the MPPDA, and formalized it in the standard exhibition contract. This agreement facilitated the adoption of the self-censorship system, which depended, for its functioning, on well-oiled mechanisms of self-regulation at all levels of the industrial and commercial structure.

But almost a year passed and only the threat of a boycott by the Legion of Decency, a powerful Catholic organization, brought about the final decision to enforce the code.[23] In a sense Hays's effort to enforce the code recalls New Deal operative strategies such as mediation and counterorganization, because of the way he encouraged the struggle between different social forces, "using" the public and the industry in a game of reciprocal determination.

The Hays Code

The Hays Code sprang from the industry's will to achieve a positive rapport with *all* of its public, without causing offense to groups of different social, ethnic, cultural, and religious backgrounds. It defined its audience as "universal" in order to conceal the too generic and commercial concept of "mass"— a definition that displeases everyone. It was an apparently undifferentiated public, of all ages, gathered in families,[24] with the preliminary exclusion of a product diversification aimed at different age or target groups. In glossing over problematic cultural, political, racial, and ethnic differences, the code attempted to homogenize this public. The code and its administrators, the Production Code Administration, or PCA, also tried to accommodate the foreign market, the source of a good 30 percent of the industry's profits. The PCA hired personnel with specific competence in evaluating the possible repercussions of the representation of other cultures and traditions. Thus the universality of Hollywood films was designed on the desks of the Breen Office.

To entertain such a vast public, cinema had to be conscious of its own functioning and effects. The code was written at a time when important studies on cinema were being made public, such as the Payne Fund studies, which professed to be a scientific analysis of the psychological and sociological effects of cinema, and the Catholic analysis of the film-going experience.[25] It availed itself of these studies in developing its knowledge of the function of cinema and formulating its theories about spectatorship. The code was not just a list of prohibitions. It clearly articulated the ideological function of the cinema and affirmed a system of values, in a calibrated dosage of WASP Americanism and modern Catholicism. It declared that "theatrical motion pictures are primarily to be regarded as entertainment," adding, however, that their "moral importance has been universally recognized" and stating that cinema had become the "art of the multitudes," that is, maintaining the double standard of cinema as both entertainment and public expression.

By defining cinema as a product that is at the same time artistic, socially useful, and commercially significant, the code legitimated it as a standardized product and even appropriated the classification in genres, distinguishing the suggestions related to "serious drama" from those related to comedy. The ideological, expressive, and productive homogeneity achieved by Hollywood cinema in the 1930s encouraged the internal articulation in film genres. Some sound films of the early 1930s, such as *The Last Flight* and *Dynamite*, were characterized not only by a lack of morality and by a certain degree of anarchy but also by disorder in the narrative structure, or by an eliptical and quick editing, by the modernity of certain narrative solutions, which strangely enough, precede the "classical period." The writing of the code and its enforcement in 1934 do not coincide by chance with the development and the maturation of American film genres, because the affirmation of the Law, in Lacanian terms, created Order in the productive system and in the product.[26]

The code also referred to the star system and to the spectator's identification with the actor-personality-star, stressing: "the enthusiasm for and interest in the film actors and actresses, developed beyond anything of the sort in history, makes the audience largely sympathetic toward the characters they portray and the stories in which they figure." The decision, made immediately after Hays's arrival on the Hollywood scene, to insert clauses concerning morality into the contracts between actor and studio, private life included, reveals the awareness of the role played by film celebrities in the "culture of abundance."

The notes to the code by one of its drafters, Martin Quigley, legitimated another founding element typical of Hollywood cinema: the option for romance to the detriment of "literal realism."[27] "The argument for complete, literal recording, if that is what is meant by Mr. James Joyce and Mr. Ernest Hemingway, must presume a discriminatory approach that is not to be presumed of the commonality." "As far as possible," the code states, "life should not be misrepresented, at least not in such a way as to place in the mind of youth false values of life." The objective was to find a balancing point between a reality that could be too crude and an excessively simplistic idealization— a balance that Hollywood reached through the reduction of social conflicts into personal problems.

The desire to reconcile morality and fun, business and art, written into the code, encouraged Hollywood filmmakers to be fairly "correct" in order not to annoy the right-minded people, while exploring all the possibilities of "entertaining" them. As one of Hays's lines synthesizes: "When you show a woman crossing her legs in a film, you don't have to show how far up she can cross them and still be acceptable to the law, but rather how little she manages to lift them and still be 'interesting'." This was the challenge: to play with the limits, constructing a metaphoric system that allowed film production the stimulating ingredients Hollywood had always used, but dosed more rigorously, according to precise recipes and with the availability of conventional substitutes.

The Hays Code described and promoted a cinema of entertainment, made of genres and stars, while proclaiming its ideological function and identifying its public in the family. This document represents a founding moment in the history of American cinema, as an index of the achievement of a high degree of internal cohesion, and as a regulating order. It expresses also the projection of its new public image—the portrait of *an industry*, not a snapshot of picturesque personalities, or a collage of studios' logos.

The New Deal and Film Censorship

On many occasions Franklin Roosevelt and the New Dealers stated that they opposed the imposition of film censorship, whether federal or local. Roosevelt reaffirmed this position in his opening address to the National Board of Review Conference, in February 1936: "While necessarily conforming to the normal requirements of entertainment, I believe our motion pictures should be sane and salutary—enlightening and mentally stimulating—expressive of the best ideals of our community consciousness." This was possible, he added, without subjecting the industry to "onerous restrictions." Among the personalities present at the event were Fiorello LaGuardia, mayor of new York, the producer Harry Warner, the screenwriter and playwright Robert Sherwood, the film critic Otis Ferguson of *The New Republic,* and actors, including Edward G. Robinson and Douglas Fairbanks Jr., all of whom expressed appreciation for the results achieved by film art in relation to self-censorship. Harry Warner amended his appreciation, however, with the comment, "People who spend their time fighting pictures could spend it better fighting the slums. Criminals breed in poverty-stricken slum districts—not moving pictures."[28] (The sociological angle was an old argument, but the Warner brothers professed it with faith also in their film production.)

The Roosevelt administration never expressed a desire to interfere with the film message as such, but not all the New Dealers worked in unison on the film front. While censorship was not a conflictual issue, the Hollywood industry's way of operating did not enjoy unanimous approval. The *Paramount* case documents reveal that early in 1938 the Antitrust Division of the Justice Department intended to proceed against the Hays Office—designated as the main defendant in the antitrust action—as the organization that elaborated the conspiratorial maneuvers and exercised monopoly. The self-censorship system was an integral part of this structure, according to the Justice Department, because the majors, by administrating the code, controlled access to the screens by requiring every producer-distributor to submit script and film to the PCA, to obtain the Hays Office's seal, in order to show films in the theaters controlled by MPPDA members, that is, in the best outlets.

The Explanatory Statement of the case also argued that the PCA discriminated against the small independent producers by "ordering certain scenes or sections deleted from their productions but permitting similar scenes to remain uncensored in the pictures of the eight major companies." It specified that this censorship referred "not always to immoral scenes but principally sections showing charging horses, Indian fighting, realistic frontier warfare and the like." Thus the PCA attacked the very attractions of the B westerns, which constituted the bulk of the small independents' product, while films like Paramount's *Lives of a Bengal Lancer* and Warner Bros.' *Charge of the Light Brigade* obtained the censors' seal, even though they showed what the document described as "mass killings and brutality." Whereas for the majors, self-censorship served the purpose of guaranteeing the studio investment and minimizing the risks, in cases like this, the PCA deprived independent cinema of its spectacular potential, with little ethical or ideological justification. The Explanatory Statement argued further that the PCA had printed its seal of approval on MGM's *Sadie Thompson* and on Paramount's Mae West films, "portraying the type of sex lewdness and vulgarity which the Hays organization permits to the major companies to produce and exhibit, but which the independent producers are afraid to make because of said discriminatory censorship."[29]

The Antitrust Division was aware, however, that to include the Hays Office among the defendants in the *Paramount* case could be a tactical error, because "censorship is always a controversial issue." This inclusion could have weakened the government's position in a trial in which the main objective was the separation of exhibition from production.[30] Once again, and in this instance in a decisive way, economic monopoly and monopoly of discourse were linked. But, as Hays had guessed, not many in America wanted to take on the role of censor, much less a government that was continually under attack for its "interference" in the country's institutional life. At the very last minute, two days before the case was opened, the division dropped the Hays Office from the case, to avoid the uncomfortable question of film censorship.

The link between monopoly and censorship re-emerged in 1948. In the context of the *Paramount* case decision, the Supreme Court granted the protection of the First Amendment to film, starting the process of revision of the system of self-censorship. In the meantime, film audiences had changed, because the distribution of foreign films on the American market had affected the taste of metropolitan audiences, while television had started capturing the family audience, which up to that time had been controlled by cinema. The end of vertical integration contributed to the decline of the studio system. In 1968 the code was abandoned and replaced by an age classification system.

Federal Trade Commission v. Paramount

The Federal Trade Commission (FTC) of the Justice Department was the agency designated to supervise the application of antitrust legislation (the Sherman and Clayton Acts), investigating and prosecuting those trade practices that limited competition on the market. Throughout the 1920s the commission investigated Famous Players-Lasky (from which Paramount subsequently developed), accusing it of holding a monopolistic control of the market.[31] This proceeding has been called "the first" *Paramount* case because it dealt with the same question: the control of the film market. As in the *Paramount* case, the FTC concentrated its attention on exhibition, dealing with specific trade practices such as block booking, identifying a risk of market monopoly in the vertical integration of the production companies, and indicating, as a remedy, the separation between exhibition and the other two branches of the industry (that is, the same penalty requested by the Antitrust Division in the *Paramount* case). For the inquiry related to this proceeding, which went on from 1921 to 1932, the FTC collected "17,000 pages of sworn testimony and 15,000 pages of evidence."[32] For the most part, the material dealt with the first phase of the inquiry, before 1925, and therefore its usefulness soon became limited because of developments in field. The "battle for the theaters" and the introduction of sound, which induced closer relations with Wall Street, radically changed the industry structure. But the central role attributed by the FTC to the trade practice of block booking in the interpretation of market control, in a vertically integrated industrial organization, did not change in time. Given that the studios produced better-quality films and availed themselves of first-run theaters in which to show them, they imposed on the small exhibitors, as a condition for obtaining their product, rental of the entire season production in block. They also covered the whole range of film programming, without giving any alternatives to the exhibitors or space to the independent producers.

In 1927 the FTC ordered the industry *to cease and desist* from block booking, defining it as an "unfair" commercial strategy that hampered fair competition by hindering the independent producers in their access to the screens and preventing the independent exhibitors from choosing the programming that was most pleasing to the communities they served. But a court of appeals overturned the FTC decision, ruling that block booking did not have monopolistic effects.

The historical and economic literature on the industry attributes a regulatory function to this intervention by the FTC, because it deterred Adolf Zukor, for example, from acquiring additional influence in the affairs of the First National theater chain he was attempting to take over.[33] It is important, however, to understand the meaning of the term "regulatory" in relation to antitrust proceedings. Presented as a restraint imposed by the government on the industry's excessive expansion, the antitrust laws tend instead to create a widespread state of alarm, which sharpens the attention of the entrepreneurs to their commercial strategies, involuntarily pushing them into distinguishing between trade practices that are disagreeable to the political-judiciary power and practices that could guarantee the same results with less risk. According to Thurman Arnold, antitrust legislation, far from being repressive, "promoted the growth of great industrial organizations, by deflecting the attack on them into purely moral and ceremonial channels."[34]

The film industry in fact reacted to the FTC antitrust proceeding by proposing to negotiate reforms of its trade practices through self-regulation. Representatives of all three branches of the film industry convened to discuss problems related to exhibition and to try to mitigate the conflict between distributors and exhibitors provoked mostly by block booking.[35] Abram Myers of the FTC, the agency then examining the complaints about the film industry trade practices, presided over these negotiations. (Myers later became the legal representative of the small independent exhibitors, united in the Allied States Association.)[36]

The FTC did not succeed in denting the film industry's integrated structure much less "regulating" its development away from cartelization. Instead, the industry used the court of appeals ruling that rejected the commission's decision as a judiciary acquittal for its monopolistic sins in the numerous administrative and judiciary proceedings it underwent in the 1930s. This inquiry, however, constituted an important precedent, outlining a disturbing profile of a highly concentrated communication industry and producing an enormous bulk of information and sworn testimony about the functioning of exhibition and the abuses of the majors—enough to attract the attention of the Justice Department.

The NRA Code of Fair Competition

The elaboration and discussion of the NRA code reopened the conflict between producer-distributors and exhibitors.[37] The first New Deal proposed to heal the economy through cooperation between industry and government, allowing the economic world the opportunity to regulate itself and adopting written codes to regulate industrial activity and trade practices. These codes coordinated an industry's operative patterns, confronted internal tensions such as union activities, and rationalized production methods, under the leadership of the trade organization and with the supervision of the federal authority, the NRA. If approved these codes would suspend the application of antitrust legislation.

The NRA code of fair competition for the film industry was anomalous in that it was the only code, out of six hundred, that did not distinguish between "buyers" and "sellers" and included the entire industry.[38] In August 1933 the deputy administrator of this code, Sol A. Rosenblatt, held a meeting in New York to set up committees to produce an acceptable document. Because producers and distributors had common economic interests, these two components formed a committee, but the exhibitors were unable to reconcile the divergent interests of the independents and "affiliated" groups, and therefore the Motion Picture Theater Owners Association (MPTOA) and Allied maintained different positions. This unbalanced situation gave the producer-distributors more control in the writing of the code. In September public hearings were held in Washington: 206 witnesses, representing "producers, distributors, exhibitors, affiliated and unaffiliated interests,

117

labor, the public, social and welfare groups, and other interested parties" had their say.[39]

The drafting of the code was no simple process. In a confidential letter to Steven Early written in October on behalf of the independent exhibitors, Abram Myers revealed that whereas there was no disagreement among the negotiating parties about the regulation of "hours and salaries," they were at an impasse on the question of trade practices.[40] After multiple revisions, the NRA code for the film industry was ready for Roosevelt's signature on November 27, 1933. In the final phase, however, the independent exhibitors, unsatisfied with the formulation of the provisions affecting their business, had abandoned the negotiation table. In another strong letter to Early, Myers expressed his disappointment, stating that this favoritism toward the majors was an "obvious outcome," for reasons he enumerated.

1. The newsreel is a valuable medium of publicity and the Administration will want to sew it up.

2. H. M. Warner made one of the largest single contributions to the Democratic campaign fund and will expect a *quid pro quo*.

3. Frank Walker, Treasurer of the National Committee and the holder of a responsible position in the Administration, was an officer of the Comerford (Paramount-Publix) Circuit of theaters and cooperated with the Hays' Office in exhibitor matters.

4. Sol Rosenblatt, appointed deputy administrator for amusements was an employee of Nathan Burkan, motion picture lawyer, in some way connected with the Loew MGM Company, and was therefore, "handpicked."

5. No. 4 was strengthened by the fact that Mr. Burkan participated in the Code proceedings as attorney for the producers, more especially Loew MGM.

6. Mr. [Marvin] McIntyre and yourself were former newsreel men, representing Pathé and Paramount, respectively, and would see that our case was not presented at the White House after we had been kicked around by NRA.

7. General [Hugh] Johnson's executive assistant and guardian of the outer chamber, Miss Robbins, was a former employee of RKO lent by that company to the Democratic Committee.

8. Assistant Administrator R. W. Lea was formerly an official of a Chicago bank that lent a lot of money to Paramount-Publix a few years ago and was supposed, therefore, to be interested in the last mentioned company.

9. Harold Phillips, a former newspaper man employed by Will Hays had virtually taken charge of publicity matters in Rosenblatt's office.[41]

Beyond these personal attacks, which, however, justify the impression that the administration did have reasons for favoring the majors, the polemics related to the code did not stop. Finally, Hugh Johnson, the administrator of the NRA, intervened to settle the question. After an investigation, he declared the complaints of the independents "groundless."[42] But the National Recovery Review Board, or Darrow Board, which later reviewed NRA activities, was not of the same opinion: reexamining the fair competition codes in April 1934, it identified the film industry code as one of the least balanced.[43]

Like every other NRA code, the film industry code contained a description of the industry, a definition of the authority administrating the code, and a list of regulations for labor relations and trade practices. But unlike other codes, this one did not call for particular care in reference to unionization. There was little need. According to a report on the code compiled by Daniel Bertrand, Hollywood workers received "higher wages than workers of the same level working outside the studios." In the report Rosenblatt was quoted as stating that "the Motion Picture Industry had less major labor trouble than any other comparable industry during the Code period."[44] (Actually, the majors had solved their problems in this area by keeping the labor force fragmented and by paying off two officials of the International Alliance of Theatrical Stage Employees (IATSE), George Browne and William Bioff, who, in their stronghold in Chicago, were in business with Al Capone's heir, Frank Nitti.[45])

The conflict developing in those years between the creative personnel and the producers emerged in the text with the institution of a writer-producer committee and an actor-producer committee in reference to the services of the more restless employees in Hollywood, who, in 1933, had organized into guilds. The report also discusses the question of excessive salaries, which received more attention in a separate inquiry ordered by Roosevelt himself. This inquiry, which aimed at the heart of Hollywood "extravagance," was viewed favorably by some elements of the industry, especially after the general salary cut that followed the bank holiday proclaimed by Roosevelt in March 1933 to stem the tide of bank closures. An employee of RKO wrote to McIntyre, as FDR's secretary:

> I think that it would be a safe estimate to say that 75% of the total studio salaries paid goes to not more than 5% of the employees—executives, directors, and stars. . . . The supervisors are drawing anywhere from 2500 to 5000 a week. Those at the top of course get plenty more—larger salaries and in addition options on the company's stock, bonuses, etc., which brings them up into the real money. . . . And at the same time some of these very companies have run up huge deficits—one of them fifteen million in the past two years.

The social lives of some of these big salaried ones could well remind us of the days preceeding the French revolution—parties costing thousands of dollars an evening, and everyone trying to outdo the last affair in novelty and costliness. ([Darryl] Zanuck just gave an affair to 400 or so last week in a specially built improvised Bower setting in Hollywood. And not to be outdone [Irving] Thalberg announces a day or so later that he is chartering a private yacht to take 50 friends to a football game in San Francisco.)

Naturally this, and living in the style to which none of them were ever accustomed, calls for large weekly checks. These salaries are of course charged to the pictures—and on the last two I have been on the overhead charges have been as high as 60% of the total budget. And this surely doesn't leave much to spend around among ordinary studio workers—who total about 95% of picture employees.[46]

After a conversation by FDR and the popular actor Eddie Cantor, with the producer Joseph Schenck and Will Hays, the question simmered down.[47] The investigation into excessive salaries did not produce any relevant outcomes. On the contrary, the report written by Rosenblatt on the subject recommended the reintegration of this type of salary after the pay cut for the bank holiday.[48] Despite being in marked contrast to the gravity of the country's economic situation during the Depression, Hollywood's extravagance had in fact the collateral effect of promoting optimism. Moreover the public associated the high salaries of Hollywood personalities with a "special environment," which was then notorious for the paucity of its sense of social responsibility.

Polemics on the NRA Code

Most of the polemics involving the film industry's NRA code were not about the question of labor but about the conflict between the producer-distributors and the exhibitors. The most heated discussions revolved around trade practices such as block booking, the "score charge," and the double bill. But precisely because these practices were controversial, the NRA code did not regulate them. The code limited itself to instituting an arbitration board to settle questions related to "clearances" (the period of time elapsing between one showing and the next, in a given zone), and "runs" (the sequence of different showings of a feature picture in a zone).[49]

Bertrand's report on the NRA code for the film industry begins with a detailed analysis of the structure of the industry and then, unexpectedly, states that the film industry functioned within a regime of competition. The competition existed on the inside between producers, studios, and independents, and between affiliated groups and the independents, and outside with other media.[50] The report interprets this competition as a corrective to the "natural monopolistic tendency of the industry, [which was] encouraged by the protection granted to it by the copyright laws." But despite this statement, the report lists a series of trade practices in clear contrast to the image of a competitive industry. These include "overbuying," the practice by an exhibitor of renting an excessive number of films to keep a theater in competition from using them, and "unusually long clearance," an unreasonably long period between the first showing of a film and the next. On the subject of clearance Bertrand points out, "It is claimed that 40% of distributors' revenue is derived from first run accounts in 100 key cities," and that "all the major film-producing companies consider at least 50% of the cost of a negative film should be amortized within three months after release"—in fact, "Paramount amortizes 80% of the cost of a negative film" in 12 weeks."[51] Thus, the financial debt of the majors contributed to the importance the first-run theater in their economy, rendering it necessary to collect a good quota of the takings in a short time. For this reason, the majors did not favor long run exploitation of a film even at that time.

In addition, the majors required that shorts and newsreels be rented in a single block with the films. This trade practice demonstrates how the majors had organized themselves to protect their commercial hegemony by saturating the entire programming of a theater, leaving no space to competition or chance for the independent producer to build a professional competence in this sector. Another source of tension was the practice by the producer-distributors of sometimes fixing in the contract the days of the week on which the film had to be shown, to maximize the profits in case of percentage rentals. Exhibitors also contested film distribution, outside the legitimate theater, in schools and churches, for example, when used as a device to annoy a recalcitrant competitor.

Bertrand's report also describes exhibition practices that had developed during the Depression but were abrogated by the code because they were unpopular with the producer-distributors. To stimulate box office sales in the most acute phase of the economic crisis, small exhibitors had begun offering "discounts" and prizes ranging from "valueless gadgets to automobiles." The producers considered these practices totally "foreign" to the film business and "demoralizing" to the industry, and so they put strong pressure on the code authority to eliminate them. On the other side of the issue, the small exhibitors received the support of pottery manufacturers, who had been selling them large numbers of china sets and expressed the exaggerated fear that the abolition of premiums in the theaters would induce unemployment in the field.[52] The NRA code had little to say about inexpensive giveaways but condemned resolutely other methods of "discount" that involved the element of fortune. Among the most popular were "Bank Night" (a bank account would be opened for the winner of a draw from among the ticket-holders), "Race Night" (on the basis of the number of the ticket one could participate in a contest to identify some products appearing in a short), and "Screeno" (a type of lottery). According to Bertrand, the phenomenon was stimulated by national advertising, and at that time, the public seemed to be particularly responsive to giveaways, whether offered over radio or by the motion picture theater. There was a risk, however, in this practice, because people always asked for more: "One small exhibitor tried one device after another and finally decided to give away a Ford car. That set the community agog with excitement until the small exhibitor's chain competitor countered with the offer of a Pierce Arrow."[53] These discounts and prizes appeared, Bertrand points out, "exclusively in areas where there was strong competition" and therefore represented the small exhibitors' reaction to crushing competition or to unjust clearances or zoning. They were in fact the last resource to lure away clients from theaters that could offer good programming instead because they were "affiliated" with the majors or belonged to a large circuit. By threatening to stop the distribution of films to the theaters that offered these lotteries, the producers succeeded in obtaining an ordinance against them. But as soon as the NRA was declared unconstitutional, this form of commercialization reemerged, assuming new features.

These efforts to stimulate consumption during the crisis occurred against the backdrop of a contradictory relationship between overproduction and poverty. The film industry maintained a detached attitude toward such low-profile manifestations of the "culture of abundance" as china premiums. In the 1930s, consumer materialism "contaminated" the film industry, however, through the sale of pop corn and drinks in the theaters, destined to become a business unto itself. Within production, Hollywood chose not to merge its destiny with that of publicity and stimulation of consumption as radio had done, giving up, for example, the production of publicity shorts, perhaps because exhibitors felt that this type of advertisement annoyed moviegoers. The studios did turn to more subtle commercialization formulas, with the presentation of electrical appliances, cars, typewriters, drinks, to viewers able to spot them in the context of the films themselves. They also signed contracts with the large department stores to sell clothing designed by Hollywood costume designers. These choices of the film industry in the realm of consumer culture confirm that Hollywood was preparing itself for a higher and more complex mediating role with respect to the "culture of abundance," placing service and entertainment before sales, and showing a strong commitment only to the promotion of itself.

Unresolved Problems

A considerable section of the NRA report is devoted to a complicated issue—block booking. After a summary of the controversy, from the FTC proceedings to the bills then pending in Congress to eliminate block booking, Bertrand discusses the solution elaborated within the NRA code, which permitted the "cancellation" of 10 percent of the films rented in block. But this option had been rendered almost impracticable by complex clauses of application in the NRA code. Nonetheless, the exhibitors affiliated with the MP-TOA saw this provision as a victory and subsequently tried to obtain more consistent and flexible conditions of cancellation. Allied instead wanted the elimination not necessarily of block booking itself but of its compulsory character.

The report points out that block booking angered civic groups because its inflexibility limited their influence on exhibitors. The organization leader in this field, the Motion Picture Research Council (MPRC), demanded that President Roosevelt insert in the NRA code "provisions essential to the public welfare, which it might otherwise take years to obtain; and keep out of it provisions that, if they go in, will still further strengthen the existing monopoly." The MPRC recommended that the clause preventing "schools, churches, museums and other non-theatrical agencies" from showing films be deleted and that block booking and blind selling be eliminated and their ill effects "corrected" by the institution of a system of trade shows and the diffusion of "written descriptions" of the film's content. In addition, the MPRC insisted on a revision of the criteria in the establishment of clearances and runs, stating, "The fundamental principle that the motion picture art belongs to the public rather than to the producers of entertainment films must be established and maintained." It thus committed itself to fight against the monopoly, because "it is useless to hope or to work for better films until, by the ending of these oppressive and monopolistic trade practices, the film market is opened to independent producers."[54] The Council assumed the role of the great reformer, aiming to modify both film content and the economic structure of the industry, while hoping "to revive the film industry, now fittingly prostrate under the displeasure of the American people."

Between the Hays Code and the NRA code for the film industry there was not only a nominal and chronological superimposition, which in itself is emblematic of the interaction between the two, but also an analogous function of mediation between different hypothesis of control of the means of communication.

In its conclusions, Bertrand's report deals especially with exhibition, calling attention to the development of the large independent circuits—a problem that returned in the *Paramount* case. Block booking, because it is an issue involving interstate commerce and therefore falls under federal jurisdiction, is the first item under the heading "Suggested Points of Application for Federal Power."[55] The report points out that because of these trade practices, the majors had been acting like a monopoly for years, but the competent authorities had never taken an official position on the legality of these operations. There is no specific suggestion of possible correctives, only an emphasis on the need for a "thorough study" of the structure of the movie industry by "a Federal agency with adequate facilities and authority"—a suggestion that was realized in the Antitrust Division investigation of 1936.

The NRA code of fair competition did not introduce relevant modifications in the functioning of the industry; it did not address the controversial question of block booking, which favored the majors; it forbade instead the lotteries and premiums used by the small exhibitors to help overcome the crisis. Initially the producers had asked the government to eliminate double features, but the committee writing the code was overwhelmed by exhibitors' protests and, probably in exchange for silence on the issue of block booking, avoided the issue. The practice was widespread, they reasoned, and it had already modified the production system.

In 1935 the NRA Division of Review published *Evidence Study no. 25,* prepared like the earlier report, by Daniel Bertrand. The report points out that in the film industry "production, distribution and exhibition are both horizontally and vertically integrated and . . . the concentration of corporate ownership in the hands of a few large companies provides an economic division of the Industry between what are known as 'major' and 'independent' interests." It then follows up the stringent comment that "the economic consequences of this concentration are reflected in nearly all problems of the Industry," with reams of economic figures, collected from diverse sources, to compose a detailed portrait of the industry's structure.[56]

A very different tone characterizes the March 1934 report by the Ward Commission, which begins: "Monopolistic practices in this industry are bold and aggressive and its small enterprise is cruelly oppressed." Furthermore, the NRA code for the film industry "was made by representatives of the large producing companies," and contains "with other unusual and unjust features, provisions that named the members of the Code Authority to administer the Code and other provisions to make the Authority so constituted self-perpetuating. . . . The Authority consists of ten members of whom eight are shown to be directly or indirectly connected with the eight large companies." (Administration officials therefore shared in part Abram Myers's remarks.) The report records the protests of small exhibitors, who, even if numerically representing the majority of the industry, did not really participate in the writing of the document. It underlines the point that the code did not confront the central issue of the trade practices, especially of block booking, re-marking that "the motion picture industry is unique in that it is probably the only industry in which many of its members do not have absolute right to buy the products necessary for the conduct of their business."[57] The Ward Commission believed that the "evil" of block booking could be corrected only with the cooperation of the entire industry, and it therefore suggested the institution of a joint commission to deal with the problem at the negotiating table, and, absent that, it recommended amending the code with anti–block booking clauses.

In May 1934 President Roosevelt received a report from the NRA with a section on the movie industry that refuted the accusations of the Review Board, stating that the "board acted solely on the basis of a disorderly mess of unsworn and largely false testimony of a few malcontents."[58] But the Review Board responded to the challenge by insisting on the abolition of block booking and making numerous references to the movement of "millions of outraged citizens" who "have joined under the leadership of various religious bodies, in putting into effect a nation-wide boycott directed against objectionable pictures."[59] It is not surprising that the neopopulists on the Review Board used the pressure of these reform groups as political lever—the same pressure that had brought about the enforcement of the self-censorship code.

This dispute between two federal agencies, the NRA and the Darrow Board, representing two different aspects of the New Deal—economic interventionism and the neopopulist defense of small enterprise—was not unusual. The New Deal often functioned through such "counterorganization."[60] Leaning on diverse interest groups, it created clashes between different ideological positions, different strategies, and different aims, thus producing both information and counterinformation, mobilizing all the social forces in the field in the process of reform.

In 1933, however, Hollywood credited the New Deal, mostly because of the NRA code, with its recovery. The *Motion Picture Herald* of May 20, 1933, for example, ran a headline that read: "Business Aided by Roosevelt Bills." In the 1934 edition of the *Film Daily Yearbook*, many of the statements issued by film executives thanked the administration or expressed pro-Roosevelt sentiments. Adolph Zukor's, for example, was entitled "Faith in NRA," and Albert Warner tied the amelioration of the industry's conditions "to the leadership of President Roosevelt and to the stimulating influence of NRA."

The correspondence directed to the White House from Hollywood confirms this positive trend in the relationship between the movie industry and the administration in the first phase of the New Deal—a trend that deeply affected the interaction between the two throughout the Roosevelt years.

NRA Materials as a Source for Economic Film History

From a historiographic point of view the NRA report affords us the possibility of a more scientific study of film economics because it is not limited to data supplied by the industry, which is notoriously inclined to transform the costs of production into publicity material and is always in need of concealing the levels of concentration and market control.

In an often-cited article on the film industry NRA code, Douglas Gomery holds that "the US federal government through the NIRA openly sanctioned the monopolistic behavior of the large firms in the motion picture industry."[61] Later he corrected this interpretation, arguing instead that "in the longer run, the publicity generated and information gathered during the NRA concerning the motion picture industry, coupled with a change in the Roosevelt administration's strategy to combat hard times, led to antitrust action against the film industry's monopoly capitalists."[62] On the contrary, Robert Sklar writes that this code "ended up strengthening the small businessman at the expense of the major producer-distributors."[63] Both interpretations are justified. The NRA code represents the phase in which all forces took a position in the field, reconfirming the choice of self-regulation, in business matters as well as in film content.

This code demonstrated that it was possible to transform a system of industrial self-government typical of a producer-capitalist mentality into a New Dealist model. The preface to Bertrand's second report, *NRA Work Materials no. 34,* states in fact: "This contribution to self-regulation by industry under the eye of the Government is of high importance to the student of industrial progress."[64] The exemplary nature of the self-regulation system carried out by the Hays Office attracted the attention of New Dealers like Raymond Moley;[65] the same "exemplariness," but of an opposed sign, attracted the attention of the Antitrust Division when it opened the *Paramount* case.

The Unionization of Hollywood

According to current historiographic interpretation, through Section 7A of the NRA and, most of all, through legislation such as the Wagner Act, the New Deal affirmed the institutional role of the union. Or, as Steve Fraser puts it, "Somehow the political chemistry of the New Deal worked a double transformation: the ascendency of labor and the eclipse of the 'labor question.'"[66] This consideration seems particularly appropriate with respect to Hollywood.

126

As the first report on the NRA code notes and most literature suggests, the studio workers did not appear particularly combative. But this is one of many legends in need of reconsideration. The growth of the labor movement in Hollywood was slow because Los Angeles for the most part adhered to an open shop policy, which discouraged collective bargaining. In 1926 the MPPDA and the unions representing various categories of studio workers signed the Studio Basic Agreement (SBA), which established an open shop, while centralizing labor negotiations. The entry of investment banking on the Hollywood scene, because of the theater expansion and the introduction of sound, in addition to the early attempts at self-censorship, made the industry more aware not only of its public image but also of the necessity of guaranteeing its profits as efficiently as possible, by controlling production costs. Labor remained fragmented, because, through the SBA, the majors recognized five unions, but without promising to hire their members. Instead they favored IATSE, selecting the large international unions in preference to rank-and-file or local initiatives.

In July 1933, however, given the growing complexity of the division of labor caused by the introduction of sound, IATSE went on strike in an effort to impose its jurisdiction over competing craft unions. Although the attempt to escalate the agitation to the entire industry caused it to fail, the leaders of IATSE did succeed in obtaining exclusive representation of the projectionists, though their methods were unorthodox.[67] In 1934, Browne and Bioff of IATSE decided to "make a deal" with the powerful theater chain of Balaban and Katz, in Chicago. The deal was "protected" by Nitti's gang. Tommy Maloy of IA Projectionist Local 110, entertaining "business relations" with Balaban, or, more specifically, extorting $150 a week for "protection," was machine-gunned in 1935.[68]

After the introduction of a second wave of New Deal legislation brought passage of the Wagner Act and with it the establishment of the National Labor Relation Board to actively support labor's right to organize, in 1936 IATSE conquered a closed shop in the studios. Through their "payoff" to IATSE, motion picture executives were not actually defending production costs, in that wages did not constitute a large portion of these costs (12 to 22 percent of yearly production costs),[69] and were controlled by hiring workers short term and raising wages only for certain groups. A labor strike like the one called by IATSE in 1933 could, however, again increase production costs by lengthening production schedules or hindering a film's completion.

In 1937 the Federated Motion Picture Crafts (FMPC) went on strike, demanding a union shop, recognition of the federation, and separate contracts for the affiliated crafts (painters, draftsmen, make-up artists, hairdressers, and scenic workers).[70] This strike lasted six weeks and met with violent reactions at the picket lines. When it was over, the FMPC had been wiped out.

The producers in cooperation with IATSE (and the Painters International) had thwarted its attempt at organizing local crafts and gaining access to the SBA. While IATSE's jurisdictional motivations and ambition to represent all amusement workers can be easily understood, it is important to stress that producers always preferred granting minor benefits or wage increases to the local unaffiliated crafts rather than including them in the SBA, keeping them fragmented and favoring instead negotiations with the centralized, international unions. In this instance centralization, a national trend in the 1930s, highly benefited management at the expense of the workers.

In 1940 IATSE leaders, Browne and Bioff were tried and convicted for extortion. By that time the industry had given over $2.5 million to union and syndicate leaders. And yet this unholly alliance had saved the industry as much as $15 million.[71] The IATSE earned this money by keeping studio locals from negotiating directly with management. By selectively raising wages it had undermined solidarity among Hollywood workers, and by refusing to grant lower or flat rates to independent producers of low budget films it had also contributed to the consolidation of the monopolistic power of the majors.[72] This type of tamed union activity and widespread acquiescence to the organization of labor imposed by the studios undoubtedly favored the industry's economic stability in the second half of the 1930s.

In the mid-1930s the film community went through a period of intense unionization, particularly in the area of creative work. This movement can be ascribed to a general tendency toward political participation in the American culture of those years, but the process in Hollywood remains peculiar.

Efforts to organize creative personnel gave rise to bitter struggles, especially involving actors and screenwriters (but directors did their part too). In March 1933, in reaction to the bank holiday proclaimed by Roosevelt, film executives declared a 50 percent salary cut, which hit everyone except, of course, the producers. This unpopular decision stirred discontent in groups that already felt oppressed by the studio system and limited in their creativity and professional expression.[73] High salaries and the stability guaranteed by working under contract could compensate the Hollywood intellectuals only in part for the limitations on their creative freedom and the contradictions inherent in their role in the film industry. Many screenwriters were politically active, and when they began to organize, the industry reacted immediately. Through the Academy of Motion Pictures, the studios instituted a sort of company union for the creative personnel. The antilabor techniques adopted by the industry and the fervent atmosphere of those years created a strong internal tension in Hollywood and a wave of "red baiting" that set the stage for the anticommunist witch-hunts of the 1950s.

The Screen Writers Guild (SWG) and the Screen Actors Guild (SAG) were founded in 1933. Although the NRA code implicitly recognized them, it entrusted the discussion of specific contractual issues to the screenwriters and producers and the actors and producers committees. When the NRA was declared unconstitutional in 1935, these guilds suffered a counterblow when the producers, in a united front, refused to recognize them.[74] In 1936, under pressure from the producers, another screenwriters guild was instituted, the Screen Playwrights, which included, for the most part, the highest ranking playwrights, that is, those who already enjoyed a privileged relationship with the front office and certainly did not need union protection. When the producers used all their power to force the screenwriters under contract to adhere to this "friendly" organization, the SWG was almost disbanded.[75] Not until 1940, after a protracted clandestine effort, did the SWG reorganize itself.

In 1937 the SAG threatened to go on strike and joined the FMPC picket lines in sympathy. IATSE, afraid of losing its grip on the crafts to the rival FMPC, mediated the guild's interests with the producers, who were extremely worried about the damage that could result from a strike by such irreplaceable workers. Robert Montgomery, president of SAG, publicly acknowledged that because of the help of IATSE, the guild won recognition as a bargaining agent for all actors and a ten-year agreement with the producers.[76]

Labor conflicts were intense but carefully camouflaged in 1930s Hollywood. Beneath the monolithic and glamorous surface of the dream industry were continuous tensions and struggles that allow us to see the studio system, not as a static model, but as a dynamic process of adaptation to many different pressures.

The Block Booking Hearings

The first NRA report defined block booking as "the most controversial problem troubling the motion picture industry."[77] Encouraged by the 1927 Federal Trade Commission ruling that had ordered its abolition, the small exhibitors fought against this distribution system with every means and at every level: from the Justice Department to the trade press, from the negotiating table to the Congress, where, between 1928 and 1939 they presented different legislative proposals for its abolition.

The voluminous publications of the hearings on these bills,[78] in addition to expressing old and new prejudices about cinema and media culture, allow us to reconstruct the daily functioning of exhibition—the least studied branch of the studio system.[79] We learn, for example, how film programs worked. Through vertical integration the majors controlled many first-run theaters and reinforced this market position by programming them with a selection of the better films produced by their studio or by the other majors.

Their theaters, then, were not obliged to rent and screen *all* of the films produced by a studio in that year—not even their own. The small exhibitors, in contrast, in order to get the good pictures produced by one of the majors, had to rent its entire output, including films of low quality. Considering that the Big Eight each produced about forty films a year, and that the majority of the independent theaters operated on a double-feature program, with fairly frequent changes (an average of three changes each week), to secure the film titles for the season program, an exhibitor rented the "blocks" of three studios, on the basis of past performance at the box office, or rotation. The small exhibitor therefore could not rent films from other companies or from the independents, because his programming space was saturated; nor could he choose which films to show, because he paid for the entire block, even for the unscreened pictures.

For the independent exhibitor compulsory block booking constituted the nucleus of the Big Eight's monopolistic power, because it put him at the mercy of the producer, who was often at the same time his supplier of goods—the seller—and, if the studio managed a theater circuit, his competitor.

One might assume that block booking was a matter of interest mostly for the independent exhibitor, and for economic reasons. But actually the fiercest opponents of this practice were civic groups, who initiated the legislative projects. They constituted a faithful ally for the independent exhibitor in all the battles against the movie industry—in court, in Congress, and in the Justice Department. It was only by "marrying" the issue of economic monopoly to those of censorship, film content, and quality of film product (related to the question of "monopoly of discourse") that the anti–block booking front became effective.

The pressure group that inspired these legislative proposals was the (MPRC), sponsor of the Payne Fund studies on the psycho-sociological effects of cinema published in the early 1930s. The MPRC proposed three bills on the abolition of compulsory block booking: in 1928 the Brookhart Bill, in 1936 the Pettingill Bill, and in 1939–40 the Neely Bill. These last two legislative proposals passed the scrutiny of a special commission but did not succeed in obtaining the approval of both houses.

In the 1936 hearings, the MPRC representative outlined "three negative effects" of block booking combined with "blind selling": the first was on the exhibitor, who "under this vicious trade practice was powerless"; the second on "the Community," which "had no selection in what it shall see." "The evil of this," he argues, "is clear. When poor pictures are shown the welfare of the community and of the children suffers. The seeds of these noxious weeds are sown." (He also made the ritual accusation that gangster films produce juvenile delinquency.)[80] His apocalyptic tones are typical of the reformist discourse on cinema, but in this context they are mixed with liberal reformism, defending freedom of expression from the risks of centralization and standardization induced by mass production of cultural forms. The third effect is on the quality of film art. On this topic, the MPRC cites Walter Lippman: "The lack of competition from independent experimental, and, occasionally, from first rate enterprises, the sterilizing effect of monopoly, can be seen among the writers in Hollywood. . . . Hollywood is an artistic parasite living upon the talents evoked in the healthier open competition of the older arts." Pare Lorentz and Morris Ernst in their book *Censored,* many intellectuals on the left, and even some creative talents in Hollywood would agree. The issue of film quality moves away from content and morality, into the economy of production, favoring a less standardized and centralized system.

In 1939, in the hearings on the Neely Bill—a carbon copy of the previous legislative proposals—the same negative effects of block booking were brought up.

It has undermined the morals of part of a generation of American youth; it has resulted in a loss of independence and initiative on the part of local welfare groups; it has created a highly centralized propaganda power which at any time may be thrown into gear in order to emotionalize the American people.[81]

Reformist groups expressed particular fear of the "monopoly of discourse" and quoted Frank Capra as having said: "About six producers today pass upon 90% of the scripts and cut and edit 90% of the pictures."[82] The film production process had become, in their words, a diabolical machination.

First, the producer or financial backer provides the original idea; second, the writers translate this idea into a story; third, the director transmits it to the screen; fourth, the designers provide the scenery, costumes, and so forth; fifth, exigencies in the course of production may modify the product; and finally . . . the idea provided by the producer, through the producer-controlled compulsory block booking and blind selling distribution system, is implanted in the minds of 85,000,000 people almost simultaneously. This entire process from the original idea to the mind of the consumer is under centralized totalitarian control.[83]

Pressure groups promoted this image of the studio system as a great autocratic machine that "from afar," from exotic California, exercised its decidedly "un-American" control over the thought of the entire nation.

The arguments in support of the 1939–40 Neely Bill defended "community freedom in the selection of films" in order to uphold "the regional and local differences in morals and tastes; the superiority of national taste to Hollywood; and . . . home rule, with the preservation of liberty in this country in contrast to the bigotry and brutality of National Socialist Germany."[84] The assertion of local community values against the national diffusion of a cultural product expressed a populist (or neopopulist) resistance to centralization. At the end of the thirties, dictatorial regimes in Europe and some New Deal reforms provoked (if ever there was a need) antifederalist reactions and localistic phobias in sectors of the middle class. During the hearings, the juxtaposition Hollywood/small community oscillated between neopopulist defense and more conservative positions.

Because of their populist matrix, pressure groups and independent exhibitors defended the small town as a value in itself. A member of Allied, Sidney Samuelson, painted a vivid picture at the hearings of a provincial town.

> Newton is in northern New Jersey. It is the county seat of Sussex County. It has a population of about 5,000. It takes pride in its town square, with the old trees [and] historic monuments. . . . It is the center of an agricultural community. It has a few small industries. . . . I also want to leave with the committee this thought: That the "Newtons" in America outnumber the large cities greatly; that the "Newtons" mold public opinion; and that the "Newtons" are providing the driving force for this legislation because of the necessity to protect those types of communities.[85]

The small town evoked in these hearings reminds us of that projected on the screens, in Capra's films, for example. But it is not always as idyllic. At times, it resembles more the narrow-minded community of *Miracle Woman* than the community of *It's a Wonderful Life*: it is a small town where there is too short a step between gossip and lynching.

The historiographic re-evaluation of populism in reference to redistribution of wealth and power is an important corrective to our view of the 1930s, and indeed these reformist groups produce a very lucid analysis of the studio system. But the hearings also reveal the obtuseness of some members of these groups, reflected in their disturbingly racist remarks.[86]

Pressure groups opposed any centralized form of censorship, whether it was entrusted to a federal office or self-administered by the industry through the Hays Office. They identified the Hays organization as the institution through which Hollywood exercised its monopoly of discourse, and always insisted that censorship be left to the local community.[87] In contrast, the independent exhibitors proposed entrusting control of the industry's ideological and commercial operations to an outside agency, possibly federal. Control of the ideological function of cinema occupied a key position in the discourse of these groups: "The children of the entire nation are taught life according to the ideas and wishes of distant directors of one vast entertainment business. . . . The children are taught 'reel' life and not real life."[88] This concept, used against cinema from its origins, expressed the typically reformist and paternalistic concern that so-called less mature people (that is, less educated classes and children) could confuse the screen with reality. These right-thinking people wanted to protect the "28,000,000 children" who weekly watched the films produced by the majors "from germs which destroy their minds."[89]

Fears about cinema also had political connotations: "The motion picture group has power to carry an election as it wishes, unless it is restrained by this bill."[90] Ethnic and racial prejudices fed suspicions about Hollywood and about the movie moguls, who, as Sklar has emphasized, threatened, with their cultural heterogeneity, WASP hegemony.[91] Sentences like "The freedom of the screen must be wrested from the strange grasp of the few irresponsible and covetous men who dominate the industry" and "When the creative force, the group that sits in judgment, upon all screen production gets down to eight men far off in Hollywood, with its peculiarly vivid and distorted background, the mothers of America are powerless" confirm the persistence of these prejudices.[92] The falsity and the exoticism attributed to Hollywood—a place of "waste and extravagance" even according to Thurman Arnold—were transformed into a label of anti-Americanism by this provincial bigotry.[93]

Actually the attack on the censorship front was not unwelcomed by the movie industry, because it stimulated the atavic American antipathy for this institution. It should be noted that the main Catholic groups and the Parent Teachers Association did not support anti–block booking legislation. Probably coopted by the MPPDA, they held that it was much easier to fight on a single front (that of Hollywood, putting pressure of the PCA, the office supervising the application of the Hays Code) than on twelve thousand fronts constituted of so many small local theaters.[94]

The importance of the small theater in the economy of the studio system is not obvious and these hearings offer an occasion to reconsider it. In the 1930s the small theater constituted numerically a significant part of the business, but the limited price of the ticket did not make it an "interesting" market for the majors. It is true, however, that the long-run market and thus the small theater guaranteed the production risk, in that every film, even the worst, received distribution because of block booking and covered beforehand production costs through blind selling. The interdependence between that which rendered this market profitable and the distribution practices contested in these hearings constituted the nucleus of the studio system.[95] In the hearings, Charles Pettijohn, legal counsel for the MPPDA promoted the industry's point of view toward the small exhibitor.

> We make no pretense of being in the business of education, and we make no pretense of being in the business of religion. We are in the entertain-

ment business, and our problem is to make pictures which the public like, and to keep this business down to mass entertainment so that it can reach the greatest number of people. . . . at a price which they can pay. And we are doing it.

The same identical pictures, the good pictures, go to the smallest, humblest village in the land, and under the same plan of distribution these villages get, many times, pictures for which the large distributing houses have to pay thousands of dollars for first runs, delivered to them for 6, 8, 12, or 15 dollars. In other words, we are delivering a Rolls Royce at the present time cheaper than a Ford. . . . You say why are we distributing them at a loss? Well, after they have been run by the bigger houses, they are still good, but we keep them running and that results, necessarily, in new customers for our business, and that keeps our entertainment down, mass entertainment of the people, to a price which the people can afford to pay.[96]

Pettijohn exalted the industry's nobility.

We are confronted with the physical task of distributing 25 to 30 thousand miles of film every day to 16,500 theaters located in 9,187 cities, towns, villages and hamlets. And, gentlemen of the committee, that is done every day of the year, and has been done every day. That has been done during snow and storms, when films have been flown by airplane to little theaters where the price paid for the films would not pay for the gasoline used in the flight, under the tradition of the stage and screen that "the show must go on."[97]

This trite phrase on the mission of cinema conceals the complex issues of blind selling, block booking, runs, and clearances, that is, the distribution methods by which the industry maximized its profits in the field of exhibition. The small theater was the place where the scarce productivity of the sector came to be "traded" with its ideological function. The industry's abuses in distribution were supposedly redeemed by the good action it accomplished in supplying a Rolls Royce "cheaper than a Ford" and in guaranteeing that the "humblest village in America" could see Hollywood's greatest pictures. The small exhibitors saw it in a different way: "One would necessarily be led to believe that the producers have no need for the small exhibitors. . . . We are continually reminded or impressed that they can very easily get along without our business."[98]Like the double feature and block booking, which nobody seemed to want but everyone imposed, the small theater played an ambiguous role, of determination and of dependence, in reference to the studio system.

The anti–block booking hearings dealt with Hollywood's "monopoly of discourse" also from the point of view of the small independent producers.

Speaking for those producers, I. E. Chadwich testified that the independent producers had to face such a closed market that sometimes they offered to reimburse the exhibitors for a picture rented in block, to be able to show one of their films in its place. In his opinion, the independents had practically quit making films because they were no longer able to invest in production. While in the past there had been thirty-four "truly independent" production companies (unlike those of a large caliber, like Goldwyn or Selznick, which distributed their films through the majors and belonged to the studio system), in 1940 there remained only eleven of them, and even these were rapidly on their way to extinction. The control of the first-run market allowed the majors to exclude them from the publicity factor connected to the release in these theaters. Dealing with a transformation still in progress, Chadwick observed that the majors had further weakened the independents' position by beginning the production of B-movies to be inserted in the bottom part of a double bill—an area previously occupied at times by the independents' product.[99]

The independent producers were mentioned in these hearings as well as in the *Paramount* case, but they were never given proper consideration. The role of the independent producer was crucial to any demonstration of the negative effects of the Big Eight's monopoly on the film product, but it was difficult to explain in what terms an independent producer like Goldwyn differed from Chadwick, without entering into less "scientific" or judicially weak disquisitions on what is a "good" film. The cause of the "real" independent producers was weakened by the modest quality of their low-budget products, for the most part serials, westerns, exploitation films of a sensationalistic character—indefensible from the point of view of civic groups.

Although they were an interest group, the independent producers lacked an ideological position that could impress public opinion over and above the generic consideration that they represented a type of small enterprise, threatened in its survival by a combative trust. Nor was it a numerous group or powerful enough to constitute a lobby that could disturb a trade organization such as the MPPDA.

Hollywood opposed the anti–block booking bills by mobilizing all of its financial and human resources in the halls of Congress and undertaking a vast promotional campaign. The MPPDA began by trying to sensitize the pressure groups it had already been able to co-opt in the self-censorship debate.[100] In this campaign the majors argued against the elimination of block booking by stressing the technical difficulties implicit in the enactment of the law: increased distribution costs, problems supplying the small isolated exhibitor, and the impossibility of supplying accurate "plot descriptions" of the films beforehand as requested by the bill in order to "correct" blind selling. (Allied, in a gesture of good will, emended this clause to try to meet the producers' objections, but they gave no ground themselves, stating that they would never agree to write this type of synopsis, even "if you attached a jail sentence to its accuracy."[101]

In 1939–40, during the discussion of the Neely Bill, the MPPDA launched a full-scale attack, inviting the studio personnel to write to their representatives expressing their opposition to the anti–block booking bills because they would cause unemployment and higher distribution costs.[102]

In the discussion of the Neely Bill, the industry tried to postpone any solution to the block booking problem until after an agreement was reached in the *Paramount* case. At the same time, within the antitrust suit, they held that, because the question of the trade practices was under discussion in the hearings, and because they hoped to arrive at a form of self-regulation of the matter, the Antitrust Division of the Justice Department should postpone this aspect of the negotiations. Abram Myers of Allied, weary of the dilatory tactics of the movie industry's legal staff, warned both the Antitrust Division and the congressional committee that the Big Eight tended to promise radical transformations of their activities when public opinion or judicial and administrative agencies investigated them, only to let them drop as soon as the agitation ceased, and, most of all, as soon as the government turned its back.[103] In fact, while the Neely Bill hearings were taking place, in 1940, the trial for the *Paramount* case opened in New York. The next day the hearings were interrupted and would not have been reconvened even if the bill had been approved by the Senate. Negotiations for the consent decree, which involved distribution methods, had already begun, and so the battlefront was definitely transferred to the Justice Department. This transfer was welcomed by the groups that had proposed the Neely Bill, because Thurman Arnold had drastically stigmatized the movie industry. No other industry, he pointed out, approached the movie industry in its control of the market: "It is the inevitable result of the vertical cartel or vertical trust—the product of these vast combinations. It is something that is apparent from top to bottom. That is the characteristic fear, bitterness, and suspicion—even hatred, that prevail. . . . Something that I feel is distinctly un-American."[104] But the international crisis modified the equilibrium in the field.[105] At the hearings the film executives immediately played on the fact that they stood to lose their foreign market, and spokesman reminded the government of the function cinema could perform if the situation worsened.

> The Government has had occasion to use us in the past, and I want to say briefly that in the trying days which we seem to be facing, I am sure that the Government is going to find an increasing use of the American screen and that the screen is again going to cooperate with the Government to the utmost of its ability. I therefore . . . beg you not to raise any obstacle to the development of the motion picture industry at this time, and do not

136

do anything that would even close one screen because we are going to
need the screen in protecting the American rights in the troublesome
days to come.[106]

This was the argument that convinced the government to sign a consent decree in the *Paramount* case and to drop the Neely Bill. Even if the Antitrust Division insisted on the need to break up vertical integration, the decree proposed a three-year trial period, during which the industry had to modify its
more controversial trade practices, in particular block booking. The decree
proposed booking groups of no more than five films, but this solution did not
satisfy anyone: it is was too different from legislative proposals like the Neely
Bill to meet the demands of the independent exhibitors and pressure groups.

In addition, it opened a new front because of the reaction by the Three
Little companies (Columbia, Universal, and United Artists), which were deprived of the distributive method, block booking, that was essential to their
fortune. They therefore refused to sign the consent decree, causing the accord to fail. When the *Paramount* case was reopened, in 1944, block booking
was declared illegal.

At the end of the 1930s, however, American film exhibition underwent a
complex transformation. National improvements in the highway system and
the bettering of economic conditions made it easier for people from small
country communities to ride into town for better theaters and a wider film
selection. At the same time, the old metropolitan movie palaces, situated in
central zones where it was hard to park a car and characterized by high operating costs began an inexorable decline. They were replaced by the modern suburban film theater, of average size, and with functional architecture
and low operating costs. The war slowed this transformation, but the signs of
change were clear enough to the industry that it modified its commercial
strategies.[107]

The Propaganda Hearings (Clark-Nye Committee)

In 1940 film issues were much debated on Capitol Hill. In addition to the
anti–block booking hearings there were two committees that were interested
in cinema, from a predominantly ideological point of view: the House Un-
American Activities Committee (HUAC), which investigated "communist subversion" in Hollywood, and the Senate Subcommittee on Propaganda in Motion Pictures and Radio, chaired by Senator Worth Clark, which analyzed the
"premature antifascism" of these media.[108] The hearings held by the two committees reached the front pages of the newspapers, revealing a notable degree
of anti-Semitism, and anti-Hollywood prejudices, bringing out phobias similar

to those that emerged in the anti–block booking hearings. But the investigations of the HUAC and of the Clark Committee, largely unpopular, revealed no subversive plot in Hollywood, gave rise to no legislative proposal, and produced no relevant information (something the block booking hearings had at least succeeded in doing). Instead they opened the door to incursions by much better trained inquisitors in the years ahead, during the Cold War.

In an opening statement in the propaganda hearings, Senator Clark defined cinema and radio as "the most potent instruments of communication of ideas" but stigmatized them for using their ideological power to "influence the public mind in the direction of participation in the European war."[109] In the background, one can perceive echoes of the contemporary debate around the concepts of information and propaganda as Senator Clark attacks Hollywood's monopoly of discourse.

> Any man or any group of men who can get control of the screen can reach every week in this country an audience of 80,000,000 people. If there is a great debate before the Nation involving its economic life or even its liberties, no man can get a syllable in the sound pictures save by the grace of the men who control sound pictures. . . . There are 17,000 moving-picture theatres in the United States. They do not belong to a handful of men, of course, but the pictures that appear on the screens of those theatres are produced by a handful of man and that handful of men can open or close those 17,000 theaters to ideas at their sweet will. They hold the power of life and death over those motion-picture houses because by their block booking system, blind selling system, and other devices they can close almost any house that they please on any day and at any time.
>
> At the present time they have opened those 17,000 theatres to the idea of war, to the glorification of war, to the glorification of England's imperialism, to the creation of hatred of the people of Germany and now of France, to the hatred of those in America who disagree with them. Does anyone see a pictorial representation of life in Russia under "Bloody Joe" Stalin? They do not. In other words, they are turning these 17,000 theaters into 17,000 daily and nightly mass meetings for war. I say this is a monopoly."[110]

This argument sounds like that of the pressure groups during the anti–block booking hearings and thus repeats the equation of economic monopoly and monopoly of discourse. The official title of the propaganda hearings was in fact, "A Resolution Authorizing an Investigation on War Propaganda Disseminated by the Motion Picture Industry and of Any Monopoly in the Production, Distribution, or Exhibition of Motion Pictures." Senator Nye worked documents and data from the *Paramount* case into his opening statement in order to present as a foregone conclusion that the Big Eight controlled the theaters and therefore maintained an economic dictatorship—a key argument in his attack on Hollywood's ideological dictatorship.[111]

Will Hays had long before understood that the majority of Americans and the administration itself opposed the ideological regulation of cinema. On this occasion, too, the Hays Organization in an effort to divert attention from the issues inherent in the economic structure, emphasized the censorial aspect of the attacks against the industry. As in the block booking hearings, nonsensical and bigoted speeches by the detractors of Hollywood cinema overwhelmed the evidence of the Big Eight's monopoly.

Senator Nye tried to defend himself and the committee from the accusation that it was motivated by racist sentiments. At the hearing he quoted an article published in the Democratic press, which he felt distorted comments he had made at a meeting of the America First Committee, a conservative anti-interventionist association.[112] The reporting, he said, was an "effort to misrepresent our purpose and to prejudice the public mind and your mind by dragging this racial issue to the front" and obscuring the real objectives of the committee, that is, the censorship of the interventionist message emanating from Hollywood. But, to avoid contradicting himself, he added that those spreading this kind of propaganda through the cinema were indeed Jews, born in foreign lands. As Sklar notes, for Nye, "the moviemakers were insufficiently American in origin, intellect and character" to run such an important communication medium at a moment of international crisis.[113]

During the Clark Committee hearings, forty-eight films were "investigated" (twenty-five were American, thirteen were foreign, for the most part English, and ten were issues of *The March of Time*). All of the studios appeared on this list, but Warner Bros., with seven films, was the most prominent. This investigation of film texts was no close analysis of their expressive and ideological functioning. Far from it—congressmen frequently cited films they had not even seen. The fact that Hollywood films were scrutinized in the hearings had the unexpected collateral effect of revealing the existence of a committed Hollywood, dealing with "serious" issues.

Suggestions were made before these hearings that the order to spread an interventionist message had been issued by the New Deal administration—such an innovative form of government as to be defined "anti-American" by the more conservative element. Senator Burton Wheeler accused the movie industry of conspiring with the Roosevelt administration to "carry on a violent propaganda campaign intending to incite the American people to the point where they will become involved in this war."[114] But American foreign policy in the late 1930s was not linear: the President himself had publicly taken isolationist positions, even though he never hid his anti-Nazism.[115] Thus the accusations moved by the Clark Committee were easily refutable, because there was not a clear enough foreign policy to allow the administration to issue precise orders in this respect.

Wendell Willkie, the Republican presidential candidate just defeated by

FDR, defended the industry with great eloquence and ability. There was a certain incongruity in his taking this role, because he had begun the presidential campaign supporting the necessity of the country's preparedness for war and only later moved to the opposite side, defining Roosevelt as "a warmonger."[116] His performance during the hearings, however, positively impressed even the Democrats in the MPPDA.[117]

Movie moguls, including Joseph Schenck and Harry Warner, defended Hollywood's intervention as part of the "public service" role of cinema. Warner forcefully expressed his American patriotism and anti-Nazism.

> I believe nazi-ism is a world revolution whose ultimate objective is to destroy our democracy, wipe out all religion, and enslave our people—just as Germany has destroyed and enslaved Poland, Belgium, Holland, France and all the other countries. I am ready to give myself and my personal resources to aid in the defeat of the Nazi menace to the American people.[118]

Modestly Warner left to President Roosevelt the decision to declare war. On his side, however, he firmly refuted the accusation that the films produced by his studio were propagandistic and incited war hysteria. In defense of the films cited in the hearings (*Sergeant York, Confessions of a Nazi Spy, Underground*) Warner cited their box office success: "They have enjoyed wide popularity and have been profitable to our company. In short, these pictures have been judged by the public and the judgment has been favorable"—that is, according to the Hollywood philosophy that the public is always right. He also used the Warner trademark depiction of contemporary reality as an argument in its defense.

> These pictures were carefully prepared on the basis of factual happenings and they were not twisted to serve any other ulterior purpose. In truth, the only sin of which Warner Bros. is guilty is that of accurately recording on the screen the world as it is or as it has been. Unfortunately, we cannot change the facts of the world today. If the committee will permit, we will present witnesses to show that these pictures are true to life.[119]

In conclusion he transformed the Warner Bros. style into a profession of faith and service: "I have no apology to make to the committee for the fact for many years Warner Bros. has been attempting to record history in the making." In his testimony Harry Warner did not go beyond the contamination among films, production methods, and internal and foreign political messages to describe the direct experience his company had of Nazism: some representatives of the German offices of the studio had in fact been victims of Nazi persecution.[120] This silence could be associated with the ambiguity of early anti-Nazi films, which dealt with Nazism by revealing its crimes but underestimating its purport. Leaving aside the complex issue of the behavior of the American Jews in relation to their European counterparts, we observe that Harry Warner—in the same statement in which he held the adhesion of his company to an aesthetic of spectacularization of information—did not use the forum of the propaganda hearings to inform the American public about the actual experience the Warner Bros. studio had of Nazism.

While the industry, through the voices of its representatives Hays and Willkie, defended itself and refuted the accusations mostly on an ideological front, the more leftist-oriented intellectuals, alarmed by incursions in Hollywood by the HUAC and the Clark Committee, attempted a counteroffensive, accusing them of unconstitutionality. On this occasion Hollywood succeeded in clearing itself, by boasting high civic ideals while turning attention away from its trade practices. This result was encouraged also by the fact that these committees, with their phobic behavior, did not gain the support of the press.

The hearings had just ended when the attack on Pearl Harbor made the entire matter moot. But Congress did not turn its attention away from the movie industry's operations: in 1943 the Truman Committee examined Hollywood's commitment in the war effort, investigating how much of this "patriotism" was lucrative and convenient for the movie industry.[121]

Study by the Temporary National Economic Committee (TNEC)

In the 1930s the U.S. government scrutinized the film industry through different lenses but always with the same rigor, to the point that one could say that a more "scientific" historiography on Hollywood developed from these efforts. The publication in 1941 of the TNEC study on the movie industry represents the synthesis of previous studies; Daniel Bertrand, drafter of the reports on the NRA code, was its co-author.[122]

On the wave of antimonopolistic fervor in 1937–38, FDR instituted the TNEC, with analytical functions. This committee did not depend on the Justice Department; its activities had limited practical weight and were in "competition" with those of other federal agencies, in particular with Arnold's Antitrust Division.[123] In the study of the film industry, however, there was a notable collaboration between the Antitrust Division and the TNEC. Bertrand and W. Duane Evans, who had worked on the materials and statistics collected for the NRA code reports, were consulted by the division for the *Paramount* case and asked to supply an economic elaboration of the data, maps and graphics, and so on.[124] On its part, the TNEC monograph on the film industry quoted a considerable amount of information derived from the *Paramount* case, showing that between the two institutions there could be an efficient exchange of expertise.

The TNEC monograph analyzes the industry's structure in detail, dwelling on crucial points such as the role of the Hays Office, the relationship between the control of the theaters and the trade practices, and the financial relations and the interdependence of the studios. On the issue of economic concentration, it states: "An even higher degree of concentration may be found in some other industries. But in many of these industries it can be demonstrated that the combination has resulted in real economic benefits to the consumer." This was not true with the film industry, where the consumer was instead damaged by this economic concentration because of block booking and the studios' overproduction. The monograph boldly defines the Big Eight's control of the market as "monopolistic" but suggests no specific correctives. Released after the signing of the consent decree in the *Paramount* case, it warns against an excessive faith in miraculous cures, such as the divorce of production from exhibition and the stimulation of competition in the field of production. Noting the development of cinema into an "important social and cultural force," the monograph suggests measuring its role "in terms other than the conventional one of dollars and cents." Beyond the economic analysis, the TNEC acknowledges cinema's ideological function and the larger implications involved in an eventual modification of the industry's structure. The monograph concludes by recommending "an intelligent and sympathetic study of the industry."[125] The careful wording of these final observations, after such a lucid analysis of the studio system, makes them fairly unconvincing. The TNEC should have undertaken this very "intelligent and sympathetic" analysis, summing up years of research conducted by the government on the film industry. But the monograph was published about the same time as the consent decree, at a moment that discouraged proposing inflexible punishments to an industry essential to the war effort. This was implicitly recognized in the statement that cinema "provides a common denominator to the feelings and aspirations of an entire people."[126]

The history of the institutional relations (and clashes) between Hollywood and Washington revolves around monopoly of discourse, prevalent in the elaboration of the Hays Code and in the discussion of the monopoly of production, and the economic monopoly, investigating the structural relations between vertical integration and trade practices. In this duel there was an exchange of plunges, retreats, and thrusts, but only the *Paramount* case, with its institutional authority, broad scope, and head-on attack aims for a final resolution of the conflicts.

5

The Paramount Case

The *Paramount* case, the antitrust suit filed in 1938 by the Antitrust Division of the Justice Department against eight film companies (Paramount, Loew-MGM, RKO, Warner Bros., Twentieth Century–Fox, Columbia, Universal, and United Artists) ended in 1948 with the Supreme Court decision that separated production and distribution from exhibition, when restraining trade.[1] Until now, scholars have concentrated on this conclusion and its implications, rather than on the development of the case as a *process*, a complex interplay of different factors, subject to different tensions.

Studying the *Paramount* case as a process allows us to clarify how the Supreme Court decision was reached, what issues the Antitrust Division articulated in order to argue for divestiture, and their relevance to the development of legal theory.[2] Indeed, this antitrust case posed a significant challenge to the Justice Department because it required a redefinition of monopoly. The government was faced with demonstrating that the market control by the eight film companies constituted a monopoly—though together they controlled only 13 percent of exhibition, and three companies did not even control any theaters.

To argue for the existence of a monopoly power by the majors, the government had to demonstrate a deep interdependence between the integrated structure of the industry and its trade practices. If the majors did control the market through this interdependence, then it was "reasonable" and "effective" to remedy the situation through divestiture, an economic relief seldom (if ever) granted in an antitrust suit. In 1948 the Supreme Court decided that this interdependence and control in fact existed and that the characteristics of the film market proved the requisite *intent of monopolizing*, which was enforced by the unfair trade practices of the majors. This opinion played an important role in the discussion of monopoly within legal theory.[3]

The demand for divestiture implied that this remedy was in the *public interest*. But demonstrating the existence of this public interest posed a problem for the government because in the film industry "the consumer" would not have benefited in direct economic terms (e.g., admission prices) from the separation of production and distribution from exhibition and would not have benefited in any way from a divestiture of distribution (because the national system of distribution maintained by the eight companies was very cost-effective). The best argument for public interest would have been that the monopoly conditions of the production branch of the industry limited access to the market for the small businessmen, the independent producers. Public groups had argued that public interest was behind criticism of the studio system for producing standardized pictures and of trade practices such as block booking, which limited the freedom of choice for the local exhibitor and the community. Small business, public groups, and local communities together did compose a reasonable public interest.

The government prepared the early stage of the *Paramount* case with this view of public interest, on both fronts—the monopoly of production and of distribution—but soon realized that this interpretation involved a discussion of film quality and of federal censorship, two very controversial issues. The film industry, however, seemed to invite this interpretation, because its trade association, the Motion Picture Producer Distributor Association (MPPDA), incorporated both the self-regulative function, standardizing trade practices and trying to achieve an internal accord, which suggested a typical monopoly conspiracy, and the self-censorship system, which tended to standardize film discourse. The Hays organization was named as the main defendant in the *Paramount* case shortly before its filing but was "dropped" only at the very last moment because of the "technical advantage" of excluding the censorship issue from such a complex case. The decision not to attack the problem of monopoly of discourse, in terms of either monopoly of production or monopoly of distribution, made it increasingly difficult to insist on studying these two branches of the industry and suggested focusing on exhibition and on the system of market control. At the same time, the New Dealers could appreciate and understand an argument that tied economic monopoly to monopoly of discourse.[4] They could not, however, drive this legal action with such an argument, for it touched the very sensitive area of censorship. Nonetheless, this hope of reforming the studio system and influencing the quality of its production—the films—through an alteration of its structure was indeed a key motivation for the filing of the suit.

An important trait of the *Paramount* case is its national scope and the inclusion of the entire industry. There were, in fact, other antitrust cases involving the film industry, but this was the only one that was not limited geographically and that did not focus on only one aspect of the industry (usually film exhibition). The case started as a "general investigation" of the film industry, which included the unaffiliated (so-called independent) theater chains. And though specific suits were later filed against independent the-ater circuits, these issues found an ideal re-unification in a series of Supreme Court decisions in 1948.

The Antitrust Motion Picture Cases

Descriptions of the film industry's structure as "monopoly" or "oligopoly" of-ten ignore the technical and legal implications of the term *monopoly* as de-fined in 1890 by the Sherman Act and its later interpretations. The defini-tion of monopoly is historical: it is elaborated by the courts within their relationship to the other powers, political, legislative, and executive. By ini-tiating a vast antitrust program, the New Deal activated the processes of re-defining monopoly, which was supported by a coeval development of legal theory.

Studies of the economic and institutional history of the film industry should take into account the "larger picture," of which the *Paramount* case represented a microcosm whose significance derived from the great atten-tion devoted to the film industry by the Roosevelt administration. The *Para-mount* case activated behaviors and concepts typical of the New Deal, espe-cially in the intricate interdependence of its components—the neopopulists and the economic planners. The theme of an octopus controlling not only a market but also a mass medium was typically neopopulist. The case implied an interest on behalf of the small businessman (the independent producer or exhibitor) against the "Big Boys," and, in parallel, a defense of the local community characteristicly championed by neopopulists. For the economic planners, the *Paramount* case raised important issues, such as the efficiency of a business structure, the role of interest groups, the cooperation between government and business, and the need to reform—and thus rationalize—business practices. The scrutiny of the studio system and the system of self-regulation through the MPPDA were testing grounds on which the New Deal measured its economic theories and interpretations, carried out through a series of investigations, committee hearings, and trials and culminating in the *Paramount* case. In this sense, this case articulates also a significant inter-pretation of New Deal history.

The *Paramount* case lasted more than ten years and turned on complex ju-ridical and economic issues that resulted in an enormous amount of docu-mentation—about 450 boxes, stored with the Justice Department. This vast collection of primary sources has not yet been fully explored. Historians and scholars have concentrated on the legal issues posed by the case, focusing mostly on the Supreme Court decision and the economic effects, analyzing the impact of the rupture of vertical integration on the functioning of the film industry. In particular, Michael Conant, in the authoritative work on this case, *Antitrust in the Motion Picture Industry,* has attempted to "report critically on the impact on industry structure, behavior and performance of the antitrust actions." These "effects" are actually difficult to establish, in view of the complex economic conjunction of the postwar period and the entry of television.[5]

Beginning in 1911 the doctrine of antitrust defined "monopolizing" through the *rule of reason*: that is, in their decisions, the courts had to consider behavior in the market that constituted "undue" or "unreasonable" restraints of trade. While Justice Oliver Wendell Holmes Jr. argued that the Sherman Act had "nothing to do with competition, but that its purpose was to prevent the ruthless and exclusionary tactics of robber barons," Justice Edward D. White, author of the opinion on the *rule of reason,* argued that the purpose of the act was to protect the public against any "acts which, although they did not constitute a monopoly, were thought to produce some of its baneful effects." According to Eugene Rostow, this produced a "duality of reasoning":

> There is a recurring emphasis on intent and purpose to violate the act by gaining "economic mastery," evidenced by trade practices which the Court calls "new," "oppressive," "predatory," or "not normal" or "usual" means of growth. Nevertheless there is equally a recognition that "economic mastery" once achieved, and by whatever means achieved, "gives rise, in and of itself, in the absence of countervailing circumstances, to say the least, to the *prima facie* presumption of intent and purpose to maintain the dominancy over" the industry in question.[6]

The question of *intent*, of the subjective element in the behavior of an economic organization, became crucial in the discussion of market control. As Alfred Chandler notes, by the 1920s, American industrial structures had developed into integrated multidepartmental enterprises, through combinations and consolidations.[7] Thus the economic system had changed, and a small group of firms, through their trade associations, held a high degree of market control. For legal doctrine, the issues were not "trusts" and "mergers" anymore, or "predatory" business practices, but the relationship of the structure of the industry (e.g., vertical integration) to trade practices. In the *Paramount* case, the degree of monopolization of the market had to be defined, established, and subjected to judicial opinion.

In his much-quoted analysis of the *Paramount* decision, Walter Adams calls the 1948 settlement of the film industry case "probably the Government's greatest economic victory in the . . . history of antitrust enforcement."

> Throughout, the major question in the motion picture cases was not the guilt or innocence of the defendants but rather the finding of a suitable

remedy to prevent future violations. And on this question, the district court was adamant; it stated that, while vertical integration is not a *per se* violation of the Sherman Act, vertical integration does become illegal if conceived with a *specific intent* to control the market or if used to create a power to control the market.[8]

According to Adams, the lower courts had exhibited "a disinclination to undertake drastic reorganization of a monopolized industry . . . from a lack of training in the economic problems involved in monopoly cases." This is why the Paramount decision appears as a unique instance, a "victory" for the government, a successful case of antitrust enforcement.

The motivations for the granting of such an extreme legal remedy reside in the development of the *Paramount* case and in the analysis of the industry structure conducted by the Antitrust Division.

Since the 1910s there have been numerous legal battles between the government and the film industry on the question of monopoly.[9] To a certain extent, the St. Louis case against Warner Bros. was a rehearsal for the *Paramount* case. In February 1936, having lost the jury trial, the Justice Department began civil action, but in the meantime Warner Bros. retreated from the exhibition market in St. Louis.[10] During the block booking hearings of 1936, pressure groups made frequent references to this trial, which, in their opinion, was a tangible demonstration of the foundation of their complaints, while the industry minimized its importance, stating that it involved only three companies and not the entire industry, and that the existence of an accusation did not prove anything more.[11]

The Origins of the *Paramount* Case

The *Paramount* case started effectively in the spring of 1936 when the Justice Department began working on an investigation, or "economic study," of the structure of the film industry and of its trade practices while the St. Louis trial and the block booking hearings were taking place.

Among the earliest materials in the department's boxes labeled "Paramount Case" are letters of complaint addressed to Rep. Francis D. Culkin, who had proposed legislation against block booking, and signed by an independent producer, "Mr." Powers, president of Celebrity Productions. In one of these letters Powers accuses the "Hays Group" of monopolizing both production and exhibition; in others he attacks the whole studio system, stating that directors and writers "at present in the employ of this group" and "controlled" by it, "with an open market, would make their own pictures," allowing for "more originality in the production of pictures."[12] The economic ar-

147

gument of market control was therefore connected to an esthetic and social discussion of cinema. These letters and many others from local exhibitors or pressure groups, addressed to congressmen who had proposed legislation against block booking or to the Antitrust Division, contain suggestions, interpretations, and information that, indirectly, prompted the action of the Justice Department. Local exhibitors complain about the arbitration of matters under the jurisdiction of the National Recovery Administration (NRA). Small businessmen, such as independent producers and exhibitors, complain about the difficulty of entering the film market. Public groups complain about block booking and blind selling because they limited the freedom of choice of the local community. These letters, all of which press for legislation regulating the film industry, reveal that economic monopoly and monopoly of discourse were interrelated at the very origins of the *Paramount* case.

The close interaction between the block booking hearings and the antimonopoly investigation is documented by an official statement by Attorney General Homer Cummings to Rep. Samuel B. Pettingill, dated April 1935. Cummings admits that, in view of the decision about the FTC investigation "it would be incumbent upon the plaintiff to demonstrate concerted action" among the studios, but he acknowledges that the trade practices in question did "place the exhibitors at a disadvantage." He accompanied his answer with a copy of the petition for the *Warner* case.[13]

This correspondence indicates not only that the Justice Department was "after" the film industry, as the dates of other motion picture cases confirm, but also that it is difficult to separate the *Paramount* case from all the legal skirmishes on other fronts—congressional hearings, antitrust private litigation, antitrust federal "local" trials, and so on. These ancillary matters keep returning and interfering with the case, either as sources of evidence and witnesses, or as areas of political interrelations, including lobbying and compromises. The institutional background of the case encompasses a plurality of political, administrative, and legal activities, as well as judicial and legislative powers, in addition to the Roosevelt administration. The *Paramount* case tends nevertheless to include and appropriate the legal and governmental issues that arose in the local venues, because it was national in scope and represented the official position of the government in the antimonopoly wars against the film industry.

The Preparation of the Case

William Benham, special assistant to the attorney general and one of the government attorneys in the St. Louis trial, was in charge of preparing the case against the film industry. The wording in a memo he sent in September 1936 signaled that it was going to be an investigation related to the second article of the Sherman Act, one in which *intent* had to be particularly scrutinized.[14]

> As a result of many complaints having been made to the Department, it was decided in May 1936, to make a comprehensive investigation of the motion picture industry. . . . The complaints as to the manner in which the industry is being conducted charge that the major producing and distributing companies, members of the Hays organization, *have monopolized and are monopolizing* the production, distribution and exhibition of motion pictures."[15]

From the records it is evident that Benham investigated the MPPDA, or Hays organization, in both New York and Los Angeles.[16] The first area to be "studied" was that of production, for which Benham said he had interviewed "a representative number of independent producers at Los Angeles." The majors were accused of monopolizing production by excluding the independent producers from the market through the operations of the Hays organization and by the administration of the self-censorship code. The Antitrust Division also planned investigations of the economic functioning of the majors (in order "to elicit corporate and statistical information") and of exhibition practices. It suggested that a similar examination be made of the "acquisition records of certain other chains," that is, the big so-called independent chains.[17] The study encompassed practically the entire industry. The profile of the antitrust case was already established when the Justice Department began its work under the title "General Motion Picture Investigation."

Paul Williams, special assistant to the attorney general (at that time, John Dickinson) coordinated the whole investigation up to the trial. Taking an early hard-line position in favor of divorcement, he set the tone of the case. After the consent decree, which momentarily closed the case in 1940, favorably to the majors, he was no longer officially involved with the case, signaling with his exit a definite change in the strategy of the Justice Department. Symptomatically, his name reappeared in the "Brief on Behalf of the American Theatres Association," appealing to the Supreme Court for divorcement in December 1947.

In a memo entitled "Work for Summer of 1936," Williams suggests that questionnaires be submitted to the Hays organization and to "the chief executives of the several motion picture companies" in New York in order to collect the necessary "corporate and statistical information." He also proposes that he proceed to California to study "the various complaints that have been made by the independent motion picture producers and exhibitors, in an effort to correlate them upon a national scale." Very detailed questionnaires were sent to the film companies on June 16, 1936 asking for copies of contracts and minute and specific information about their corporate structures, the number of feature films produced and distributed, and their operations in production, distribution, and exhibition. At the MPPDA, Williams and Benham discussed the questionnaires with attorneys Gabriel L. Hess and Sidney Schribner, representing the Hays organization, and, later, with the lawyers of individual companies. These lawyers, Williams explained in a memo, were "generally favorable to cooperating fully with the Department," but they felt that supplying "information concerning the leases and ownership of theaters" would be "unreasonably difficult and burdensome."[18]

Behind the facade, the counterposed forces had already identified the crucial issue: theater control. The film companies' strategy was established: stated cooperation on one hand, delays and legalistic maneuvers on the other. This cooperation, far from being a spontaneous or disinterested manifestation of self-regulation under government control, was offered in the hope that the companies might receive, if not immunity, at least "fair warning." The site of this "cooperation" was the Hays organization, with its seemingly omnipresent and omniscient attorneys.[19] An early action by the Justice Department against a theater chain elicited an indignant response from Hess. The Hays organization, he said, understood that before instituting a suit against it or any of the major distributors, the Justice Department would give them an opportunity to discuss the matter with a "view to voluntarily eliminating such violations of law as were found to exist." Irritated, Williams made clear that the department "could not be placed in the position of agreeing 'or even seem to be in a position of agreeing' to submit cases to the Hays organization before instituting a suit."[20] This, however, was probably Hays's expectation. This misunderstanding is just the first in a long series and demonstrates the impossibility of communication between the "meddlers" of the MPPDA and the Justice Department in a case that required delicate political handling.

Although clearly the film industry was aware that the Justice Department was interested in its affairs and aware of the implications of that interest,[21] the first phase of the *Paramount* case seems to have been suppressed in the official "memory" of the film industry.

In 1936 the film industry cooperated with this "study" of its structure by the Justice Department, furnishing the information, the evidence, that later, in the trial, was used against it. At that time, the industry did not seem to worry. The Roosevelt administration had not yet started its antimonopoly campaigns, and even though the NRA had been declared unconstitutional, the spirit of its economic policy was still alive, encouraging self-regulation under government supervision. Nonetheless, this investigation by the Justice Department was not isolated: together with the proposal of anti–block booking bills in Congress, the St. Louis antitrust suit, and other cases against theater circuits, it opened hostilities between the government and the film industry.

In January 1937, Williams, restrained by budgetary limitations from hiring professional economists, offered his own economic interpretation of the case in a memorandum to the FBI.

> In my opinion, the question of theatre control by the major producers presents one of the most disturbing problems now confronting the administration of the antitrust laws in so far as the motion picture industry is concerned. Whether the dual relationship of producer-exhibitor imposes illegal restraints upon commerce in motion picture films, or whether such restraints as are imposed as a result of this relationship are only those that may be reasonably expected in the lawful exercise of property rights, presents a question that can only be solved after a careful consideration of all relevant facts.[22]

Williams was implicitly referring to the *rule of reason* in discussing the complex relationship between trade practices and the structure of the industry, that is, its vertical integration—a key juridical question since the twenties, when vertical integration and bigness ceased being considered evil. He therefore suggested that the FBI, the agency in charge of the investigative work for the Justice Department, collect data on three classes of theater: (1) "de luxe" first-run theaters in metropolitan areas ("These theatres are of the utmost importance in the exploitation of motion pictures for all subsequent runs wherever exhibited."), (2) affiliated theater chains, that is, chains in which a major producer has some interest, and (3) unaffiliated theater chains, with buying power large enough to command contracts with major distributors, making it difficult for independent exhibitors to exist. Williams suggested that the FBI focus specifically on showing that, "with a few possible exceptions, this de luxe department of the exhibition field is practically controlled by certain of the major producers, and that, in the main, only pictures distributed by them have access to the de luxe theatre market." He suggested further that they investigate whether "the pictures produced by the owners of these de luxe theatres obtain playing time irrespective of the quality of the pictures and that they are in no ways subjected to competition with the product of others."

Prompted by Williams's memos the Justice Department began to shift its interest in an eventual monopoly of production to the issue of theater control, identifying as the crucial aspects of the case: the role of the first-run theater in market control, the privileged position their buying power granted to theater chains, and the relationship of this structure of the market to a monopoly that limited access to other producers and exhibitors. When the MPPDA was informed of this new phase of the investigation and film companies began to receive questionnaires, the industry started show-ing signs of nervousness. This nervousness was intensified when an article in the *Motion Picture Daily* quoted an assistant to the attorney general say-ing the Justice Department "would resort to criminal prosecution if the charges of flagrant antitrust law violations were true."[23] The reference was probably to the St. Louis case, but Williams reassured the companies by telling them that he knew of "no departure from this cooperative accord." But beneath the surface of this cooperative attitude, there were recurrent signs of reciprocal distrust. The majors adopted a strategy of delay, as a memo for the files signed by Williams in April indicates: "The feeling has arisen that various of the distributors, particularly Paramount and Warner, are attempting to inaugurate a dilatory attitude; while they are courteous at all times, the material requested is not being furnished quite as rapidly as seems desirable."[24]

The memos of this period, addressed mostly to the FBI indicating areas of investigation, reveal a patient and thorough collection of data. All economic aspects of the film industry were analyzed; all possible sources tapped, from the Securities and Exchange Commission to the Internal Revenue Service, the National Labor Relations Board, transcripts of hearings and trials, and even books and industry publications. While all of this data was being col-lected in 1936 and 1937, the Justice Department was beginning a series of an-titrust litigations against department stores and systems of chain distribution. Aware of some similarities in the structural models, the film industry grew alarmed.[25]

On October 27, 1937, Williams proposed a petition against the motion picture industry. He identified "the principal evil" in the "theatre domina-tion and control by producers" and proposed divorcement as a remedy, along with "some Federal regulation." This proposed bill in equity was signed by the attorney general, Robert Jackson, on November 5.[26] The study of the film industry had thus become an indictment. J. Edgar Hoover, director of the FBI, decided to put more FBI agents to work on the case and promised the attorney general that "every effort will be made to complete this investi-gation by November 15."[27] But the suit was not filed, perhaps because the Jus-tice Department felt the need for more investigation, and perhaps because the government had not yet signaled its intention to move toward antimo-nopolism.

In late November, Williams informed Jackson that "two major problems" remained that involved "probable violations" of federal antitrust laws. He re-ferred to the Production Code Administration and to "the monopolization of exhibition by independent theatre chains in various sections of the coun-try."[28] Williams argued for the need of "a test of the legality of monopoliza-tion of exhibition by independent theatre chains" in case "the main objective of the petition is reached"—that is, divorcement of exhibition from production and distribution—"for, this separation, unless carefully supervised by the Court, may result in a series of large chains, which will just as effectively monopolize exhibition as do the major producer-owned chains under existing conditions." He perceived with precision the interrelationship of the two types of monopoly in exhibition, that is, the monopoly exercised by the affiliated theaters (those theaters owned or controlled by the producer-distributors), and the monopoly power of the big "independent" circuits. Historians have noted that the lack of enforcement of the divorcement recommended in the area of the independent circuits weakened the impact of the Paramount decision. Williams anticipated this risk in 1937.

In 1939 the Justice Department began a series of federal antitrust actions against independent theater chains. The main suits were brought against the Schine and the Griffith circuits, the two largest in the country, with about 150 theaters each, and against the Crescent circuit. These cases were filed after the *Paramount* case was filed. *Crescent* was settled by the Supreme Court in 1944, and *Schine* and *Griffith* on the same day as the Paramount decision in 1948. From the documents on the *Paramount* case, it is clear that these three suits filed in 1939 originated within the same "General Motion Picture Investigation" that became the *Paramount* case, but, in keeping with Williams's suggestion, they were tried separately. Exhibition issues were involved also in two other local federal antitrust actions against affiliated chains, in the *Fox West Coast* case and the *Balaban and Katz* case, instituted in 1928. Another suit against an affiliated chain was *United States v. Interstate Circuit*, filed in Texas in 1936.[29] The interrelationship between these exhibition antitrust cases and the Paramount suit, in terms of personnel, evidence, and interpretations, was very tight, though this fact emerges only sporadically in the documents.

In addition to the theater chains, Williams had left the issue of the code authority out of the first petition. But he brought it up in his November memo to Jackson.

> As a result of the domination and control of the motion picture industry
> by the Hays Organization and its membership, independent producers are
> compelled to submit their product to and obtain the approval of the Production Code Administration in order to successfully operate. . . . The
> power thus vested in the Production Code Administration gives it complete control of production under the guise of censorship.

Williams understood that the interrelationship between the system of self-censorship and monopoly raised complex questions and that the Hays organization was, in effect, "usurping a power of censorship which properly should be lodged only with the people themselves or with their various governmental agencies, either local, State or Federal."[30] Echoing the pressure groups' arguments, Williams proposed that an external agency, possibly a federal authority, supervise the film industry. His project was to start a separate case against the MPPDA that did not involve the issue of censorship.

> In the drafting of the proposed petition submitted with my memorandum of October 27, 1937, I considered fully the advisability of testing in that case the legality, under the antitrust laws, of the Production Code Administration and its operation. However, upon reflection, I concluded that to do so might prove to be a mistake from a tactical point of view. Censorship is always a contentious subject and might afford the ground to seriously prejudice the Government's main case if attacked by the Government in the same case. For this reason I decided that it probably would be unwise to attempt to incorporate a cause of action testing the self-censorship imposed by the Hays Organization in the proposed petition whereby a divestiture of theatres by major producers is the main objective.

The case against the theater chains was later filed, but the suit Williams proposed against the Code Administration did not materialize, perhaps because it touched such a delicate issue, perhaps because the MPPDA lobbied against it; or perhaps because the Justice Department believed that regulating economic monopoly would necessarily affect this monopoly of discourse.

Thurman Arnold at the Antitrust Division

The legal theories of the 1930s were strongly influenced by the coeval development of the social sciences, specifically by currents of thought emphasizing the economic determination of the ideological apparatus.[31] The school of legal realism in particular studied the interrelationship between social and economic processes. Although not a representative of this school—even an opponent of it in his writings—Thurman Arnold was a key figure in the development of a legal theory sensitive to sociopsychological and economic factors.

In March 1938, Franklin Roosevelt, dissatisfied with the slow economic recovery, increased the use of fiscal policy and moved toward an antimonopolistic policy, "to restore fluidity in the market place."[32] The President appointed Arnold to head the Antitrust Division. The choice of Arnold as chief trust-buster was in no way obvious and probably reflected the New Deal's contradictory attitude about antitrust. Arnold had in fact written a sarcastic chapter, entitled "The Effects of Antitrust Laws in Encouraging Large Corporations," in *The Folklore of Capitalism*, and though this cast some shadows on his intentions about enforcing the same laws, he was actually "the most effective director in the history of the Antitrust Division."[33] As head of the division be-

154

tween 1938 and 1941, he expanded budget and staff and adopted new policies (for example, in the area of consent decrees)[34], while redefining the issues of antitrust in legal theory and filing (and winning) more antitrust cases than the Justice Department had filed in its previous history. His dual role, as an analyst of ideological production and an enforcer of antitrust legislation, makes it particularly significant that he was the signatory of the *Paramount* case petition, because it suggests a precise relation between this intervention in an economic structure (the antitrust suit) and the expectation of a modification of the (ideological) product—the films.

When Arnold arrived at the Antitrust division, the "motion picture case" was in an advanced stage of preparation. Significantly, one of the first letters related to this case that Arnold received was signed by Abram F. Myers, head of the Allied States Association of Motion Picture Exhibitors, the organization that represented the interests of the small independent exhibitor. Arnold was attentive to the consumer and the public as well as small businessmen, the ones more likely to profit from the restoration of unfettered competition,[35] and so he allowed Allied to play an important role in the *Paramount* case by supplying the government with witnesses and evidence against the majors. In this instance, Myers can be seen as the head of an organized pressure group. (Organized groups were privileged interlocutors for the New Deal, which tried to respond to society's needs by selecting those issues that had found vocal supporters.) Myers, a fierce antagonist of the majors and of the Hays organization, was particularly afraid of the monopolization of so important a medium of communication as cinema; this fear was a neopopulist theme frequently discussed in the thirties.[36] In an address before the Twentieth Century Club in Boston, a copy of which he sent to Arnold, Myers described the majors' control over the industry as "comparable in degree and kind with the power exerted by foreign political dictators over their subjects."[37] He equated political dictatorship with economic monopoly; it was a concept with which Arnold would have agreed, given its implications for industrial democracy, the only belief shared by all New Dealers.[38] Myers and Allied were natural allies for Arnold. Their views and interpretations often coincided, as did their interests, counterposed to the "Hays group," which Myers further attacked, in the same address, for getting help "from whichever party was in power," and for having "practically unlimited" financial resources to combat unwanted legislation.[39]

In the preparation of the petition for the *Paramount* case, the Antitrust Division gave careful consideration to the issue of the inclusion of the Hays organization among the defendants. A decision was made only on July 18, two days before the official filing of the suit, to exclude the organization because of its minor role—a sort of clearing house—in the acquisition of theaters. Nonetheless:

> The principal activities of the Hays organization which the Department
> desired to test was one which exercised censorship over all pictures which
> went further than suppression of pornography, for example, the suppres-
> sion of "It Can't Happen Here."[40] This was considered to be a practice
> which the Department was very much interested in stopping. Secondly,
> the Hays organization offers a sort of insurance against antitrust suits in
> that it gives a central defense for any company to its violations of law.[41]
> This practice the Department should not tolerate.[42]

The division thought that "it would confuse the issues to permit" these two
complaints in a suit "primarily aimed at divestiture—because the suit might
be deflected into some sort of a trial of the right to suppress salacious pictures and keep the public pure." It was therefore decided to raise these issues
"in a separate suit or in a supplemental bill," as Williams had already suggested but which was never done. The memo concludes in a self-reflective
mode seldom to be found in this kind of material: "The question was of such
importance that it was reduced to writing." Maybe this was a way to anticipate
the accusation of having dropped the Hays organization because of its powerful lobby.

The question whether the case was of general public importance was also
discussed in preparation for the petition. That cinema was not covered by the
First Amendment made things more complicated, because, if film was, as the
Supreme Court had stated in 1915, "a business, pure and simple," it would
be necessary to argue for eventual federal interference with its structure, using appropriate legal concepts.[43] "Public interest" was in fact the legal basis
on which to request divestiture in an antitrust case. In its final form the petition insists on the national scope of the case, in that film business was an
"interstate commerce," and thus of "general public importance": "The Department receives more complaints from persons in the motion picture business located in all parts of the country, of restraint and oppression like dealt
in this case, than any other industry in the country, thus indicating that the
defendants and others are guilty of the same conduct on a national scale."[44]
(This hard statement about the film industry was confirmed by the number
and length of antitrust suits in which it was involved.)

The FBI had prepared a long (89 pages) and very detailed report on the
results of its investigation. It was a technically specific description of the issues and evidence of the case, discussing the monopoly of production and
exhibition, the role of the first-run theater, the interlocking relationship
among the companies, and the position of the MPPDA, giving specific information about every item in the petition.[45]

By the time the FBI report was completed the preparatory stage of the
Paramount case was almost finished. Earlier in June, Arnold had written to
the President: "Both the Attorney General and I feel that the Moving Picture

prosecution should not be started without conferring with you." Despite the intensive investigation by the Antitrust Division to prepare a case that was supported by many complaints from exhibitors and public groups, Arnold felt the need for the President's approval. He was afraid that "sooner or later some sort of story is coming out that the Moving Picture prosecution is being stopped."[46] There were many reasons why the news of the filing of the antitrust suit against the eight companies might be unexpected: the rumors that had circulated concerning the administration's involvement with film business, the fact that it had favored the majors in the NRA code, the power and lobbying of the Hays organization, and, above all, the power of the film medium, and in particular the control of the newsreels by the majors. Immediately, in fact, the press interpreted the decision to proceed with a civil rather than a criminal suit as a concession to the film industry, in exchange for such favors as "pro-administration attitudes and cash," referring to the "recent unadvertised visit of Gen. Will Hays and a platoon of prominent executives" at the White House.[47]

The Petition of the *Paramount* Case

The suit was filed at the Southern District Court of New York on July 20, 1938. The judge assigned to the case was Henry Goddard.[48] The petition begins by describing the defendants, the eight film companies—that is, the five majors, integrating production, distribution, and exhibition; the two producer-distributors, Universal and Columbia; and the distribution company United Artists. The petition then discusses the companies' histories, focusing on the process of vertical integration. The sections entitled "Competitive Conditions in the Industry" and "Offenses Charged" articulate the core of the case. The offenses include: (1) *Monopoly of exhibition in first-run metropolitan theaters* (by owning first-run theaters in key cities of the United States, the defendants excluded other producers, exhibiting their own product or the products of other defendants in their theaters); (2) *Nationwide monopoly of exhibition by producer-exhibitor defendants* (affiliated circuits, the division of territory between the defendants, preferred runs, and cross licensing); (3) *Monopoly of production* (eight companies monopolized the production of films "of better grade and quality" through contracts that tied up most of the "valuable stars, players, directors, and technicians," who could not work for the independent producers, while they were "loaned" among the defendants); (4) *Trade practices imposed upon independent exhibitors* (such as block booking, forcing of shorts and newsreels, arbitrary designation of play dates, clearance and zoning, overbuying, arbitrary film rentals, prohibition of double features, minimum admission prices, that is, all those trade practices that had long created conflicts between independent exhibitors and majors); and (5) *Benefits, favors, and advantages extended by the defendants to each other* (such as the favorable conditions granted reciprocally by the defendants, in sharing advertising costs, in contract modifications, and so on).

The "Prayer" asked: (1) that a preliminary injunction be issued "restraining the defendants . . . from building, buying, leasing, or otherwise acquiring any additional theaters," (2) that "the contracts, combinations, and conspiracies . . . be declared illegal," (3) that the defendants be "perpetually enjoined" from their monopolistic practices, (4) that vertical integration be declared "unlawful," (5) that divestiture in theater holdings be ordered for the producer-distributors, (6) that divestiture from production be ordered to the exhibitors, (7) that the pooling of assets and loaning of stars be enjoined,[49] and (8) that the unfair trade practices be "permanently enjoined."

The Explanatory Statement

Arnold prepared an Explanatory Statement specific to the *Paramount* case and planned to do the same for all the antitrust cases. This innovative policy of issuing official statements was meant to clarify the antitrust issues involved for the public, for the industry party in the trial, and for any business or industry that had a similar structure or analogous operational mode.

There are at least three versions of the Explanatory Statement for the *Paramount* case: the first, undated and unsigned, refers to a "suit in equity under the Sherman Act against the MPPDA and its principal constituent members"; the second describes a suit against "the major motion picture companies" and includes the Hays organization among the defendants; and the third, dated July 20, 1938, and issued as a press release the day of the filing of the suit, does not include the MPPDA among the defendants, according to the decision made two days before.[50] There are remarkable differences among these texts, even though many of the concepts and phrases in the first one reappear in the second and third, which, in particular, are very similar. The three versions come across as phases in a process. The most striking example is the movement away from considering film as a medium toward discussing it as a product in a market situation, from "the people" as public (film audience) toward the people as consumers and small businessmen—a movement that parallels the diminishing role assigned to the MPPDA, from its being a defendant in the first version to its absence in the third. The first version was probably prepared in June for the discussion between Hays, the film executives, and Roosevelt. Then Hays probably lobbied at the White House, and the White House put pressure on Arnold to eliminate the MPPDA. Whatever process resulted in eliminating the MPPDA, the cautious memo of July 18 by the Antitrust Division indicates very clearly that the department was concerned about introducing into the case, together with the MPPDA, issues such as film regulation and censorship and general considerations about the control of mass media.

The first version of the Explanatory Statement, under the title "Public Interest," contains a section not included in the later versions that names among the interested parties not only the independent exhibitors and producers and "the theatre-going public" but also "the members of the consuming public" who "were concerned about the highly centralized control of so powerful a medium of entertainment and of education as motion pictures." Echoing the protests of pressure groups, it also argues: "No other industry exerts so powerful an influence on the manners, morals and customs of the people. There is a widespread demand for localized public control rather than centralized private control over the operating policies of the theatres."

The three versions vary in their descriptions of the monopoly situation. The first insists on the monopoly in production as much as on the exhibition monopoly, identifying distribution as the specific site of control.[51] It deals also with the standardization imposed by the studio system, suggesting that anyone making "only an occasional experimental picture" must market his product through "some established distributing agency. This means that he must entrust the marketing of his pictures to a concern that is primarily interested in marketing its own competitive products."

The later drafts omit any mention of "occasional experimental pictures" but concentrate on the issue of market control. The following extract from the third version is reproduced at length to demonstrate how the Antitrust Division prepared to move its legal attack.

Producer-Exhibitor Combinations. The public theatres constitute the only market for the commercial distribution of motion picture films. The finer theatres and theatre chains are now dominated by five of the major companies . . . [that], together with the three other major companies, United Artists, Columbia Pictures Corporation and Universal Corporation, control about 65% of all pictures produced from the selection of the story to the final showing at the theatre.

The actual control of product is even greater than would appear from this figure, because from 80 to 90% of the quality feature films upon which exhibitors are dependent for the successful operation of their theatres are produced or distributed by the eight major companies.

Absence of Competition between Major Companies. In acquiring theatres and chains of theatres, the major companies have not occupied, to any great extent, the same territory. Indeed, there appears to be a virtual division of territory. Operating in their separate divisions of territory, the theatres of each major company afford a market for the pictures produced by the others. . . . So effective is the combination that these companies in the production of pictures have pooled their most valuable assets and made them available to each other. These assets consist of stars and feature players of known drawing power, as well as directors, technicians and physical properties such as sets and scenes. Seldom are these facilities made available to independent producers.

Suppression of Independent Theatres. So far as ownership is concerned, there are enough independent theatres to furnish the basis for substantial competition with the theatres controlled by the major companies. This competition, however, is prevented by the major companies by denying to independents equal access to the films distributed by them. A theatre affiliated with a major company is given first access to the product of all the major companies before the independent is permitted to exhibit it on any terms. Thus, in a territory where an independent exhibitor is in competition with a theatre affiliated with a major producer, he may not be able to obtain first-run pictures. He must wait until the affiliated theatre has exhibited the choice films. This is true regardless of the price which the independent might be willing to pay for the film. . . .

The control of the finer theatres by the five major producer-exhibitors has given them the actual power to exclude other producers from these markets. This in the judgment of the Department constitutes monopolistic power forbidden by the Sherman Act.

The conclusions of the draft statements differ greatly. Whereas in the third version Arnold anticipates the restoration of competition, in the first, under "Hoped for Results," he indulges in less focused rhetoric.

A look forward rather than a glance backwards has prompted this suit. The aim is not to assess blame but to make effective the mandates of public policy. At present, the conduct of the motion picture industry appears to be out of accord with American ideals and traditions. In the current structure there is little place for individual initiative, free enterprise, or the play of market forces. The manager of the local theatre has lost his freedom of selection and his control over the details of his business. He has become a vendor of packaged goods and can no longer accommodate his product to his distinctive clientele.

The impact upon the interests of the movie fan is apparent. In books, in painting, in music, an art in all its variety is made to serve many different groups. In motion pictures the chance to reach many distinct audiences is gone. A community cannot even choose from the pictures which are available as its taste or need dictates. Instead the industry has avidly sought the least common denominator; and on the level of mass appeal, individual and group and locality have been forgotten. As matters now go, the studio cannot be brought into touch with the demands of the movie-going public. Opinion passes only in the crude coin of type and star, while the appeal of the exceptional picture rests upon an artistry too subtle for so easy a classification. The line from scenario to screen is a one-way wire; in reverse the voice of the spectator dies away long before it reaches the producer. A popular art quickly becomes sterile unless it is constantly refreshed by creative contact with the people. The channel to its sources must be broken open, if the most democratic of our arts is to serve the common folk.

This condemnation of the studio system has an intense and harsh tone that we can trace back to Arnold's discussions of the collective unconscious and popular mythologies in *The Folklore of Capitalism*. Arnold was an intellectual who could appreciate the value of cinema in the public sphere. He was an attentive cinephile too,[52] and this might explain his defense of an "experimental" picture, his interest in a "democratic art serving the common folk." But Arnold was also a small-town lawyer, tenaciously holding onto his values—a neopopulist defense of the local community, and of the interests of the small entrepreneur against big business.[53] In the final section of the first version of the Explanatory Statement, Arnold includes among the "hoped for results" that producers would compete in an "unfettered market," according to the merit of their films, that operators would freely choose films according to the taste of their clientele, and that local communities would be able to hold exhibitors accountable for their choices and practices. Although this segment was not used in the final version of the Explanatory Statement, it points to the result that the Antitrust Division really "hoped for": an end to the monopoly of the Hollywood discourse, modification of the way films were made in the studio system. Despite being omitted from the final public statement, this objective was always active and traceable in the later phases of the case.

Attorney General Cummings was particularly satisfied with the favorable reactions in the press to the filing of the Paramount suit and publication of the Explanatory Statement.[54] Independent exhibitors filed statements and supplied further evidence against the majors; common citizens suggested that the Justice Department investigate the monopoly of "every phase of the popular music industry" held by the same film companies.[55] Even the film industry responded favorably by issuing a press release headlined: "Industry Welcomes Opportunity for Clarification of Film Trade Customs, Says Will H. Hays." In his statement, Hays develops a subtle argument, emphasizing the issue of trade practices (defined as "inherent in the development" of the industry), and, to dispel anticipation of the industry's guilt, insisting: "Courts clarify and explain the meaning of law. Such a suit as this can do just that."[56]

But despite the cooperative tone that publicly greeted the suit, the work behind the curtains and the lobbying activities became feverish.[57] Attempts were made to have some names "dropped" from the case, such as that of

David Sarnoff on the charge that he had been "made a party defendant [only] because he [was] the director of the parent company defendant RKO." Universal investigated "the possibility of a separate stipulation or consent decree."

Early in February 1939 the Antitrust Division was embarrassed by a new development: James Roosevelt, the President's son, was a member of the Board of Directors of United Artists and therefore had to be listed as a party defendant in the case.

Preparation for the Trial

The Antitrust Division asked the FBI in preparing the evidence for the trial to update the data and find prospective witnesses by interrogating the key men in the regional associations of independent exhibitors (Allied and Independent Theater Owners) and to re-examine complaints filed by congressmen, or by local exhibitors and complaints taken in the investigation of other motion picture cases or hearings. At this stage, the specific areas of investigation were those of exhibition, in particular unfair trade practices, and "distress methods in the acquisition of theatres." The department was in fact working toward the preliminary injunction requested in the petition to maintain the status quo in terms of theater control and ownership. The film companies immediately resisted the proposed injunction. After lengthy negotiations, they reached an agreement, stating that they were not involved in any program of expansion of theater holdings, and that they would inform the division about changes in theater ownership or control.

While the FBI was acquiring evidence, the Antitrust Division was busy collecting data and affidavits, tabulating information from trade publications such as the *Motion Picture Almanac* and the *Film Daily Year Book* and Census Bureau and IRS documents, and studying motion picture antitrust private litigations. It tried also to secure the services of Daniel Bertrand, who had studied the structure of the film industry for the NRA Division of Review and was working on an analogous study for the Temporary National Emergency Committee (TNEC). For "budgetary reasons" this was not possible, but W. Duane Evans, co-author of the TNEC report on the industry, did supply some assistance. He scrutinized the development of the economic structure of the industry, re-examining the *Famous Players–Lasky* case, to help clarify the reasons for vertical integration.[58] Evans suggested working on a mostly economic demonstration that the proposed remedy—divestiture—was "reasonable, effective, and the simplest means of achieving the desired end." But in fact the courts rarely (if ever) ordered a measure as drastic as divestiture because of the likely economic effects.[59] Furthermore, the three drafts of the Explanatory Statement reveal that the division had not elaborated a legal justification for requesting divestiture. The concept "public interest" still identified the audience as "public" more than "consumers." Even the third version gives only vague reasons for requesting divorcement, stating only that "public interest will be served by restoring free enterprise to an industry which affects so vitally the welfare and morals of large sections of our citizenship."

The best economic argument for divorcement was to demonstrate that vertical integration was the basis for market control, that is, the functioning of exhibition. Most of the work in this phase went into preparing this argument. Evans proposed, in particular, retabulating the data "to show the different situation of small town markets and metropolitan areas." He devoted special attention to the dual role of the first-run theater,[60] as a showcase, crucial in the exploitation of a picture, and as the source of "the cream of the profits." He also emphasized the need to show that when an affiliated chain assumed management of a theater, there was seldom, if ever, a drop in admission prices, and in fact there was more often an increase. He used this example "to show a marked and vicious difference" between the operation of theaters and of "other types of retail chains." While normally a chain organization benefits the consumer with lower prices, the opposite was happening in film exhibition.[61] Evans's argument echoed Arnold's in *Bottlenecks of Business*. Neither opposed "bigness" or vertical integration unless the advantages of the "structural efficiency" were not passed on to the consumer.

While Williams and Arnold were busy preparing the legal arguments for the case and resisting the majors' stalling tactics, FBI agents and the division attorneys were investigating film exhibition. The files are full of their colorful reports and some strong complaints by independent exhibitors, which evoke an image of business practices of old-time rugged capitalistic aggressivity. One small independent exhibitor offered "all the assistance possible in bringing this moving picture major producer octopus to justice. If they are not brought to justice soon there will be no independent exhibitors in the business to compete with them. . . . They broke me financially and physically, so I am now in a position where I have no fear of them and am free to testify without any thought of what they may do to me thereafter."[62] Seymour Krieger, one of the division attorneys investigating film exhibition, reported in a series of letters that he was discovering just how well the majors had learned to cover their tracks.

> Exchange men telephone one another and do act in concert but they
> don't seem to put much in writing nor do they tell the exhibitors about
> their conspiracy but the results of conspiracy are there and as we develop
> numerous specific instances we can put together a persuasive argument. . . .
> One very definite problem that I have run into is that independent ex-
> hibitors now in the business seem to be free to talk to me and tell me all

they know, but they frankly tell me that they might be reluctant to testify vigorously because they know the power of the defendants and how easily they can be crushed by the stroke of a pen or the lifting of a telephone. What assurance can I give them that the government will vigorously protect its witnesses from the vengeance of the defendants?[63]

Behind this image of the movie business as recklessly aggressive are the neopopulist prejudices of some of the Justice Department attorneys. Deeprooted animosities show up in the correspondence of the *Paramount* case, which is filled with references to labor problems and blacklisting,[64] in addition to examples of the traditional hostility between producers and exhibitors and the anger of vociferous public groups.

In the fall of 1938, Arnold and Williams were resisting the eight companies' attempt to delay the trial by applying for a bill of particulars, that is, a list of instances of the alleged violations, and by opposing the preliminary injunction against theater acquisition. The majors opposed the injunction on the grounds that theaters had to be regularly relocated in response to a constant shift in the places the public would go for entertainment and "to changing ideas of comfort and convenience."[65] But Arnold countered that not proceeding toward a preliminary injunction in no way implied the department's approval of any proposed acquisition.[66] The majors' actions in later phases of the case suggest that this specification went unnoticed.

The division also implicated the "Little Three"—Columbia, Universal, and United Artists—in the case. Although these companies did not operate theater chains, the division's "organic" interpretation of market control lumped them into the general picture—"the monopolistic condition which has grown up in the motion picture industry."[67]

Some of the ambiguity that appears in the development of the *Paramount* case can be attributed to the differences—in size and function and how they relate to vertical integration—between the "Little Three" and the majors, despite their participation to the same trade practices.[68] For example, when offered a separate consent decree to stop the litigation, Universal rejected it. The war in Europe limited the distribution of their films and they would take no steps that might anger the majors, who controlled their American outlets.[69]

Negotiations

When stalling tactics failed, the majors resorted to their traditional strategy of self-regulation. On December 3, 1938, they informed the Justice Department about "proposals resulting from the conferences between the distributors and the various exhibitors groups."[70] But Arnold rejected the film industry's offers of agreements and self-regulative efforts, just as the Antitrust

Division was at this time consistently rejecting proposals for self-regulation associated with the block booking hearings.[71]

In January 1939, Sol Rosenblatt, who had drafted the NRA Code of Fair Competition for the Motion Picture Industry (generally interpreted as favorable to the interests of the majors), offered his services for the *Paramount* case. Some of the moves and events of this phase suggest that Rosenblatt started working toward a consent decree, though whether in good or bad faith is unclear. The division was in an embarrassing situation. The plan proposed by Rosenblatt provided for local boards that would hear complaints on block booking, unreasonable clearances, and other unfair practices. Compliance would be enforced by prosecution for violation of the consent decree. According to division attorney Seymour Krieger, this plan had the positive element of offering "some of the flexibility of control that the industry needs."[72] Williams instead opposed Rosenblatt's project on the grounds that the independent producers and distributors distrusted him, according to the "opinion that he worked, under the NRA code, in the interests of the major companies." Rosenblatt's plan, however, signals that negotiations to avoid going to trial had started.[73]

As expected, Allied reacted immediately: "Mr. Myers stated that, in his opinion, any connection of Mr. Rosenblatt with the case would seriously affect the confidence of the independent exhibitor in the Government's suit."[74] Myers supplied the division with the records of the Darrow Board of 1935, strongly critical of the Motion Picture Code, as influenced by the majors. Not only did Rosenblatt embody the typical New Deal contradiction between a NRA mentality and neobrandeisan antimonopolism, but he was suspected of having "come off very well financially out of that experience."[75] No official position was taken about hiring him regularly, but he stayed in touch with the division.

As preparations for the trial continued, the Antitrust Division grew doubtful that divestiture, if it was even obtainable, would effectively correct monopolistic trade practices. In January 1939, Williams suggested in a memorandum to Arnold that they apply to Congress "for the purpose of securing remedial legislation."[76] Quoting the position he had taken in 1937 favoring "some Federal regulation," Williams reproposed his suggestion.[77] (Federal regulation or supervision had already been applied to radio, in the same period, and this was reason enough for the film industry to be jumpy.)[78] Williams had not changed his mind about the need for a rapid legal proceeding and about divestiture, but he felt that it was important to respond to the majors' stubborn and dilatory behavior and reintroduced the hypothesis of a federal supervision.[79]

In those very days Congress was examining various anti–block booking bills, about which Williams punctually reported to Arnold, in detail. When the hearings on the Neely Bill began, all the action moved to that front. While Williams was working to prepare for the trial, and Arnold was applying for funds to start "ten new cases against the motion picture trust,"[80] "rumors" of a possible consent decree materialized, having been hinted at in a report about a conversation with the industry's lawyers, among which Bill Donovan played an important role. With talk of local arbitration, flexibility of control, and a consent decree, the negotiations had entered a new, operational phase. Words like "negotiations," "cooperation," and "consent decree" started appearing regularly in the correspondence, as early as February 1939.

Encouraging this development in the case, Harry Warner wrote to the secretary of commerce (and Roosevelt's most faithful collaborator), Harry Hopkins, on March 6, 1939. In his ten-page letter, Warner discusses the role of the film industry and its problems, in terms reminiscent of Will Hays. This letter deserves close attention, because it was instrumental in originating the consent decree. In it Warner points out that the film industry was responsible for a "$150,000,000 annual export trade without benefit of subsidy or protective customs duties . . . built up slowly and steadily . . . until today the American motion pictures dominate the film markets of the world."[81] Warner argued that divorcement from theater ownership would limit the studios' ability to make risky big-budget "quality films" and jeopardize both its export trade and international dominance. Linking the depiction of American standards of living to the worldwide demand for consumer goods, Warner upheld films as "America's greatest salesman. . . . Our films fairly shriek Buy American."

Warner also stressed the good-will and propaganda function of motion pictures in a phase in which this issue had acquired a new relevance that was due to the international situation, but he emphatically returned to the question of the first-run theaters—the theaters to be divested in case of the government's victory in court: "The financial success of quality pictures depends to a great extent upon the manner and the place of their initial exhibition and exploitation."[82] In Warner's formulation, good pictures were expensive; cheaper films would bring in less foreign and domestic revenue, making quality pictures more scarce. The reduced appeal of Hollywood films would, in the end, hurt all. Hopkins must have been impressed, since it was through the good offices of the Department of Commerce that the consent decree was reached. Warner's letter suggests the ways that film's ideological role in the coming war and the "hollywoodization" of the planet fostered the survival of the studio system. In a sense, it was the "monopoly of discourse," the great power of mobilization of Hollywood cinema, that allowed the industry to maintain its economic monopoly for ten more years.[83]

THE PARAMOUNT CASE

In View of the Trial

While the film industry had begun working toward a consent decree, under the pressure of the approval of the Neely Bill by the Senate in the summer of 1939, it kept the Antitrust Division busy answering bills of particular as preparation for the trial continued. In a memorandum to the attorney general in June 1939, Arnold worried that outsiders, unaware of the difficulties he was encountering in having a judge assigned and starting the case before 1940, might blame the division for the delay.[84] He wanted to go to court as soon as possible and was against "soft" consent decrees in principle.[85]

In this delicate phase of the case, the President was informed of the situation. He insisted on the need to find a solution that would satisfy the Justice Department's requirements of real change in the operations of the film industry, but he gave the Departments of Commerce and Justice responsibility for effecting it. In particular he took this position in an exchange of letters with Will Hays that are quoted extensively here because they also document the tone of their relationship. Hays informed the President about the negotiations for the consent decree.

> The study of the Motion Picture Industry being made by the Department of Commerce has progressed during the last months as planned. They have been most thorough in their investigation and our companies have literally given them everything. Whatever their report and recommendations may be, they are certainly going to be reached by them with a full knowledge of all the facts. They are evidently almost finished, and I am worried about the next step. You will remember that the whole plan, as discussed with you and Secretary Hopkins, depended upon their conclusions being the reasoned judgment of the Commerce Department and the Secretary so that you would personally have the best judgment of unprejudiced agencies; then, the industry will join in effectuating those recommendations and a big, constructive job would be done.
>
> It has been the plan, always, of course, that the Department of Justice would be related into it, and the final result must be satisfactory to them. However, if Mr. Arnold still projects himself into the Commerce Department's own study before they make their own recommendations, which will be based on proper business and practical necessities and not solely on legalistic theories, then progress will be very much more difficult. There is danger of Mr. Arnold doing that very thing right now because of Harry's illness [i.e., continuing problems since his operation for stomach cancer], and I am very anxious that nothing happens prejudicial to our obligations to him. The whole study has been under his aegis, and his personal influence has guaranteed its thoroughness and integrity. The final recommendations should have his personal endorsement. This will give

you the additional assurance of confidence in the recommendations and
will keep him personally a party in what I am sure will be a very creditable
conclusion.

Hays insists that the Commerce Department plan was a serious attempt to
reform the industry's trade practices, that the recommendations would be
"very severe" and "far-reaching." He acknowledges that the Commerce and
Justice Departments would have to work together on "the final solution."
"But," he continues, "if we do not get the recommendations of the Department of Commerce really without 'combative and prejudicial pressure,' it
defeats the purpose of giving the effort the benefit of the Department of
Commerce's thorough and impartial study." Hays emphasizes the tension
between the two federal agencies in relation to the project, reminding the
President of his involvement with the plan, with the evident purpose to encourage him to lean toward the position that was more favorable to the industry: the Department of Commerce's.

> I am sure that the steps we discussed in March and the amplified efforts of
> these past months will finally result in a most comprehensive and con-
> structive readjustment of the whole business. This is really a tremendous
> thing and *should* end litigation and all *contested* legislation. I worry about
> any mistake now and want your advice. We can get the industry's complete
> cooperation on the entire plan we discussed. These recommendations of
> the Department of Commerce which our people know will have grown out
> of an impartial study conducted by Government experts under the aus-
> pices of Harry Hopkins and your own encouragement, these recommen-
> dations will have tremendous weight and are the *next step*. They will give
> the *basis* for the most major readjustments going farther, no doubt, than
> you and I discussed; and they should be gotten to you with Harry's ap-
> proval as soon as possible. Then Commerce and Justice can do their dis-
> cussing and then with your help the answer can be found. Your own inter-
> est in finding the *right* has been, of course, the principal causative element
> in preparing our people to go to the most extreme length for the same ob-
> jective. Be assured the industry will do its full part. Please let me know in
> some way any suggestion. I know your continued interest in the success of
> the effort. I am determined that it not fail and success is not possible with-
> out you. I am afraid of what may be done if we don't watch within the next
> little while. (original italics)[86]

The coded references and little nuances of Hays's subtle blackmailing tone
is typical of his epistolary style, in this instance to make the President face his
responsibilities by referring to his continued interest in it. In this struggle between two political titans, Roosevelt was, however, second to none; his answer
flings back the attack.

I have noted carefully what you say in regard to the situation in the motion picture industry. I am, of course, greatly interested in reaching a constructive solution and I have high hopes that the study now being made in the Department of Commerce will be productive of good results.

At the same time, I do not feel that the activities of the Department of Commerce could, or should, restrict the Department of Justice in fulfilling its duty to enforce the antitrust laws. I see no necessary inconsistency between the activities of the Department of Commerce on the one hand and the prosecution by the Department of Justice of the pending suit against the motion picture industry on the other. If the study now being made in the Department of Commerce should result in an economically desirable solution of the problems of the motion picture industry, it is conceivable that such a solution might furnish a basis for settlement of the pending equity suit. But the Attorney General tells me that unless or until a settlement is proposed which the Department of Justice believes is in the public interest, he would not be warranted in delaying or otherwise altering the normal course of litigation involving the film industry. I concur in the view of the Attorney General on this point.

The only suggestion that I might offer would be that you do not regard the pendency of litigation as a bar to the economic solution of the problems of your industry. The Department of Justice could not, of course, approve any plan which in its judgment violates the antitrust laws. If a plan should be worked out, however, with or without the help of the Department of Commerce, which meets the legal objections to the present formation and operation of the film industry, I am quite certain that it will be accorded a reasonable reception both in the Department of Justice and in the courts.[87]

Roosevelt never lost sight of "public interest," nor did he bypass the proper agencies or force administration representatives to act contrary to their opinions. The next step was for the two sides—Hays and the Warners on one, Roosevelt, Hopkins, and Walker on the other—to work together preparing the way for the consent decree.

The Monopoly of Production

A year after the Paramount suit was filed, preparation for the trial continued, but the actual court proceedings were not yet in sight. To help document the actual working of the industry, from the point of view of the monopoly of production the Antitrust Division approached film executives and Hollywood personalities who had approved the filing of the suit, trying to transform old animosities and personal problems into sworn statements, necessary for the trial. But it did not find a very receptive Hollywood.

Williams asked two federal attorneys on the West Coast, Albert Law and David Podell,[88] to check the names of independent producers quoted by Benham in his 1936 report and to contact "other persons such as directors, writers, or actors" who could testify in the trial, or supply evidence or file statements critical of the studio system. He referred, for example, to an interview he had had with the screenwriter Donald Ogdon Stewart, "who indicated a sympathetic understanding of the Government's suit."[89] But despite the bitter struggles for the institution of the actors', directors', and screenwriters' guilds, and the politicized atmosphere of those years, the records suggest that film personalities did not respond to the opportunity "to go on record as a part of this case in no uncertain terms." Perhaps the people in Hollywood did not realize the political potential of the case, or perhaps the government avoided getting involved in such peculiarly conflictual areas as Hollywood guilds, and the artist's natural resentments against the industrial aspects of the "dream factory."[90]

Carl Leammle of Universal and Samuel Goldwyn of United Artists, who managed a nonintegrated system, without a direct outlet into the market, and had long fought against the power of the majors, could well take an official stand for divestiture. Samuel Goldwyn, for example, according to Williams was "sore" at the industry. When Warner Bros. backed out of a deal to release a Goldwyn film because United Artists objected, Goldwyn tried unsuccessfully to be relieved of his contract with United Artists. This was an excellent example to Williams of the Antitrust Division's complaint that producers cannot "get into the market except at the sufferance of the major companies."

But the government wanted statements and evidence, not the usual complaints and personal resentments. Williams wanted Goldwyn to "illustrate the reasons why it is important, from the viewpoint of free enterprise and open competition, to have theatres divorced from producers and distributors so that they and each of them would stand as a part of an independent market to which all distributors should have access."[91]

Frank Capra was another Hollywood personality who had always defended the ideal of the little man, of "small business," in his pictures, and was personally involved in the affirmation of the creative (and productive) autonomy of the director against the front office. But in those very days his contractual situation made his position less appropriate to the division's needs.[92]

The intricacies of contract agreements made it difficult to get a straightforward definition of independent producer. In the block booking hearings of 1940, Chadwick discussed the problem.

> [Some of these companies] are merely subsidiary corporations of other
> majors. In other words, let us take Frank Capra Productions. He just left

170

Columbia and has gone with Warner Bros. Well, Frank Capra Productions are now, instead of calling him a director, an employee, they have set up a separate unit for him, but it is owned and controlled by Warner Bros., and merely designated Frank Capra as a producer and distributor. In a sense he may be called an independent producer, but actually and in effect he is an employee, just as much as he ever was. He draws a salary. He has a share of the profits, that is true, of the picture he makes; but in the end, conceding that he is an independent producer, he is still an integral portion of the major company.[93]

A letter from Podell documents the disappointing reaction from the West Coast.

I have managed to interview both [Walter] Wanger [at United Artists] and Goldwyn; the latter is strongly with us but extremely reluctant to take the stand, saying that he has to live with these people; Wanger, too, is bounden to them in many ways. I have an understanding with Wanger however that Silverstone, who I believe is either Chairman of the Board of United Artists or the President, will speak very definitely and emphatically for United Artists. . . . They are both naturally very eager to see the matter adjusted before trial, if possible, and I would suggest that you say nothing to discourage that attitude, except, of course, that we want a real housecleaning in the industry and no mere pro forma decree, and that it is our purpose to fight until we can open up the industry; that nothing would please us better than if they did the housecleaning themselves. . . . All of the three gentlemen feel that divorce alone, while necessary, will not solve the problem; indeed, it is apt to create even a worse situation if the exhibitors are permitted to function as a group of powerful chains; that to get real relief, the chains must likewise be broken up.[94]

Williams started growing skeptical about the help that the independent producers could give the Antitrust Division. He observed that "these so-called independent producers and all persons who are dependent upon them for their livelihood are so much a part of the thing against which we are complaining that it is and will be a complete waste of time to try to develop anything from them which will be helpful to the Government or to the New York suit. Each of them is an integral part of the industry as it now operates and each is dependent upon the present structure and operation of the industry for the maintenance of their respective positions." The solution, he felt, was that the government's suit should be "waged as an attack against the present organizations and operation of the industry. This attack should be objective and should be separated, as far as that may be possible, from the strife of divergent interests and divergent personalities that seem to hold such a prominent position on the stage of the industry."[95] The division could not communicate with these Hollywood personalities, let alone collaborate with them. The position of the independent producers in the case had become less obvious. Their interests seemed to be too intertwined with those of the majors. Lacking powerful allies for a frontal attack against the studio system weakened the government's case, from the point of view of the monopoly of production.

Stipulations for the Trial

Finally, in New York, a tentative date for the trial was agreed upon: February or March 1940, soon delayed to May. Within the discussion about the stipulation of a date between the Justice Department and the film companies, the majors, citing the difficulty of preparing for so many trials at the same time, negotiated the postponement of other trials, including the *Fox–West Coast* case. After the stipulation, the film companies' lawyers insisted to the judge that their agreement to go to trial on May 1 was based on two things: that "(1) all other action involving the defendants be postponed until after the completion of this action, including criminal action on the West Coast, and (2) that the Government would answer fully their interrogatories as served at least sixty days before the trial." Answering "interrogatories" meant that the Justice Department would have to reveal its witnesses and this further weaken the presentation of the case.[96] In addition to this delaying tactic, the film industry insisted on interpreting the postponement of the theater chains suits as a virtual cancellation.

The twenty-page "History of the Suit to February 1, 1940," presents a technical description with specific dates and stipulations, of the lengthy negotiations between the government and the film companies, the preliminary injunction on theater acquisition, and various bills of particulars and sets of interrogatories. It mirrors the tiresome process behind the trial and reveals how the stated "cooperation" of the industry must have appeared, in the end, to the government, only as a stalling maneuvre.

Toward the Consent Decree

The idea of a consent decree became more concrete. The problem was its efficiency and articulation, not its stipulation. Arnold asked Paul Williams and Robert Wright (the government counsel in the future Paramount trial of 1944, who was involved sporadically with the case in this phase),[97] to express their opinions about the plan of reformation of trade practices, developed out of the "study" by the Commerce Department, which had been, at first, rejected. Both Williams and Wright criticized the Commerce Department plan for lacking a mechanism of enforcement of the reforms, insisting that current practices were inherent in the industry's structure and that a decree would not change the relationship of exhibitors and producers. In order to argue for divestiture, the Antitrust Division had to move into a terrain practically never covered before: this ground-breaking role of the *Paramount* case should not be underestimated. The decree would have to be backed up with an innovative mechanism for enforcement.[98] Wright concluded that the Commerce Department should propose such a mechanism. If the plan seemed likely to succeed, the move toward divorcement could be postponed and perhaps eventually set aside. But without such a plan, the divorcement should proceed. This was in fact the course that events followed.

The division was preparing for the trial, as a memo by Arnold to the FBI, with detailed instruction for the pretrial work, indicates. It also decided to orally examine the film executives at an early date (February or March). In reference to this examination, special attorney William Farnsworth proposed the names of the Paramount executives, because he felt that "practically every allegation in the complaint can be proved through the history of Paramount and its various affiliations."[99] The profiles of the seven executives are more reminiscent of shyster figures than of professional businessmen.

> Sam Katz, assisted by Dembow, appears to have been the master mind in the development of the Paramount-Publix chain of theatres. Coercion of practically all varieties was used upon competing exhibitors forcing them into the Paramount-Publix chain. Ralph Kohn was treasurer of Paramount before the bankruptcy, and I believe he evolved the unique system for buying interests in theatres. Publix would buy a 50% interest in a theatre, using instead of money stock at a certain valuation guaranteed by the company. When the crash came, and the price of Paramount securities hit the toboggan slide, the company was unable to make good on its guarantee. This was the big push that sent them into bankruptcy. S. A. Lynch was one of the early Paramount-Publix men and apparently is an able businessman. When they got into trouble, they called him back from retirement and put him in charge of all of their real estate problems. As you know, they came out of bankruptcy still hanging on to over one thousand theatres. Y. Frank Freeman took over the job from Lynch after Paramount came out of bankruptcy.

Farnsworth's allegations are confirmed in authoritative texts such as Benjamin Hampton's *The History of the American Film Industry,* in which the Paramount men who fought the "battle for the theatres" are labeled "dynamite gang" and "wrecking crew."[100] In Farnsworth's judgment, the examination of these executives would have supplied the division with "a very complete story"—a history of vertical integration. He also implicated Frank Walker, Roosevelt's friend and the administration's Grey Eminence, in the murky details of a deal between Comerford and Paramount, hinting that behind-the-scenes maneuvers protected the Comerford chain when Paramount filed bankruptcy. Even if it is hard to believe that Farnsworth did not know who Walker was the profile he draws is quite disturbing, but, associated with Hays' remarks, it casts Walker in a protagonist's role. Farnsworth saw Warner Bros. in an "exemplary position" in the history of vertical integration: "Warners apparently have the dubious honor of running second to Paramount as pressure boys in the acquisition of theatres. Joe Bernhard, in charge of theatres, should be able to develop the picture. If we take him step by step from the first Warner theatre through the various acquisitions, it may be a great help in building up the case."

The Trial Strategy

The Antitrust Division was devising a trial strategy that closely followed the structure of the petition, with a historical section, on the development of vertical integration, and a descriptive one, on the organization and operations of the film industry. Among the witnesses from the West Coast that Williams wanted for the trial were film industry personalities such as Thomas Tally, William Hodkinson, Richard Rowland, and I. E. Chadwick. They were expected to be sympathetic to the government's position and provide testimony about the historical development of either independent production or independent exhibition.

In February 1940, the government suffered some embarrassment in the hearings when Judge Goddard dismissed its objections to Columbia's interrogatories. To Farnsworth, the government "took quite a licking." In this instance, Judge Goddard, who was going to sit on the case, seemed to Farnsworth to be "completely unsympathetic to the position of the Government."[101]

On the other scene, at the Department of Commerce, Ernest Tupper was working on a trade practices code, referred to as the Code of Fair Competition, with an obvious reference to the NRA codes.[102] Tupper was convinced that the proposal was "revolutionary" and would "meet all the objections of the public spirited groups and the independent exhibitors" and "provide a real opportunity for the producers to place the industry on a much firmer economic basis than it has been in the past."[103]

The Commerce Department's code, entitled "Proposal for a Consent Decree as a Basis of Settlement of Suits Against the Motion Picture Industry" provided for the elimination of blind selling (through trade showings), substituted block booking with groups of (5–8) pictures, forbade the imposition of shorts, newsreels, trailers, and so on, and allowed for the cancellation "of any picture which is legally offensive on moral, religious or racial grounds." It regulated questions of clearance and run and conflictual situations between independent exhibitors and majors, through a system of arbitration. The proposal was similar to the Neely Bill, then under discussion in the House, and whose fate was tied to the outcome of these negotiations. The Commerce Department plan reproposed the idea of blocks and did not allow for a real selectivity. To "correct" blind selling, it proposed trade shows, which were an inconvenience for the small-town exhibitor (but they were no worse a solution than the synopsis requested by the Neely Bill).

Despite Tupper's optimism, the Justice Department rejected the plan, mostly because it made no reference to divestiture and to the situation in theater acquisitions. Nonetheless it continued to circulate among the interested parties, in an endless process of negotiations, coming finally to a standstill because of opposition from Allied. At the request of the Antitrust Division, Myers, on behalf of Allied, the interested party, analyzed the plan in detail and gave his criticism on specific items. Allied opposed trade showings, preferring the Neely Bill proposal of synopses, adequate cancellation privilege, and selective contracts. It disliked arbitration, particularly by the American Arbitration Society ("supported by big business interests"), and resented the inclusion of a representative of the Commerce Department, "because of a long history of dissatisfaction with the Motion Picture Division of that Department."[104]

The Neely Bill hearings were resumed. In this phase, the Justice Department worked in tight collaboration with Allied. This relationship was in keeping with the New Deal tactic of drawing on organized interest groups able to support their positions with an articulated ideological motivation. What counted for the administration was the size of the interests represented and the organized nature of the group. Joseph Hazen, counsel for Warner Bros., hinted to Tupper that the Allied States Association's membership figure had been "grossly exaggerated."[105] At this crucial stage of the negotiations, the administration was assessing the parties involved to identify with a figure the interests that would benefit from this reform. The decreasing interest in the independent producers—the weakest among the interest groups—is not surprising then.

The discussion of the specific terms of the consent decree continued. Columbia refused an offer to "step out of the case" by "taking a decree," stating that it was "vitally interested in block booking" and if it were abolished, it "would fold up."[106] The diverse interests of the minors, that is, their reliance on the established trade practices in the absence of vertical integration, discouraged them from "taking a decree," while the government probably favored their dismissal from the case, being aware that they constituted the weak side of the monopoly argument, in that they did not control any theaters.

When the possibility of a consent decree seemed to vanish, the division went back to work on the trial, notwithstanding the increasing difficulties. "The Government is now being subjected to flank attacks by the defendants in hope of further delays," wrote Williams, in April 1940, but he kept a firm stand on the date of the trial, even if, by then, he had realized that it was going to be "an uphill battle with [Judge] Goddard."[107]

When Williams left for New York to prepare for the trial, a new character entered the scene. It was James Hayes, special assistant to the attorney general, who took charge of the case in Washington. It is unclear why a new person was introduced in the case in such an advanced stage of preparation and given such a prominent role, when it was evident that he was not familiar or sympathetic with it. Hayes immediately criticized the preparation for the trial, expressing doubts about the solidity of the government's position in the case. In a memorandum he stated that legal arguments on important questions such as the evidence necessary to prove a conspiracy among the majors or on the legal limitations on a copyright monopoly were insufficient. He questioned the definition of independent producer and the entire issue of the monopoly of production.[108] Given the massive documentation collected by the Antitrust Division and all the work done by Williams, his criticism seems unjustified, especially coming from a newcomer. It is not surprising, however, that having critically reviewed the preparation for the trial, he concluded that the trial should be avoided in favor of a negotiated solution.

> A decree ordering divorcement would have to be supported by strong, convincing evidence of monopoly from both independent chains and independent producers. Such evidence is not presently available, nor does any reasonable hope of obtaining it appear to exist. Further, the picture of monopoly painted by the bill gets most of its color not from the integration of certain of the defendants but from the alleged discriminatory trade practices imposed on the independents to the advantage of the defendants. Eliminate the discriminatory trade practices from the bill and the picture disclosed is not a huge monopoly established by eight powerful corporations acting in concert, but of eight competing companies seeking the favor and patronage of thousands of independents.

Hayes was questioning the very foundation of the case—the relationship Williams firmly believed in between vertical integration and trade practices. He even questioned the existence of a monopoly.

At this point, the Justice Department was developing reasons to negotiate a consent decree. In the meantime the date for the trial was postponed again, to June, coinciding with the final phase of the block booking hearings, which contain frequent references to this trial where all the issues related to the control of the film market were to be discussed and decided.

As the trial date approached, Williams prepared a document entitled "Trial Brief," which seemed to ignore Hayes's criticism. He also sent Arnold a copy of a speech delivered by Stanton Griffis of Paramount. In the speech Griffis boasts about the political and ideological power of cinema. Griffis states that the film industry was an "Art Industry" that "entertains and educates in the United States . . . more than 80 million people weekly and approximately 150 million people abroad." And adds:

> This is an industry, too, that consistently, even if not quietly, stick to its knitting of furnishing amusement, laughter, entertainment and escape; spends [its] far-flung energy in making the world a happier place to live in; resolutely endeavors to keep out of the field of politics and propaganda; although I sincerely believe that if the motion picture companies should so desire, and would for the moment stray from this principle, within a very short time could so influence public opinion as to elect a Congress and a President; and probably has more influence on the lives of the younger generation—and this is a broad statement—than most of our schools and colleges put together.[109]

Williams underlined this section of the document. The filing of this material within the case demonstrates both the kind of implicit blackmail posed by the industry to the political-legal establishment, and the division's attention to the ideological function of the medium. A few days later, during the trial, Arnold referred to this "address," but he did not stress the point, in keeping with the tested strategy of masking the ideological contents of the *Paramount* case behind the economic-legal discussion.[110]

The Trial (June 3–7, 1940)

On June 3 the trial began in the Southern District court of New York, Judge Goddard presiding. The government was represented by Thurman Arnold and Paul Williams, the industry by lawyers representing each major, individually; since the MPPDA had no part in the case, there were no representatives on its behalf.

After a few procedural details, Arnold took the stand and tried to link the case to his general policy of antitrust. His statement, generic and in a sense digressive, included a historical excursus on American antimonopoly legislation, defined as "a general principle of industrial democracy" and "a law which prevents the private seizure of industrial power." He offered his interpretation of the rule of reason: a combination that dominates the market is illegal unless it "is justified by considerations of necessity in order to get goods around, distribute goods to the consumers," or "put its savings on the efficiency of mass production on to the consumer." (Later in the trial, counsels for the majors tried to demonstrate this "necessity" precisely.) In this statement (as in his writings), Arnold analyzed the psychology of businessmen and the mentality of the leaders of trade organizations, side-tracking into recent German history and referring to other antitrust cases undertaken by the Antitrust Division. For this case, he said, the government was suing the majors "as examples of the kind of things that happen when an industry gets this overwhelming domination." He added that their monopolistic power had led to a "situation of terror," a "notorious waste," and a "situation in which people are not free to introduce new ideas." When the court asked him not to digress and to keep to the main points of discussion, Arnold declared that the case had been started because it fell "within the broad general type of situation" and that the division's "prosecution policy is directed at picking out and freeing the market first of all in those necessities which low income groups must have. Among those are foods, fuel, milk and amusement." The first point confirmed the importance of the study of the film industry structure within the legal and economic debate of the New Deal; the second, by defining cinema as "a necessity," implicitly recognized the social function of cinema. To the court, however, these were not legal bases for an antitrust case. Arnold further stated that, while some might refer to the film industry "as a marvelous combination of art and industry," to him, this combination had the detrimental effect of controling the public taste. Not surprisingly, the industry's lawyers criticized Arnold's statement for being ambiguous when it could instead have defined the objectives of the case.[111]

It fell to Williams to explain the Justice Department's position more precisely. Williams began with a detailed history of the film industry and a list of the witnesses who would speak about the specific phases. He illustrated his statement with a map that clearly delineated the territorial divisions among the majors. The map had been drawn according to data from FBI investigations and information supplied by the companies in their interrogatories, and Williams used it to explain his definition of "conspiracy" (an essential element in this case). Whether this geographic division, he said, "came about by accident or design or by intent on non-intent can make no difference on the economic situation which has resulted from it." Thus, "a film made by a house is projected in theatres of all the houses and has its first showing in all areas," and therefore "regardless of who produced the film, everyone benefits." This innovative interpretation of the rule of reason minimized the intentionality of the practice, while concentrating on the effects. But there was the risk that the same interpretation could be used against the government: if, in the absence of concrete evidence of conspiracy, it could be demonstrated that this situation was due to entrepreneurial necessities, the complaint would have been dropped. (And, in fact, this was the argument developed later by the defense.)

Williams described exhibition and distribution as forms of interstate commerce, that is, as activities that could be regulated by a federal authority. But when he delved deeper into the question of block booking, the court interrupted him to ask: "Now why is that wrong, for a manufacturer of films or any other article, to try to sell his year's output if he can?'"—a question that showed little understanding of the government's line of argument.

To illustrate the monopolic control of production, Williams boldly asked why high-quality films were so scarce and responded with the rhetorical question: "Is that because of a lack of creative genius amongst Americans, or is it because of some organization and commercial situation that has been developed that will not permit the free play of those forces?" This set up the defense to argue later in the trial that obviously the industry had no reason whatsoever *not* to produce quality films: their very "rarity" confirmed the special ability of the majors, who knew how to make good pictures.

Concerning the three minor companies, Williams stated that they were involved in the case because "they joined with these producer companies in giving them a monopoly of exhibition . . . by making their products available to them before it is made available to any others" and had adopted the same trade practices, but, he added, "they might be a reluctant party to this conspiracy." It was obvious that the lawyers for Universal, United Artists, and Columbia tried, at this point, to have their companies acquitted already in the courtroom.

Williams ended by emphasizing how many complaints the division had received against the film industry from all parts of the country—complaints he called symptoms of the "illness" that infected the industry. In the entire statement, he never used the word *monopoly*.[112]

The word then passed to the defense. Judge Thomas T. Thacher, the attorney for Paramount, opened by stating that the industry welcomed the trial because it provided a forum for publicly clarifying the industry's mode of operating.

He said that all the problems described by the government's representatives were the results of "the underlying and controlling economic forces" by which the industry had always been "freely competitive." The industry's current trade practices had come about, not as the result of a conspiracy, but as "the necessary and normal result of economic factors, business considerations and competitive struggle." He contested the division's assumption that vertical integration was "unlawful *per se*" and, above all, the fact that Arnold and Williams had not stated to the court whether they charged the industry with *being a monopoly* or *attempting to monopolize*.

He accused the division of serving, not the "public interest," but the interest of only a small group of dissatisfied exhibitors, whereas the industry it-self actually served the public interest by making films available to all. To con-firm this positive image of the industry, Thacher read the Federal Trade Commission decision that there was "free competition between producers and distributors" and "lack of monopolization." He reconstructed the history of Paramount to show how it had fought against monopoly—first through Adolf Zukor's project of imposing a better-quality product and then through vertical integration—and how intense competition between the studios was maintained to guarantee larger profits.[113]

The trial continued with statements by the other defense lawyers repre-senting the various companies. They in turn recounted the history of the re-spective studios, highlighting specific merits and characteristics and describ-ing the overall competition as typical of the industry. With each of them developing a particular legal angle, they all insisted that there was no con-spiracy and that trade practices and vertical integration were the results of entrepreneurial necessity. With mounting sarcasm they dismissed Arnold's and Williams's opening statements as too general. "What is the charge against us here?" asked John W. Davis, counsel for MGM. "I hope I won't be regarded as discourteous . . . but I really hope that as a result of the govern-ment's opening statements your Honor got a clearer idea of the issues in this case than I was able to obtain."[114] "Violation of law—not some vague eco-nomic theory attractively called 'industrial democracy'—must be the basis of its case," insisted Ralph Harris, attorney for Twentieth-Century–Fox.[115] Joseph Proskauer, attorney for Warner Bros., attacked Arnold with acrimony. The so-called power of monopolizing (one of the charges) did not exist at all, he said. On the contrary, it was the government that had tried to seize in-dustrial power—the same government that had earlier on approved the very trade practices it was now attacking. The New Deal could not easily have re-futed these accusations. The first Hundred Days legislation had been con-sidered an undue interference of the government in the country's economy, and the NRA code for the film industry was historical proof that the govern-ment had once approved the trade practices now under attack. Defending the industry against the antimonopolistic theory of Arnold and of the New Deal, Proskauer pointed out that the film industry "passed on the savings" obtained through structural efficiency to the consumer, "to a point that 85 million weekly visitors to the theatres . . . see any picture . . . for 10 cents" and that, in those years, the doubling in price of production costs had been ac-companied by a reduction in ticket prices.[116] Ralph S. Harris, counsel for Twentieth Century–Fox, stated that, having examined the information sup-plied to them by the Justice Department, along with interrogatories and bills of particulars, he had concluded that there was no evidence of a conspir-acy.[117] The government had reason to fear that the case could be weakened by the defendants' knowledge of the evidence in the bills of particular the government had collected against them.

The industry's attorneys moved from discrediting the government attorneys, to belittling the witnesses, describing them as "egocentrics" who, having "missed the bus" of the industry's history, were therefore envious and upset.[118] Taking a different track, and echoing Harry Warner's message to Roosevelt of the previous year, Proskauer also warned the court that a punishment such as divorcement could cause a drop in the quality films that could hurt all parties because it could disrupt exports, which represented a major part of the industry's business.

The "three minors" based their defensive strategies on those of the majors but stressed the disadvantage they had in the market because they did not own theaters. Trade practices such as block booking were essential to their functioning, allowing them to compete with the majors in production and have access to the theaters.[119] For this reason, that is, for what Williams had called "recalcitrant" participation to the conspiracy, the attorneys of the three minors announced that they would apply for dismissal for their clients.[120]

On June 6, the fourth day of heated debate, at the end of the opening statements, when the time had come to examine evidence and witnesses, Louis D. Frolich, counsel for Columbia's, interrupted Williams. He presented a motion to dismiss his company "on the ground that all the matters . . . could have been litigated . . . in the Texas suit" (that is, within the *Interstate Circuit* case).[121] Taken by surprise, Williams asked for time to read the document, while from all sides, motions to dismiss were presented to the judge. One of them concerned "an individual United Artist defendant . . . whose name I shall not mention," said Edward C. Raferty, counsel for this company, which included James Roosevelt on its board.[122]

After showing some signs of perplexity about the procedural turn of events, the judge adjourned the hearing. Faced with this counteroffensive by the industry and its unexpected legal moves, Williams sent an "urgent and confidential" telegram to Arnold, asking for advice. On June 10, all parties met before the judge and agreed to work toward a compromise, that is, to draft a consent decree.

The Drafting of the Consent Decree

The unexpected course taken by the trial accomplished what external pressures and internal doubts had not been able to do: it convinced Williams and Arnold to work on a consent decree for the time being, maintaining the possibility to petition for divestiture after a trial period, thus avoiding the risk that the court's opinion would oppose divestiture. On June 7, Williams had written to Arnold:

> My estimate of the situation is as follows: a consent decree at this time, embodying a comprehensive trade practice code and setting up a system of arbitration, would be a distinct step in advance and might possibly prove successful in eliminating forthwith many of the ills and discriminatory trade practices present in the industry. At the foot of the decree would be a provision similar to that in the *International Harvester* case whereby, after a lapse of time in which the trade practice code could be fairly tested, the Government could make application on a supplemental petition for such other relief as might be necessary to bring the industry and its operation into harmony with law, including, of course, the issue of divorcement.
>
> Secondly, the weak spots in the Government's present case could then be remedied, because, by reason of the opening statements, definite information is now available as to where the case is weakest. . . .
>
> If the case goes to trial, there is a grave question as to whether or not a decree may be had favorable to the Government upon any of the issues in the case. Yesterday noon I discussed with Judge Goddard the possibility of negotiations for a consent decree, and was amazed to find that after having listened to opening statements for four days, he had obtained no grasp of the case or of the operations of the motion picture industry, whatsoever, and frankly so stated.
>
> I therefore feel that while the Judge is upright and honest, he will not be able to grasp the minute and complex ways in which restraints of trade are brought about in this industry, and that therefore it is extremely unlikely that a decree in the Government's favor may be expected of him. . . . In truth, the whole issues of the case may be so confused by his handling of the matter that chances of success upon appeal may be greatly diminished. . . .
>
> I feel, therefore, that from the sole viewpoint of tactical advantage, a great step forward may be taken by obtaining a consent decree at this time embodying a trade practice code with the right to test the question of divorcement. . . .
>
> Whether the position that the Department has taken on divorcement can be reconciled with such a decree is, of course, a matter, that must rest with you.[123]

The Antitrust Division contacted all interested parties, in particular the independent exhibitors, in order to revise their main requests to arrive at a satisfactory stipulation. Myers insisted on the need to maintain the position on divestiture, allowing for a three-year test period with continuous surveillance by the Justice Department, with the inclusion of findings in the decree, to prevent the defendants from using the decree as a "document which, in effect, proclaims their innocence," and with an injunction against the acquisition of theaters in the test period.[124] Allied decided not to oppose trade showings and groups of five pictures but added specifications ("pictures must be completed before being sold," and be "released consecutively") and inserted a special clause not limited to the trial period, to prevent the producer-distributors from changing their leasing and distribution methods to circumvent the decree. It was generally agreed that the consent decree would be "a plan de novo." Actually the Commerce Department plan, although officially rejected, remained the basis for discussion throughout.

The discussion of a consent decree created irreconcilable differences with the three minor film companies, as shown by a memo reporting a conference between the Antitrust Division and attorneys for these companies.

> The conference started out by the representatives of the defendants announcing positively that under no circumstances would their clients enter into a consent decree [the document dryly reported]. They stated that with world conditions what they are today, it is impossible for them to undertake the expense of rearranging their business so as to trade show pictures before they are sold or to sell them in small blocks.
>
> They were then asked whether they would be willing to enter into a decree if trade showing and sales in small blocks were eliminated. They stated flatly that their companies would not enter into any consent decree, no matter what was contained therein. . . .
>
> Their position was that they wanted to be free to use every bit of economic power at their command to force the sale of their pictures wherever they could sell them, and that they did not propose to give up any rights that they had, or thought they had, unless the court should require them to desist from doing so. . . .
>
> Representatives of the defendants stated that although they under no circumstances would enter into a consent decree, they would be willing to consider a reasonable fair trade practice code. When asked what should be contained in such a code, they stated that they felt it should provide that exhibitors be required to take their pictures and pay fair rentals for them, and that any dispute as to the fairness of the rentals should be submitted to arbitration. They stressed the point that the real bad boys in the industry were the exhibitors, and that the Government was approaching the situation from the wrong end by going after the producers.

The juxtaposition of producer and exhibitor was an old story, but in the case of the non–theater-holding companies it was more conflictual. The three minors were irreducible. This memo explains why the three minors *never signed the consent decree,* thus voiding its efficacy and causing the case to be reopened. Like the independent producers, the three minors fitted into the government's comprehensive picture of monopoly. Because of their structural position in the market, working with, and in the same manner as the majors, in distribution, they were part of the monopoly, and they could not be dismissed from the case. But in the absence of vertical integration, they were "a weak spot" in the case presentation.

The division had always indicated its willingness to give the three companies a separate consent decree, but they would not accept. They were not afraid of the "remedy"—divestiture— and their acceptance could be considered an admission of guilt. Furthermore, a decree would force them to give up trade practices they believed were essential to their functioning.

Informed of the refusal of the three minors, Allied took a skeptical position, insinuating that if the majors "show real determination in putting the industry's house in shape, the [minors] will conform to the new order." As there had been a request for an "escape clause" after one year, that is, for vacating the reforms of block booking after one year, had the three minors not consented yet to the decree, the independent exhibitors suspected that the five majors were "conniving in the recalcitrancy of the three."[125] Myers insinuated that the minors were faking a resistance, in order to support the majors' interest and demonstrate that there was no conspiracy, thus no monopoly. (This was a far-fetched interpretation, but it indicates the atmosphere of general distrust, and the terrible reputation of the film industry.) The independent exhibitors evaluated the weak position of the government in a court proceeding ("the defendants have had months since the receipt of the extraordinary bill of particulars in which to work on the government's witnesses") but did not believe that the negotiations for the consent decree were an honest effort to reform trade practices. They saw them instead as another way for the industry to "escape regulatory measures." They therefore favored reproposing the Neely Bill, rather than working on the decree, and loosened their connections with the division.[126]

It was August; one month had passed and the consent decree had not yet been drafted. The division tried to develop a new document by incorporating Allied's criticism into the Commerce Department plan, along with the outcome of the negotiations with the majors, the independent exhibitors, and public groups. This draft contained significant changes and additions, especially about theater acquisition: the clause devised for the preliminary injunction was re-proposed, and theater expansion was forbidden. The most significant change, however, was the Addendum.

> It is understood that the proposals set forth above shall be given a three-year trial. During such three-year period the Government will not seek to obtain the divorcement of exhibition from production and distribution. At the end of the three-year trial period, the Government shall be free to apply to the court for divorcement if it deems such divorcement necessary to restore competitive conditions in the industry.

In this way, the issue of divestiture was reintroduced in the stipulation, giving the consent decree a clear status as a "trial period." The proposal, dated August 3, 1940, was circulated for consideration and suggestions among the interested parties as well as the pressure groups who had proposed the Neely Bill.[127]

Williams approved the draft with a weary detachment, insisting that nonetheless divestiture was the only final solution.[128] By mid-August a serious crisis developed when the division rejected Paramount's and Fox's counterproposals to the decree, and Allied called the draft "wholly inadequate from the standpoint of both independent exhibitor and public."[129] Despite Allied's opinion that the decree was slanted in favor of the majors, the division tried to keep working with the independents, to the point of compiling a 51-page report analyzing the individual independent exhibitors' complaints. These complaints referred mostly to the "proposed new method of selling pictures and of trade showing," that is, to the core of the reforms introduced by the decree, which had already been accepted by the Allied Executive Committee. According to Williams, the independents had three reasons for objecting to the provisions.

(1) The added cost and inconvenience of buying pictures, in that a great number of contracts will have to be negotiated during the year instead of, as at present, one contract upon the annual basis. It is said that the new method will increase both the costs of selling and of buying pictures, which costs ultimately the public will have to absorb.
(2) The inconvenience of attending trade showings is objected to by those independent exhibitors who live at a distance from the exchange centres where the trade showings are to be conducted.
(3) The right granted the distributors to group pictures together as they may elect in blocks of five without any cancellation privilege places the power in the distributors to force objectionable pictures on exhibitors along with the ones that might be needed or desired for their theatres. It is contended that this, in effect, is an extension of block booking in an altered form. Further, that there is no restriction, whatsoever, upon the composition of picture blocks. A group of five pictures may be made up for one exhibitor and a group of different composition be made up for another exhibitor, thus giving rise to potential discriminations in the treatment of various exhibitors.[130]

These objections to the reforms of trade practices were constantly reiterated and stood as the main criticism to the decree in this respect. According to Williams, the independent exhibitors desired "a steady flow of product arising out of annual contracts, with a reasonable cancellation privilege." He therefore insisted that "the Department should not seek to impose upon the industry the new method of selling, particularly where it will not bring relief against the restraints and discrimination aimed at the present litigation." Williams's recommendations were not taken into account in the final drafting of the consent decree, which imposed the method of selling opposed by the small independent exhibitors.

The real crisis actually took place elsewhere. By 1940, the New Deal was adopting new economic policies, inclining toward Keynesianism, and quickly abandoning its antimonopoly stance. In addition, Thurman Arnold the trust-buster was at the center of many animosities, having disturbed so-called big interests, while the international crisis was rapidly changing into a war.[131] A confidential memorandum by James Rowe, a collaborator of the White House, dated August 15, 1940, to the President, discussed Arnold's difficult personality and his intention to file antitrust civil suits against the oil companies, notwithstanding their good relation with the National Defense Commission, the agency in charge of the industry and government collaboration for the war effort. It is a revealing document that discloses the inner workings of New Deal politics and thus the larger perspective in which the *Paramount* case should be seen.

> The problem is insoluble before election unless a formula can be worked out to satisfy both Arnold and the Commission. I do not think both can be satisfied. A few days ago Arnold wrote to the Commission practically accusing them of trying to kill the antitrust laws. . . .
>
> There are two possible temporary solutions, either of which may get us past election:
>
> (1) The President. Arnold has said almost openly that if these suits are stopped he will publicly bolt to Willkie. I think this threat should be taken seriously. Normally he has a very excitable temperament. Members of his staff say that today he is facing a nervous breakdown from overwork. Arnold would undoubtedly regret such a public statement the rest of his life but that would be of little help. Bob Jackson cannot be of help in this situation because, I am told, he has reached the limit of his patience with Arnold, and Arnold thinks he is being soft. Also, Arnold believes, for some reason, that Jackson has kept him from seeing you. His constant refrain to his friends is that he never sees the President.
>
> If you could talk to Arnold privately and tell him that the President also has a few problems and that he could ease your burden by not bringing this to a head now, it might work. He claims he has some political sense and will make no stir on other antitrust suits involving national defense until after the election. Arnold does feel he is not appreciated; he claims, quite rightly, that he is the only man who ever enforced the antitrust laws and the Administration does not appreciate him. You might even indicate to Arnold he could be useful campaigning in the West.[132]
>
> These moves may not satisfy Arnold. In such case I believe a record should be prepared showing the negotiations on this matter, which can be offered to the public if Arnold bolts, proving he was just too darn difficult.

In mid-August 1940, while the consent decree was under discussion, the administration slowly withdrew its support from Arnold's trust-busting program. The film trade press immediately acknowledged this change of policy, attributing it—as rumor had it—to election-year politics and the role that films could play "in carrying through the administration's defense plans." The film medium was needed to transform the isolationist attitude of the country into preparedness to war. Movies could also help the Democratic campaign, as the press suggested, reporting that:

> State Department officials are making no secret to newsreel companies of their displeasure at the amount of space being accorded Wendell Willkie, Republican presidential nominee in newsreels. It was said that an agreement might be reached whereby the film companies would turn out before the November election several pictures dealing with Roosevelt policies, movies which might be effective in turning public sentiment to the administration.[133]

By the end of October, Williams was no longer involved in the *Paramount* case. We have no documentation of a reason, other than his noncommittal response to a complaining independent exhibitor: "It so happens that I am engaged upon other matters now and no longer have any connection with the motion picture case." He had prepared the case with the objective of requesting the divorcement of exhibition from production-distribution in court; he had continued working even when it was decided instead to develop a consent decree; but when it had become apparent that the decree would not respect the exigencies of the party it was supposed to defend, that is, the independent exhibitors, he quit the scene.

The negotiations between the Justice Department and the film companies assumed the tones of a bargaining effort, when the film companies brought the other motion picture cases in which they were involved as defendants into the stipulation of the consent decree.[134] Not only had the companies negotiated a decree that was not unduly severe in terms of trade practices, but also they had removed the other legal obstacles from their path toward war expansion. Douglas Gomery suggests, in fact, that the war period was the most prosperous era ever for the theater-owning companies.[135]

The Consent Decree

On November 14 the court examined the consent decree. The government was represented by Hayes, who described the agreement, trying to demonstrate that it was an honest attempt by the division to correct the industry's problems. As soon as Hayes finished speaking, the many opponents to the decree took the stand, heavily criticizing the entire operation.

Columbia's counsel expressed doubts about the constitutionality of the decree, since the court, by supervising the decree, would become "a kind of N.R.A. over this industry." He argued that the decree did not address the aims and that the facts were insufficient.[136] Furthermore, he argued that the government's sanction to the new distribution system would allow the majors to "blackmail" Columbia, forcing it to adopt the system that it had previously rejected, and to sign the decree, in order to have access to first run theaters.

Myers of Allied attacked the decree on the ground that it legalized and perpetuated the defendants' monopolistic practices, presenting the formal complaints of the pressure groups, who, for years, had collaborated with Allied on the legislative front. One of the independents' representatives retorted:

> Since at least 98% of the independent exhibitor group have objected,
> then it seems to me that the Attorney General ought to recognize that the
> very public he represents does not want it, and it is something he should
> give very earnest consideration to before he stands before your Honor and
> favors this kind of a decree; one representing 7,800 theatres, another one
> 2,500 or 3,000 theatres, and others, stand here and earnestly plead against
> its adoption.[137]

Robert E. Sher, one of the government's attorneys, remarked that "after listening to the gentlemen who have appeared as friends of the Court, it is apparent that the Court has more friends than the decree has" and tried to defend the division's strategy. The judge had remarked that the decree displeased the very people it was supposed to benefit and had asked why the same group was "under the impression that they have not had a chance to present their views to the Department of Justice." Sher pointed out the number of meetings Arnold had held on these issues and recalled how Allied had at first expressed a favorable opinion on the trade practices reforms.[138] Myers responded that the elimination of "many safeguards" they had discussed caused Allied to change its stance.

On November 22, 1940, the government and the five majors signed a consent decree after filing a supplemental and amended complaint, "bringing up to date the charges of the original complaint and praying for substantially similar relief in more detailed terms." The majors were forbidden expansion in exhibition, and the Justice Department would not request "divorcement" for a trial period of three years. The eventual complaints came under the jurisdiction of a national system of arbitration. Block booking and blind selling were abolished for a one-year trial period, the 1941–42 season. Features could be licensed only after they were completed and trade shown, and in groups not to exceed five. The forcing of shorts and newsreels was forbidden. This distribution method was valid for a year because an escape clause would be invoked if the three minors did not sign the decree.

The decree was not severe with the majors. The Warner brothers, in fact, wrote to Arnold and to the President, to thank them for the conclusion of the case. Harry Warner wrote to Arnold thanking him on behalf of the industry "for the courtesy and consideration which you and your associates have shown to us" and praising the work of James V. Hayes, Robert E. Sher, and Robert Dwight.[139] Jack Warner was effusive in thanking the President, a few days later.

> A year ago last March my wife and I had the extreme pleasure of visiting with you at the White House. During our talk we discussed the trials and tribulations of the motion picture industry and I mentioned to you that if some amicable arrangement affecting the entire industry could be brought about it would do so much to create harmonious feeling throughout the motion picture business.
>
> On Friday last, Judge Goddard signed the Consent Decree in the antitrust proceedings against the motion picture industry, thus ending the litigation.
>
> I want to take this opportunity to express my thanks and appreciation for your good offices in having made possible the original study of the problems of the motion picture industry by Mr. Hopkins, the then Secretary of Commerce.
>
> It was the study and recommendations of the Commerce Department that furnished the basis and plan of settlement which is embodied in the Consent Decree.
>
> I believe that with the functioning of the arbitration machinery provided for under the Consent Decree, the motion picture industry will enter upon a new era of good relationship with the exhibitors and the public.
>
> Certainly, in so far as our company is concerned, it will be our constant endeavor to make the Decree an effective and living instrument of industry peace.[140]

The "Trial Period of Three Years"

The consent decree provided for a three-year test period, in which the industry's performance was going to be controlled, to help decide whether the trial had to be resumed. The industry paid little attention to this clause, almost as if the consent decree were to be the final conclusion of the *Paramount* case; but the government kept filing material and documenting the industry's behavior, to be ready for this eventuality. It could be speculated that the division believed that this occurrence was very probable, from the care it invested in documenting the industry's faults. Or, perhaps, it never really believed in the consent decree and was just waiting for a favorable situation to resume the suit. But, in the meantime, the independent exhibitors, members of Allied, had grown skeptical about the government's intentions and were not as cooperative as before. Robert Wright, who had taken Williams's position in charge of the case, tried to reassure Myers of the government's attitude and to convince him: "Our appraisal of the divorcement question at the end of the three-year period would have to depend upon the complaints data that was built in our file during that period."[141]

The decree unit was very dissatisfied with the behavior of the exhibitors and the majors, as Wright pointed out to Arnold before preparing a press release to denounce the situation in January 1941.[142]

Theater acquisition had always been a sensitive area of discussion. The majors kept ignoring the provisions of the decree and started the forbidden "program of expansion" because exhibition was particularly profitable in this period. One year after the signing of the consent decree, in November 1941, angered by the violations to the decree, the division decided to take action; it would:

> (1) Attempt to secure immediately as early a trial date as possible in the *Schine case*—probably January 15. . . .
> (2) Proceed to trial in December, if possible, against three independent producers, Columbia, United Artists and Universal, on the question of block booking and blind-selling. Under the decree, the provision against block booking and blind-selling operates for one year only. Hence, we are under a duty to test, under the terms of the decree, the legality of this method of sale.
> (3) File a petition under the New York decree enjoining further acquisitions by Paramount and Fox and objecting to certain acquisitions already made on the ground that they were not necessary to the normal expansion of competitive market but were in furtherance of achieving a monopoly position in the areas in which purchases occurred.[143]

This counterattack was soon met with the traditional delaying tactics. Columbia's attorney, Frolich, refused to restore the case in New York, arguing that, as agreed, "the case was not to be tried until the defendants had sufficient time to prepare for trial after the termination of the *Schine* case."[144]

In an official press release, which analyzed all the aspects of the decree operation, the division expressed its dissatisfaction with the majors' disattention to the decree, warning: "The decree has certainly already supplied some relief to a substantial number of exhibitors from certain unfair trade practices. It has not yet demonstrated that film licensing discriminations inherent in the ownership of theatres by distributors may be effectively remedied by measures short of divorcement."[145] According to the Antitrust Division, the most serious charges against the film industry were related to theater expansion. In January 1942, the division decided to petition to the court for the divestiture of the theaters acquired, in its view, in violation of the consent decree. But, as Williams anticipated, the unprecise wording of the decree (or the naive concessions in this area) restrained the division's ability to react. The court took an adverse position on this petition. It "found that this expansion was, in neither case, a part of a "general program" of expansion . . . and dismissed the proceeding as to both defendants." Judge Goddard demonstrated again his weak understanding of the division's position.

At the end of the first year of testing, the general dissatisfaction with the consent decree provoked an attempt to revise the terms of the stipulation. The occasion was the expiration of the "escape clause" on the method of selling, motivated by the decision of Columbia, Universal, and United Artists not to sign the consent decree. Exhibitors and distributors met in New York, in February 1942, to devise a common plan to present to the division to substitute for the consented one. Wright discussed this proposal with the majors' counsels, taking no hard stand on the issues related to the method of selling but warning them about the division's intention to resume the trial.[146] In the discussions about the "new method of selling," Wright defended trade showings and the blocks-of-five system, because it "had resulted in the production of better pictures." Given the government's position in instituting the *Paramount* case, as indicated in the Explanatory Statement, "better pictures" was indeed an important accomplishment. The division did not explain on what grounds it classified the movies produced after the decree as "better pictures." In the files there is a copy of a trade paper article arguing that the new method of selling had produced "an improvement of the film product.,"[147] The movies in those years, 1940–41, were *Citizen Kane, How Green Was My Valley, Sargeant York, Meet John Doe,* and others. Evidently, the division believed that structural changes were able to determine an improvement of film quality.

The New Trial (1945) and the Supreme Court Decision (1948)

At the expiration of the decree, in 1944, the industry and the division began negotiating a new consent decree. It was again a lengthy process, but this time the government insisted that the divorcement of film exhibition had to be inserted in the decree because of the unsatisfactory results of the reforms of trade practices in relation to competition. The film companies refused this proviso. The negotiations were therefore interrupted and the case was brought on for trial.

On October 8, 1945, the *Paramount* case returned to court, at the Southern District court of New York.

> For twenty days Robert L. Wright hurled some three hundred documents, secretly and feliciously collected, at the startled galaxy of defendants' counsels. Letters from exhibitors, carbons of contract forms, witnesses' transcriptions, and an FBI investigation of five hundred towns of fewer than 25,000 inhabitants were included in the plaintiff's prima facie case. Concentrating on "divorcement," the government did not press charges of monopoly, but left them open for a possible appeal to the Supreme Court.[148]

The impressive material presented by Wright at the trial was an adjourned edition of the division's preparation for trial, curated by Williams, in 1940. The government's strategy was to request both divestiture of exhibition for the producer-exhibitor defendants and injunctive relief against all the eight film companies "with respect to particular distribution practices which, in themselves, unreasonably restrain competition." The main difference from the 1938 petition was that the issue of monopoly in production was dropped. The discussion of the monopoly of exhibition stressed the interdependence of the trade practices with vertical integration: the division simplified the issues, focusing on the monopoly of exhibition in order to obtain divestiture.

Even then the court's decision was adverse. It in fact established that the defendants had "unreasonably restricted trade and commerce in the distribution and exhibition of motion pictures and attempted to monopolize such trade and commerce" but only enjoined them from certain distribution practices, while allowing them to retain theater control, "since ownership of only one-sixth the theatres was not judged a potent weapon of monopoly."[149] The court had accepted neither the argument that connected the trade practices to the ownership of theaters nor the emphasis on the role of the first-run theaters controlled by the majors. In addition, instead of trying to improve the system of arbitration of the consent decree, which had produced some positive results, the court cancelled it. The court changed the method of selling, unwelcomed by the small exhibitor, into an absurd system of competitive bidding for the pictures, limited to "competitive areas." It was indeed "a whole grab bag of odd concessions."[150]

A series of appeals and cross appeals reached the Supreme Court. In May 1948 the court issued the decision about the *Paramount* case together with that of the *Schine* and *Griffith* cases, giving an overall interpretation to the "motion picture cases," which reflected the comprehensive view of the Justice Department in building these cases.

Various briefs amici curiae, filed on this occasion, accompanied the petition, signed by Wright. The American Civil Liberties Union supported divestiture "to bring about a realistic recreation of diversity in filmfare and permanent protection to the rights of the general public under the First Amendment." (The brief was signed also by Wendell Berge, who had worked on the preparation for the case, at the Antitrust Division.) Morris Ernst, who argued that divestiture would benefit the public who "will find that competition for its favor is on the basis of merit of pictures rather than the power held by reason of ownership of theatres or horizontal accords," represented the Independent Motion Picture Producers (Hughes, Chaplin, Disney, Goldwyn, Wanger, McCarey, Hal Roach, Selznick, etc.). Abram Myers signed a brief for the independent exhibitors. Thurman Arnold and Paul Williams presented a brief against competitive bidding, on behalf of the American Theaters Association. Most of these attorneys had worked on the *Paramount* case for more than ten years and did not want to miss the final act. While the petition resumed the argument developed in the trial of 1945, focusing on the economic and legal aspects of monopoly, the briefs amici curiae reintroduced the issue of film quality, that the division tactically marginalized after the 1938 petition. The qualitative aspect acquired new importance in the presentation to the Supreme Court, given the transformations in film production and in the film market in the postwar period.[151]

In its important decision, the Supreme Court affirmed the illegality of certain trade practices, insisting that price-fixing combinations were illegal per se, and that it constituted an illegal use of film copyright to fix admission prices. It reiterated the criteria for reasonable clearance, shifting to the defendants the need to demonstrate this reasonableness. It declared illegal, and thus prohibited, block booking and eliminated competitive bidding.

As the district court had tried to break the pooling agreements in film exhibition, the Supreme Court, while upholding this decision, established that the court below had erred in failing to inquire how these joint interests had been acquired, that is, if they had been acquired illegally, or adopted within the conspiracy to restrain trade. In this instance they had to be separated; it thus directed the lower court to reconsider divestiture.

On the basis of its opinion on the *Griffith* case, the court stated "that specific intent" was not necessary to establish a "purpose or intent" to create a monopoly but that the requisite "purpose or intent" to create a monopoly is present if monopoly results as a *necessary consequence* of what was done. Williams's interpretation, which the majors' counsels belittled during the 1940 trial, closely resembles this jurisprudencial decision, which created an important precedent in antitrust legislation.

According to the Supreme Court, the film industry did indulge in unfair trade practices, demonstrating "a marked proclivity for unlawful conduct." The court suggested that market structure allowed the film companies to engage in illegal trade practices, from which they derived illegal profits. This observation related the undoubtful trade abuses to the structure of the industry, allowing it to call for divestiture. It had been, in fact, the underlying thesis of the Antitrust Division in its presentation of the case.

As in the *Griffith* and *Schine* cases, the defendants were required to divest themselves only of theaters that were acquired as a result of illegal restraint of trade. The decision thus did not ask for the divorcement of exhibition from production in toto, but only in the specific instances of a monopoly situation.

In the petition for the appeal, while insisting on its economic reasoning, the Antitrust division discussed also the sociocultural function of cinema.

In our view the relief requested here which the trial court rejected is required by antitrust precedents in purely commercial fields and was so argued here. Nevertheless, the expediting court's remedy has implications affecting constitutional freedom of expression which may scarcely be ignored here. . . . Only by assurance that the distribution field is equally open to all may the fullest diversity of film content be had. . . . Certainly such a past gives little hope that they will in the future encourage production of the wide variety of films needed to satisfy the wide variety of tastes possessed by the potential American film audience, rather than a standardized mass product adapted to profitable exhibition in a controlled market.[152]

Within its decision, the Supreme Court expressed its view on this important issue: "We have no doubt that the movie pictures, like newspapers and radio, are included in the press whose freedom is guaranteed by the First Amendment." It thus opened the way to the 1952 decision in this respect, which modified the system of film censorship.

The deep ties between the monopoly of discourse and the economic monopoly, between self-censorship and industrial self-regulation, re-emerged at this crucial moment, finding their final resolution together. In his reformist attempt, Arnold had tried to fragment the monopolistic power of Hollywood cinema by analyzing and dismantling its economic structure. This led to the Supreme Court decision, headed by William O. Douglas, whose doctrinary positions were similar to those of his old friend Arnold. The 1948 decision was a victory for the reformers, who had, from the very beginning, tried to control and correct Hollywood's discourse. They succeeded in this intent not by enforcing censorship but by recognizing film as "an important medium of expression and education," that was protected by the Constitution. The promotion of cinema to a more mature and autonomous stage of expression came contextually to the modification of its productive structures.

A fairly ironic destiny is this, which disrupts Hollywood cinema not through a maneuvre, attempted for years on other fronts and with other arguments by reformers and pressure groups, but through an intervention by a judicial and political establishment, which had grown out of a New Deal perception of the relationship between economy, society, and ideology.

Another ironic element is constituted by the size of the monopoly of exhibition: while the majors held an almost total control of production and distribution, they controlled a small (but crucial) section of exhibition; and yet this was the sin for which they were punished. Reasoning in terms of interest groups, it is evident, from the *Paramount* case documents, that independent producers were not vociferous, and nobody ever attacked the key element of the monopoly, distribution. The alliance between independent exhibitors and pressure groups made exhibition politically more vulnerable. This explains why the government tried to reach the desired ideological result of a more diversified film product, through a modification of the economic structure of the film industry.

The *Paramount* case is an examplary test of the mechanism of determination: if the Hollywood cinema was determined by its mode of production—the studio system—important reforms of its operational methods and structure could not but change its product—the films. This was a reasonable expectation for a New Dealer. The resolution of the *Paramount* case is one of the many legacies of the New Deal in postwar America. It proposes the New Deal in the role of the great reformer, continuer and innovator of reformist theory-practice, defender of a modern ideal of industrial democracy, in this instance, adapted to the blooming postwar economic reality.

Conclusion

By the end of 1941 the relationship of communications to politics, that is, of Hollywood to Washington, became a synergic effort, Hollywood plus Washington. Producers, directors, and actors wore their uniforms and fought the war—on the front, at home, in the studios.[1] They participated in the war effort, not only as individuals, but as members of an industry, offering entertainment and propaganda messages, for the troops and for the American audiences. Because their involvement and performance were so outstanding, the government never asked the film industry to sacrifice its production rhythm. Supported by this privileged condition and relieved of the torment of antitrust litigations, the industry took full advantage of the war's booming conditions, reaching an average of 90 million people a week and profits of $1,692 in 1946. In addition to its successful economic performance, Hollywood could boast its patriotic role, a balanced output of propaganda film and escapist fare, both necessary, for different reasons, during the war. President Roosevelt officially addressed the Academy Awards ceremony in February 1941 to congratulate the industry for its patriotism.

It would be impossible to explain this apparently sudden militarization of the screen if it were not for the 1930s political experience. People in Hollywood were probably more aware of the nazi-fascist threat than average Americans. In addition, in the 1930s Hollywood had realized its ideological function, its sociocultural role in a destabilized society. It helped to restore faith in the American value system and perfected its discourse, even in political terms, finding balances between contested areas and learning how to adapt its language to the self-censorship code. The cinema also elaborated a new national culture, by redefining Americanism and offering a communal cultural service through a system of national distribution. (Radio had acquired, in the 1930s, the same ability to function as both a nationalizing cultural medium and a national broadcasting, and advertising, network.) This dual national role of cinema in World War II is a key element in its efficient function.

197

CONCLUSION

Many Hollywood products of the war could be labeled as propaganda. But scholars, and the industry, in self-defense, have refuted this unpleasant label, describing the films instead as a naive but sincere effort to participate in the war spirit, a spontaneous manifestation of patriotism in the age of innocence; or accusing the government of having coerced the industry into making propaganda films. According to this interpretation, the government would have coerced the industry by promising to suspend antitrust challenges,[2] or by threatening to impose new forms of censorship and control, for example, through the Office of War Information (OWI), with its manual of suggested themes and its script-supervising office.[3] But these speculations do not explain the film production of 1941–45. Here again, we should make distinctions. To begin with, there is no social space or practice *outside* politics and ideology. Hollywood was making films for a country at war. Thus, the banal view that politics dominated the media in this case is unequivocally false. In the specifics, the OWI was a government office, but it was populated by Hollywoodians, and even headed, in its foreign version, by a screenwriter, Robert Sherwood.

Washington used Hollywood talent, and paid for Hollywood's services, to make instructional films and propaganda documentaries for the front and the home screens. This was a definite change in communication strategy, in that the administration gave up its own film production, the U.S. Film Office, when the war began. It could have continued making its own documentaries: it had the structures, the personnel, and even a successful practice. But it chose instead to trust its propaganda effort to the competence of the film industry, with its national distribution system.

The implications of these choices are not so linear though. The OWI did not like Frank Capra's films for Gen. George Marshall, the *Why We Fight* series: the army, signal corps, and OWI had very different ideas of cinema, and of what constituted good propaganda. Hollywood's war mobilization did not produce only official appraisals or celebratory pictures, and, in fact, the 1943 Truman hearings looked into undue profits Hollywood could have made through the "war effort."[4] From a stylistic point of view, the war experience seriously affected the filmmakers, as John Huston's films after *The Battle of San Pietro* or George Stevens's postwar cinema reveal. Hollywood worked for Washington and was influenced by its Washington experiences.

The struggle during World War II between Hollywood and the government for control of film production is written not only in the OWI files, or in the filmmakers' biographies, but also on the films. The early forties were the time of Hollywood canteens and GI Joes, of multiracial platoons fighting in the Pacific islands, but they saw, too, the beginning of film noir, the making of *Double Indemnity* and other James Cain and Raymond Chandler adaptations, unthinkable within the regular functioning of the Hays Code. Lost innocence is not the only issue here. There is a progression to a more adult and realistic representation of life in the mid-forties product, as if the legitimation gained by making patriotic films could allow Hollywood to broaden the scope of its themes and expressive discourses.

Continuing on the line of the Hollywood-plus-Washington collaboration, after the President's death, the Roosevelt heirs tried to develop a film project on FDR's life, to be called *The Roosevelt Story*,[5] but things were different in the postwar period, and nothing materialized.

Until 1946 the film industry continued to expand and make a profit. Then everything changed, all of a sudden. The sentence of the *Paramount* case, the beginning of the television age, new demographics and new leisure spending habits disrupted business.

During the cold war witch hunts the House Un-American Activities Committee investigated Hollywood for evidence of participation in leftist politics and New Dealist inclinations (and even for having produced war propaganda). The committee politically scrutinized Hollywood personalities in the bleakest scenario ever involving politics and communications in American history.

The Motion Picture Producer Distributor Association lost its central position in the system. The New York offices were abandoned for a Washington location, as the growing foreign market, and the increasing importance of American cinema as a source of propaganda in foreign lands during the cold war, made the foreign version of the trade organization, the Motion Picture Export Association, more visible.

Cinema slowly emerged from this crisis with different products, adapting to new sociocultural conditions. As foreboded in the *Paramount* case by creative Hollywoodians, and by pressure groups throughout the 1930s, structural changes offered more space to independent production.

It was 1960 when communications and politics, Hollywood and Washington, again developed close connections, a new interaction, under John F. Kennedy. But this is another story.

Notes

Introduction

1. On politics and cinema in thirties, see Ronald Brownstein, *The Power and the Glitter: The Hollywood-Washington Connection* (New York: Vintage Books, 1992); John Hartley, *The Politics of Pictures: The Creation of the Public in the Age of Popular Media* (London and New York: Routledge, 1992); and Brian Neve, *Film and Politics in America: A Social Tradition* (London and New York: Routledge, 1992). For analysis of the relationships among politics, culture, and cinema that is less period specific but far more stimulating, see Miriam Hansen, *Babel and Babylon: Spectatorship in American Silent Film* (Cambridge, Mass.: Harvard University Press, 1991), and William Uricchio and Roberta Pearson, *Reframing Culture: The Case of Vitagraph Quality Films* (Princeton, N.J.: Princeton University Press, 1993). For a good basic study of the relationship between society and cinema, see Robert Sklar, *Movie-Made America* (New York: Vintage Books, 1994).

Hansen discusses the role of cinema as a new public sphere, arguing for "the significance of the cinema for social groups whose experience was repressed, fragmented, or alienated in systematic ways—the recently urbanized working class, new immigrants, and . . . women. These groups had either no access to existing institutions of public life or, in the case of women, only in a highly regulated and dependent form. . . . At less expense than the mainstream commercial entertainments, the cinema offered an horizon that made it possible to negotiate the historical experience of displacement in a new social form" (*Babel and Babylon*, 91–92). Hartley, discussing the public domain of the 1990s, the interaction of television and politics, notes: "The cultural sphere is . . . political, and so are pictures. They are the place where collective social action, individual identity and symbolic imagination meet—the nexus between culture and politics" *Politics of Pictures*, 1–3).

2. For general references within the traditional historiography of the New Deal, see William E. Leuchtenburg, *Franklin D. Roosevelt and the New Deal, 1932–1940* (New York: Harper, 1963); Arthur M. Schlesinger, *The Age of Roosevelt*, 3 vols. (Boston: Houghton Mifflin, 1957–60); and Frank Friedel, *Franklin D. Roosevelt*, 4 vols. (Boston:

201

Little Brown, 1952–73). For a general view of historical research in America, see Michael Kammen, *The Past Before Us: Contemporary Historical Writing in the United States* (Ithaca, N.Y.: Cornell University Press, 1980).

3. For recent historiography on the Hays Code, see Lea Jacobs, *The Wages of Sin: Censorship and the Fallen Woman Film, 1928–1942* (Madison: University of Wisconsin Press, 1991); Giuliana Muscio, ed., *Prima dei Codici* (Milan: Fabbri, 1991); and Richard Maltby, *Reforming the Movies: Hollywood, the Hays Office, and the Campaign for Censorship, 1908–1938* (New York: Oxford University Press, forthcoming).

4. In this respect, we should reread the French "new" historian Fernand Braudel: believe history can be conceived only at *n* dimensions. This generosity is indispensable: it does not reject to inferior levels, that is, outside the explicative space, the cultural point of view or dialectic materialism or any other type of analysis; it poses at the basis a concrete, multidimensional history" (*Scritti sulla storia* [Milan: Mondadori, 1973], 181–82; my translation).

5. Raymond Williams, *Marxism and Literature* (Oxford: Oxford University Press, 1977), 112. We should take into account also the aspect of commercialization that "represents a fundamental shift in the nature of the hegemony, which now operates not through the traditional authority and personalities of local elites, nor through the power of capitalist employers, middle-class reformers, and state intervention, but rather through the impersonal, even apparently 'natural' structures of corporate industries and mass markets. . . . Hegemony is the child of the marriage of corporate profits and consumer 'fun'; social control and class expression are merged in the same practices" (Richard Butsch, ed., *For Fun and Profit: The Transformation of Leisure into Consumption* [Philadelphia: Temple University Press, 1990], 19).

6. On the relationship between the New Deal and Hollywood cinema, see Nick Roddick, *A New Deal in Entertainment: Warner Brothers in the 1930s* (London: BFI, 1983); Andrew Bergman, *We're in the Money: Depression America and Its Films* (New York: Colophon, 1971); and Richard Steele, *Propaganda in an Open Society: The Roosevelt Administration and the Media, 1933–1941* (Westport, Conn.: Greenwood Press, 1985). These authors, however, reduce the relationship implied in the pairing of the New Deal and cinema by asserting a reflective determinism of the sociopolitical context over the films.

7. Lary May "Making the American Way: Modern Theatres, Audiences, and the Film Industry, 1929–1945," *Prospects* 12 (1987): 90.

8. On national, centralizing, business tendencies, see Alfred D. Chandler, *Strategy and Structure: Chapters in the History of Industrial Enterprise* (Cambridge Mass.: MIT Press, 1969). "The shift in hegemony and leisure practices accompanied the development of corporate capitalism after 1880. . . . Bureaucratic control of work displaced the personal style of direct supervision characteristic of the family firm. National mass markets superseded local markets. . . . The federal government became involved not simply in controlling working-class leisure, as local reformers had done, but in stimulating its commercialization. Copyrights laws of the late nineteenth century enhanced the commercial value of music, plays, and fiction. The government, rejecting a recommendation that it retain control of broadcasting, aided the creation of a radio patent pool and of RCA as a joint venture of General Electric, AT&T, and Westinghouse, thereby commercializing radio and future television broadcasting. Such

government intervention contributed to the twentieth-century move from locally backed entertainment to recorded or amplified performances offered by national corporations through capital-intensive technology. . . . Leisure industries of the mid- to late nineteenth century had catered to class-specific markets; local entrepeneurs successfully profited from fulfilling working-class demands for class-expressive recreation. But like the rest of the economy, leisure industries gradually came under the control of national corporations that created cross-class 'mass' markets" (Butsch, *For Fun and Profit*, 14–15).

9. On Hollywood classical cinema, see Douglas Gomery, *The Hollywood Studio System, 1930–1949* (New York: St. Martin's Press, 1986); David Bordwell, Janet Staiger, and Kristin Thompson, *The Classical Hollywood Cinema: Film Style and Mode of Production to 1960* (New York: Columbia University Press, 1985); and Tino Balio, ed., *Grand Design: Hollywood as a Modern Business Enterprise, 1930–1939* (New York: Scribner's, 1993).

10. Hansen (*Babel and Babylon*) and Uricchio and Pearson (*Reframing Culture*) discuss this process of negotiation. Hansen interprets the film-viewing experience as "a contested field of multiple positions and conflicting interests, defined (though not necessarily confined) in terms of the viewer's class and race, gender and sexual orientation" (7).

11. See Brian Taves, "The B Film: Hollywood's Other Half," in Balio, *Grand Design*, 313–50.

12. For revisionist works, see Barton Bernstein, "The New Deal: The Conservative Achievements of Liberal Reform," in Bernstein, ed., *Towards a New Past* (New York: Pantheon, 1968); Gabriel Kolko, *Main Currents in Modern American History* (New York: Pantheon, 1975); Warren Susman, *Culture as History: The Transformation of American Society in the Twentieth Century* (New York: Pantheon, 1984); Richard Pells, *Radical Visions and American Dreams* (New York: Harper and Row, 1977); and, the more radical, Gary Gerstle and Steve Fraser, eds., *The Rise and Fall of the New Deal, 1930–1980* (Princeton, N.J.: Princeton University Press, 1989), and Lizabeth Cohen, *Making a New Deal: Industrial Workers in Chicago, 1919–1939* (Cambridge: Cambridge University Press, 1990).

13. Susman, *Culture as History*, xx.

14. In the *Paramount* case, the film industry, that is, the five majors and the three small studios, were accused of holding a monopolistic control over the film market. The documents of the case are preserved at the Antitrust Division of the Justice Department in Washington, D.C. (AD). For this study, I examined several boxes of uncatalogued and unpublished materials of the period 1936–42.

15. On Thurman Arnold, see Gene Gressley, *Voltaire and the Cowboy* (Boulder: University of Colorado Press, 1971), and Edward Kearny, *Thurman W. Arnold, Social Critic: The Satyrical Challenge to Orthodoxy* (Albuquerque: University of New Mexico Press, 1970). See also Richard Hofstader, *The Age of Reform* (New York: Random House, 1959), and Pells, *Radical Visions*. The most important works by Arnold are *The Symbols of Government* (New Haven, Conn.: Yale University Press, 1935) and *The Folklore of Capitalism* (New Haven, Conn.: Yale University Press, 1937), which, at the time, was a best-seller.

16. Thomas Ferguson, "Industrial Conflict and the Coming of the New Deal: The

Triumph of Multinational Liberalism in America," in Gerstle and Fraser, *Rise and Fall of the New Deal,* 5.

17. See Marc W. Kruman, "Quotas for Blacks: The PWA and the Black Construction Worker," *Labor History* 16, 1 (1975):37–51, and W. H. Droze, "TVA and the Ordinary Farmer," *Agricultural History* 53, 1 (1979): 1988–202.

18. On this series of ideological tensions as expressions of political differences between various social pressure groups, see Ellis W. Hawley, *The New Deal and the Problem of Monopoly* (Princeton, N.J.: Princeton University Press, 1966). Bernstein's argument, however, that the New Deal was at the service of interest groups ("New Deal," 270) has encouraged the interpretation of the New Deal as "an attempt by big business to institutionalize the corporate state" (Ferguson, "Industrial Conflict," 5) and suggested the theory of "political capitalism" elaborated by Kolko in *Main Currents.*

19. In this sense, the New Deal did have a conservative function. One of the most penetrating analyses, from this point of view, is that elaborated by Bernstein: "The liberal reforms of the New Deal did not transform the American system; they conserved and protected American corporate capitalism, occasionally by absorbing parts of threatening programs. There was no significant redistribution of power in American society, only limited recognition of other organized groups, seldom of unorganized peoples. Neither the bolder programs advanced by the New Dealers nor the final legislation greatly extended the beneficence of government beyond the middle classes or drew upon the wealth of the few for the need of the many. Designed to maintain the American system, liberal activity was directed toward essentially conservative goals. . . . Never questioning private enterprise, it operated within safe channels. . . . The New Deal failed to solve the problem of depression, it failed to raise the impoverished, it failed to redistribute income, it failed to extend equality and generally countenanced racial discrimination and segregation" ("The New Deal," 264).

20. Ferguson, "Industrial Conflict," 6–7. In his essay, Ferguson argues that before World War I, the major labor-intensive industries, which opposed high tariffs and were enemies of labor, constituted the core of the Republican party, together with the banks that financed them. After the war, a wave of racial, ethnic, and labor conflicts developed. International banks, interested in the reconstruction of Europe, joined the less labor-intensive industries, which wanted lower tariffs, in order to expand consumption worldwide. The U.S. economy abruptly and definitively changed from debtor to creditor. The multinational bloc that emerged then was made up of modern and growing corporations with the most sophisticated management, an efficient relation with public opinion, and a less antagonistic attitude toward labor. Future New Dealers worked for their consulting firms. These economic forces dominated the foundations that influenced public opinion. They were able to "influence public opinion generally outside of both parties" (9) through "a newspaper stratification process that brought the free trade organ of international finance, the *New York Times,* to the top; by the growth of capital-intensive network radio in the dominant Eastern, internationally oriented environment; and by the rise of major news magazines."

The boom of the 1920s exacerbated tensions and enhanced the position of the oil companies and capital-intensive firms. Non-Morgan investment banks and Chase National Bank, out of J. P. Morgan's control and in Rockefeller's hands by 1932, moved toward the Democratic party. Rockefeller, already in FDR's orbit, moved away from banking and became more involved in oil. These banks supported the separation of investment and commercial banking. In 1935, "as the industries fought, labor stirred." FDR looked for new allies. And, at "the darkest point of the New Deal, . . . Roosevelt and part of the business community began to discover the logic of a [stable] winning political coalition. The first successful capital-intensive-led political coalition in history began dramatically to come together." This coalition accepted the Wagner Act, while FDR refused more inflation and stronger federal control on banking. "The powerful appeal of the unorthodox combination of free trade, the Wagner Act, and social welfare was evident in the 1936 election. A massive bloc of protectionist and labor-intensive industry formed to fight the New Deal" (21). But when Alf Landon moved toward protectionism, the multinationalists moved toward FDR, who started revising the treaties with France and Great Britain (25).

21. Alan Brinkley, "The New Deal and the Idea of the State," in Gerstle and Fraser, *Rise and Fall of the New Deal*, 99.

22. Michael A. Bernstein, "Why the Great Depression Was Great: Toward a New Understanding of the Interwar Economic Crisis in the United States," in Gerstle and Fraser, *Rise and Fall of the New Deal*, 46.

23. Steve Fraser, "The 'Labor Question,'" in Gerstle and Fraser, *Rise and Fall of the New Deal*, 60.

24. Ibid, 67. Fraser also notes: "The relationship between the 'second New Deal' and the 'new unionism' was organic. Above all, the 'welfare state' was expressively designed by its chief architects to encourage and stimulate mass consumptions: state intervention in the labor market, along with the state's credit policy, urban renewal, and so on, were tactical devices for achieving that larger strategic purpose" (ibid., 60).

25. See ibid., 24, for an acute analysis of the political line of the Democratic party since the 1930s. Ferguson even argues: "Cultivated by the press, nourished by increasingly affluent business groups, and fiercely protected by two generations of (often handsomely rewarded) scholars, this view of the Democrats and the New Deal left ordinary Americans. . . . to puzzle out why the party did so little to help unionize the South, protect the victims of McCarthysm, [and] promote civil rights for blacks, women, or Hispanics. . . . To such people, it always remained a mystery why the Democrats so often betrayed the ideals of the New Deal. Little they realize that, in fact, the party was only living up to them."

26. Ibid., 17–18.

27. Alan Brinkley, "The New Deal and the Idea of the State," in Gerstle and Fraser, *Rise and Fall of the New Deal*, 94. "They would rather be . . . ever vigilant referees, always ready to step into the market . . . to defend the interests of consumers, who were replacing producers as the ultimate focus of liberal concern" (ibid.).

28. Arnold, *Folklore*, 389.

29. Brinkley, "New Deal," 112.

30. On populism, see Richard Hofstader, *The American Political Tradition* (New York: Vintage Books, 1974); Lawrence Goodwyn, *Democratic Promise: The Populist Moment in America* (New York: Oxford University Press, 1976); and Jeffrey Richards, "The Ideology of Populism," in *Visions of Yesterday* (London: Routledge, Kegan Paul, 1973).

31. Hawley describes how language was used to enhance this reconciliation of

contradictions. "'Competition' became 'economic cannibalism' and 'rugged individualists' became 'industrial pirates.' . . . The time-honored practice of reducing prices to gain a larger share of the market became 'cut-throat and monopolistic price slashing,' and those engaged in this dastardly activity became 'chiselers.' Conversely, monopolistic collusion, price agreements, proration, and cartelization became 'cooperative' or 'associational' activities" (*New Deal*, 54).

32. See Sara Evans and Harry Boyte, *Free Spaces: The Sources of Democratic Change in America* (New York, Harper and Row, 1986); Craig Calhoun, "The Radicalism of Tradition," *American Journal of Sociology* 88, no. 5 (March 1983): 886–914; and Harry Boyte and Frank Reissman, eds., *The New Populism* (Philadelphia: Temple University Press, 1986).

33. William E. Leuchtenburg "The Great Depression," in C. Vann Woodward, ed., *A Comparative Approach to American History*, Voice of America lecture series (Washington, D.C., n.d.), 325–40.

34. On the relationship between nationalism and populism, see George Mosse, *The Nationalization of the Masses* (New York: Harvard Fertig, 1974).

35. See James Hay, "LUCE/Cinema/Shadows," in *Popular Film Culture in Fascist Italy* (Bloomington: Indiana University Press, 1987).

36. Clayton Koppes and Gregory Black, *Hollywood Goes to War* (New York: The Free Press, 1987); Richard W. Steele, "Preparing the Public for War: Efforts to Establish a National Propaganda Agency, 1940–41," *American Historical Review* 75 (October 1970).

37. See William Stott, *Documentary Expression and Thirties America* (New York: Oxford University Press, 1973), and Francis V. O'Connor, *Art for the Millions: Essays from the 1930s by Artists and Administrators of the WPA Federal Art Project* (Boston: New York Graphic Society, 1973).

38. Alfred Kazin, *On Native Grounds* (New York: Anchor, 1956).

39. *The Grapes of Wrath* by John Steinbeck (1939), originated as a project for a book of photographs; the film *The River* (1938), by Pare Lorentz was based on administrative reports.

40. Roosevelt had a favorite conceptualization of "the people": "Frances Perkins noted that he thought of those listening to his Fireside Chats 'individually.' He thought of them in family groups. He thought of them sitting around on a suburban porch after supper on a summer evening. . . . He never thought of them as 'the masses.'" (Stott, *Documentary Expression*, 100). On Roosevelt and public opinion, see Richard W. Steele, "The Pulse of the People: Franklin D. Roosevelt and the Gauging of American Public Opinion," *Journal of Contemporary History* 9, no. 4 (1974): 195–216.

41. Raymond Moley, in his autobiographic account of the New Deal, explains that, to Roosevelt, "a good cause does not justify any trip: a good trip justifies any cause. Campaigning for him was unadulterated joy, . . . it was crowds of friends from the half dozen who, seated on a baggage truck, waved to the cheery face at the speeding window to perspiring thousands at a race track or fairground; it was hands extended in welcome, voices warm with greeting, faces reflecting his smile along the interminable wayside. . . . Travel is to make friends and influence people" (*After Seven Years* [New York: Harper and Brothers, 1939], 52). This traveling also helped construct the image of Roosevelt as a dynamic president, despite his wheelchair.

42. Stott, *Documentary Expression,* 77. On Roosevelt's attitude toward the media, see Steven E. Schoenherr, "Selling the New Deal: Stephen T. Early's Role as Press Secretary to Franklin D. Roosevelt," Ph.D. diss., University of Delaware, 1976, and Steele, *Propaganda in an Open Society* Both confirm Roosevelt's distrust of the press.

43. Susman, *Culture as History,* 159; my italics.

44. Lindsay's definition has been reproposed by Susman, in ibid., xvii.

45. For a fundamental work on the history of radio, see Eric Barnouw, *A History of Broadcasting in the U.S.,* 3 vols. (New York: Oxford University Press, 1966–70). On the relationship of radio to cinema, see Michele Hilmes, *Hollywood and Broadcasting: From Radio to Cable* (Chicago: University of Illinois Press, 1990), and Rick B. Jewell, "Hollywood and Radio: Competition and Partnership in the 1930's," *Historical Journal of Film Radio and Television,* 4, no. 2 (1984).

46. Lary May, *Screening Out the Past: The Birth of Mass Culture and the Motion Picture Industry* (Chicago: University of Chicago Press, 1980), 238.

47. See Lawrence W. Levine, "American Cuture and the Great Depression," *Yale Review,* 74, no. 2 (1985): 196–223, Sklar, *Movie-Made America,* 204; Susman, *Culture as History,* 155.

48. Robert Ray, *A Certain Tendency of Hollywood Cinema, 1930–1980* (Princeton, N.J.: Princeton University Press, 1985); Charles Maland, *American Visions: The Films of Chaplin, Ford, Capra, and Welles, 1936–41* (New York: Arno, 1977).

49. Materials in the Roosevelt Library, Hyde Park, N.Y., document these connections. See also Robert E. Sherwood, *Roosevelt and Hopkins: An Intimate History* (New York: Harper, 1950).

50. The term "film exploitation" was used in the 1930s and 1940s to describe the advertisement of a specific film usually by a local exhibitor.

51. See Giuliana Muscio, "The Commerce of Classicism," *QRFV* 15, no. 3 (1994): 57–69. Gomery defines monopoly through a theoretical economic model, but Bordwell, Staiger, and Thompson's *Classical Hollywood Cinema* is not free of this limitation.

52. On legal realism and the interdisciplinary approach to legal studies, see Karl N. Llewellyn, *Jurisprudence: Realism in Theory and Practice* (Chicago: University of Chicago Press, 1962). On this period, see Brinkley, "The Idea of the State," in Gerstle and Fraser, *Rise and Fall of the New Deal,* 90.

CHAPTER 1

1. Thurman W. Arnold, *The Symbols of Government* (New Haven, Conn.: Yale University Press, 1935), xiii. See also Arnold, *The Folklore of Capitalism* (New Haven, Conn.: Yale University Press, 1937), and Arnold, *Bottlenecks of Business* (New York: Reynal Hitchcock, 1940).

2. "By the symbols of government we mean both the ceremonies and the theories of social institutions. Ordinarily, these ceremonies and theories are collected and studied, not as symbols, but as the fundamental principles of separate sciences of law, economics, political theory, ethics, and theology" (Arnold, *Symbols of Government,* xiv).

3. Arnold, *Folklore of Capitalism,* 2.

4. "It is considered quite a sophisticated observation in these curious times to say that both political parties are exactly alike. Few, however, understand that the reason

for this is that where the center of attention is abstractions rather than practical objectives all parties are bound to be alike" (ibid., 31).

5. In 1928 the "inventor" of the public relations industry, Edward Bernays, noted also that politics were falling behind mass consumption: "Politics was the first big business in America. Therefore there is a good deal of irony in the fact that business has learned everything that politics has had to teach, but that politics had failed to learn very much from business methods of mass distribution of ideas and products" (Robert B. Westbrook, " Politics as Consumption: Managing the Modern American Election," in Richard Wightman and T. J. Jackson Lears, eds., *The Culture of Consumption: Critical Essays in American History, 1880–1980* [New York: Pantheon, 1983], 145).

6. Arnold, *Folklore of Capitalism*, 343–45.

7. See Westbrook, "Politics as Consumption."

8. Ronald Brownstein, *The Power and the Glitter: The Hollywood-Washington Connection* (New York: Vintage Books, 1992), 74. See also Daniel Czitrom, *Media and the American Mind: From Morse to McLuhan* (Chapel Hill: University of North Carolina Press, 1982).

9. Peter Collier, *The Roosevelts: An American Saga* (New York: Simon & Schuster, 1994), 134–35. "The increasingly powerful medium of advertising used [Theodore Roosevelt's] image, without permission, to sell everything from baby powder to cigars. . . . And there was, of course, his complicity in the birth of the Teddy Bear" (ibid.). The communicative ability was "in the family," then, both in Oyster Bay and in the Hyde Park Roosevelts.

10. Cf. Becky H. Winfield, "Roosevelt and the Press," Ph.D. diss., University of Washington, 1978, and Steven E. Schoenherr, "Selling the New Deal: Stephen T. Early's Role as Press Secretary to Franklin D. Roosevelt," Ph.D. diss., University of Delaware, 1976.

11. On the American newsreels, see Raymond Fielding, *The American Newsreel 1911–1967* (Norman: University of Oklahoma Press, 1972).

12. E. W. Chester, *Radio, Television and American Politics* (New York: Sheed and Ward, 1969), 3. See also David H. Culbert, *News for Everyman: Foreign Affairs in Thirties America* (Westport, Conn.: Greenwood Press, 1976), and Robert S. Fine, "Roosevelt's Radio Chatting: Its Development and Impact During the Great Depression," Ph.D. diss., New York University, 1977, 2.

13. As Westbrook argues: "Nineteenth-century partisan culture fostered an active, rich symbolic experience of community, ethno-religious, and class solidarity, while for the modern American voter electoral politics has, by virtue of its transformation into an exercise in mass marketing, come to share with other spheres of experience the peculiar features of the culture of consumption: passivity, atomization, and spectatorship" ("Politics as Consumption," 151).

14. Schoenherr, "Selling the New Deal," 22.

15. Fine, "Roosevelt's Radio Chatting," 61. "I tried the definite experiment this year," Roosevelt explained to Walter Lippman, of "writing and delivering my speech wholly for the benefit of the radio audience and press rather than for any forensic effect" (cited in Frank Freidel, *Franklin D. Roosevelt: The Apprenticeship* [Boston: Little, Brown, 1952], 243).

16. Fine, "Roosevelt's Radio Chatting," 64.

17. William M. Moore, "F. D. Roosevelt's Image," Ph.D. diss., University of Wisconsin, 1946, 168–70. Lawrence Levine has polemically emphasized: "We have spoken and written as if the political culture of the 1930s represented all of American culture: as if Franklin Roosevelt and his advisers spoke for the vast majority of Americans" (*The Unpredictable Past: Explorations in American Cultural History* [New York: Oxford University Press, 1993], 208).

18. Arnold, *Folklore*, 392.

19. Richard Hofstader, *The American Political Tradition, and the Men Who Made It* (New York: Vintage Books, 1974), 437.

20. Fine, "Roosevelt's Radio Chatting," 187.

21. Ibid., 334–35. An interesting catalogue, rich in photographic documentation, was published on the occasion of an exhibition held at the Smithsonian Institution, Washington, D.C., January 1982: Arthur P. Molella and Elsa M. Bruton, *FDR: The Intimate Presidency, Franklin Delano Roosevelt, Communication and the Mass Media in the 1930's.* See also Greenstein, ed., *Leadership in the Modern Presidency* (Cambridge, Mass.: Harvard University Press, 1988).

22. Fine, "Roosevelt's Radio Chatting," 129–31.

23. FDR was in constant contact with his "reporters," his mobile "eyes and ears" (William Stott, *Documentary Expression and Thirties America* [New York: Oxford University Press, 1973], 94).

24. Gary Gerstle, *Working-Class Americanism: The Politics of Labor in a Textile City, 1914–1960* (Cambridge: Cambridge University Press, 1989), 8; see also p. 2.

25. On popular entertainment in different historical periods, see Richard Butsch, ed., *For Fun and Profit: The Transformation of Leisure into Consumption* (Philadelphia: Temple University Press; 1990); Roy Rosenzweig, *Eight Hours for What We Will: Workers and Leisure in an Industrial City, 1870–1920* (Cambridge and New York: Cambridge University Press, 1983); Lizabeth Cohen, *Making a New Deal: Industrial Workers in Chicago, 1919–1939* (Cambridge: Cambridge University Press, 1990); *Immigrant Women in the Land of Dollars: Life and Culture on the Lower East Side, 1890–1925* (New York: Monthly Review Press, 1985); Herbert Gutman, *Work, Culture and Society in Industrializing America* (New York: Vintage Books, 1977); Kathy Peiss, *Cheap Amusements: Working Women and Leisure in Turn-of-the-Century New York* (Philadelphia: Temple University Press, 1986).

26. Lizabeth Cohen, "The Class Experience of Mass Consumption: Workers as Consumers in Interwar America," in Richard Wightman Fox and T. J. Jackson Lears, eds., *The Power of Culture: Critical Essays in American History* (Chicago: University of Chicago Press, 1993), 138.

27. Gerstle, *Working-Class Americanism,* 7, 8, 15.

28. Daniel Boorstin, "Selling the President to the People," *Commentary* 20 (November 1955), 421; H. F. Gosnell, *Champion Campaigner: Franklin D. Roosevelt* (New York: Macmillan, 1952), 223; Moore, "F. D. Roosevelt's Image," 188; Graham J. White, *FDR and the Press* (Chicago: University of Chicago Press, 1979), 12; Winfield, "Roosevelt and the Press," 224; Schoenherr, "Selling the New Deal," 124.

29. Schoenherr, "Selling the New Deal," 145.

30. Moore, "F. D. Roosevelt's Image," 446.

31. Molella and Bruton, *FDR,* 45.

32. Fine, "Roosevelt's Radio Chatting," iv.

33. Moore, "F. D. Roosevelt's Image," 182; White, *FDR and the Press,* 21.

34. Of Roosevelt, Hofstader wrote, "No personality has ever expressed the American popular temper so articulately or with such exclusiveness," emphasizing that FDR was "a public instrument of the most delicate receptivity" (*American Political Tradition,* 410, 413).

35. Michael Kammen, *Mystic Chords of Memory: The Transformation of Tradition in American Culture* (New York: Vintage Books, 1991) 450. I found many examples of this use of history by the New Dealers in the volume published in Philadelphia on the occasion of the 1936 Democratic Convention, beginning with the choice of Philadelphia (a city of great historical-symbolical importance for its role in the formation of the nation as the site of the convention. The first page, for example, has a photograph of the Liberty Bell and, underneath the title, a motto by Thomas Jefferson. A quotation from Roosevelt—"Democracy is not a static thing"—is backed at the highest symbolic level by the reference to Jefferson's authority. The historical memory of the Democratic party is constituted as a "usable past," according to a definition by Van Wick Brooks.

36. Fine, "Roosevelt's Radio Chatting," 230.

37. Hofstader, *Americal Political Tradition,* 413; P. K. Conkin, *FDR and the Origins of the Welfare State* (New York: T. Y. Crowell, 1967), 2.

38. Hofstader, *American Political Tradition,* 411–13.

39. "Roosevelt's press conferences, his leadership of the legislative activity of the hundred days, his travels, and his broadcasting, all seem to support an image of the singular national leader who, capable of overcoming polio and near-assassination, might lead the whole country out of its paralysis" (Fine, "Roosevelt's Radio Chatting," 196).

40. Maurizio Vaudagna, *L'estetica della politica* (Rome: Laterza, 1989), 94.

41. Raymond Moley, *The First New Deal* (New York: Harcourt, Brace, 1966), 98.

42. Fine, "Roosevelt's Radio Chatting," 296.

43. According to Fine, 74 percent of Roosevelts supporters were "lower income" (ibid., 314).

44. On the uneasiness of the middle class in the thirties, see Lawrence W. Levine, "Hollywood's Washington: Film Images of National Politics During the Great Depression," *Prospects* 10 (1985): 169–95.

45. Thomas Ferguson, "Industrial Conflict and the Coming of the New Deal: The Triumph of Multinational Liberalism in America," in Gary Gerstle and Steve Fraser, eds., *The Rise and Fall of the New Deal, 1930–1980* (Princeton, N.J.: Princeton University Press, 1989), 19.

46. Schoenherr, "Selling the New Deal," 1.

47. Ibid., 2.

48. "With only a phone call he could plant favorable and unfavorable stories in the press and radio. He could arrange appointments for his friends with the President. He could, and did, ask J. Edgar Hoover to investigate a political enemy and private business firms. He could obtain favorable decisions for friends from regulatory agencies such as the [Federal Communications Commission] and the Civil Aeronautics Board. His daily visitors list was a roll call of America's financial, communications, and political elite" (ibid., 2).

49. This group was so defined because of the cuff links Roosevelt gave to each one of them after the 1920 electoral campaign, with "FDR" engraved on one side and the recipient's initials on the other. Even when they were no longer working for FDR, the members of the gang got together once a year, on Roosevelt's birthday, to reaffirm their loyalty (Schoenherr, "Selling the New Deal," 35).

50. In the chaotic first day at the White House, Early discovered that in the presidential residence there was no equipment for radio transmission, though an announcement had already been made that the President would give a radio message that same night. Working feverishly with Harry Butcher of CBS, Early succeeded in adapting the presidential studio for the broadcasting. Early had met Butcher when he was an editor at Paramount News. In 1928, in fact, Adolph Zukor, president of Paramount, had acquired 40 percent control of CBS, for which the two companies, for a brief period, worked in close contact. In particular, Paramount's sound newsreels often used CBS technicians. According to legend, it was Butcher who invented the expression "fireside chat." ibid., 110, 56, 84; Moore, "F. D. Roosevelt's Image," 287–90, 312; Winfield, "Roosevelt and the Press," 163–65.

51. Winfield, "Roosevelt and the Press," 1; Moore, "F. D. Roosevelt's Image," 282.

52. White, *FDR and the Press,* 1.

53. Moore, "F. D. Roosevelt's Image," 190, 342.

54. Winfield, "Roosevelt and the Press," 1.

55. Cited by William E. Leuchtenburg, "Franklin D. Roosevelt," in *Greenstein, Leadership in the Modern Presidency,* 18.

56. Moore, "F. D. Roosevelt's Image," 211, 265–66; Schoenherr, "Selling the New Deal," 38.

57. Winfield discusses this type of evolution in journalism in many sections of her text; see, for example, "Roosevelt and the Press," 2 and 291.

58. Early worked through a friend of Hearst's mistress, the popular film star Marion Davies, to persuade Hearst to "soften the language used in his papers" (Schoenherr, "Selling the New Deal," 59).

59. White (*FDR and the Press*) analyzes the question of the hostility that FDR imputed to the press in three chapters of his book, one of which is entitled, "The Famous Eight-Five Percent."

60. Winfield, "Roosevelt and the Press," 92.

61. Stott, *Documentary Expression,* 79. It is interesting to reread what Thurman Arnold wrote on the subject: "The elections of 1936 brought out the fact that a very large number of people, roughly representing the more illiterate and inarticulate masses of people, had lost their faith in the more prominent and respected economic preachers and writers of the time, who for the most part were aligned against the New Deal. They repudiated the advice of the newspapers which they bought and read because they were more immediately affected by the economic pressures of the time which were depriving them of security" (*Folklore of Capitalism,* 81).

62. Winfield, "Roosevelt and the Press," 201, 209. Fine, "Roosevelt's Radio Chatting," v. Roosevelt also loved the radio simply because he could stay comfortably seated while he spoke.

63. Fine, "Roosevelt's Radio Chatting," 148.

64. Schoenherr, "Selling the New Deal," 68.

65. Fine, "Roosevelt's Radio Chatting," 236.

66. Schoenherr, "Selling the New Deal," 130–31.

67. Fine, "Roosevelt's Radio Chatting," 139.

68. Schoenherr, "Selling the New Deal," 108; Winfield, "Roosevelt and the Press," 211. In the 1930s, the fireside chats were proposed as unsurpassed models of transmission of an ideological content, which the large corporations tried to appropriate in order to correct the negative image that the Depression and the New Deal had projected on them (see William L. Bird, "The Drama of Enterprise: DuPont's Cavalcade of America and the 'New Vocabulary' of Business Leadership, 1935–1940," paper presented at the annual conference of the Society of Cinema Studies, Washington, D.C., May 1990).

69. Thurman Arnold also participated in the preparation of FDR's speeches, as he tells in his autobiography: "It was planned that the President would read over the radio a special message on the problem. Cohen and I wrote drafts over and over again until we got one that was simple and comprehensible and short. I was with the President when he delivered it. Just before going on the air, he took the last draft and changed it in a way that gave it his own personal touch. He was a genius at this sort of thing" (*Fair Fights and Foul* [New York: Harcourt, 1965], 137). On the preparation of FDR's speeches, see the detailed and affectionate testimony of Robert E. Sherwood in *Roosevelt and Hopkins: An Intimate History* (New York: Harper, 1950), 121–28.

70. Fine, "Roosevelt's Radio Chatting," 125–26. Raymond Moley describes the preparation of these speeches: "Roosevelt had a sense of the general subject matter appropriate or necessary to the occasion, the timing suitable to the presentation of this or that project, and the public state of mind or emotion at the planned time of delivery. . . . He could work and think with some people. With others he was annoyed, impatient, bored. . . . After many drafts and a great deal of consultation with Roosevelt, the speech evolved. It became part of his personality; it matched his moods and met his feeling for words and style" (ibid., 124).

71. Schoenherr, "Selling the New Deal," 179. The decision to limit the speeches to twenty-five minutes was determined, according to Early, by the fact that the average American's radio attention span was not more than half an hour. Early's shrewdness went so far as to provide extra time for applause for a speech given in public.

72. He pronounced about 110 words a minute. Roosevelt divided the speeches into five-minute segments, cutting paragraphs into brief phrases of five or six words. Roosevelt attributed so much importance to his radio performances that after the transmission he would spend thirty to forty minutes discussing his presentation (Winfield, "Roosevelt and the Press," 204).

73. Schoenherr, "Selling the New Deal," 123–24.

74. Sociologist Robert Merton uses the phrase "episodic plebiscite" to describe how public support was designed to help Roosevelt govern in the interval between elections" (ibid., 131).

75. Ibid., 168.

76. Ibid., 188.

77. For a discussion of Lazarsfeld's study, see Stott, *Documentary Expression*, 81.

78. In 1936 "FDR won only 42 percent of the upper-income share of the two-party vote, but 80 percent of union members and 84 percent of relief recipients" (Leuchtenburg, "Franklin D. Roosevelt," 21).

79. This is the Middletown studied by Robert S. Lynd and Helen Merrell Lynd in their *Middletown: A Study in American Culture* (New York: Harcourt, Brace and World, 1929). Mandrake Falls is the mythical "little town" that appears in Capra's films.

80. Fine, "Roosevelt's Radio Chatting," 206.

81. For a full discussion of the fireside chat on the dustbowl, see ibid., 247–60.

82. Ibid., 70.

83. Ibid., 216–17.

84. Schoenherr, "Selling the New Deal," 107.

85. Samuel Rosenman, *Working with Roosevelt* (New York: Harper and Brothers, 1952), 6–10.

86. Dorothy Thompson, in *Look*, April 22, 1941, 16–17; quoted in Moore, "F. D. Roosevelt's Image," 158. "Roosevelt on the stump still stirs me as he stirred me that day when he appeared before the Chicago convention. Then I first knew the characteristic toss of the head. Then I first knew that confidential look with upraised eyebrow he gives his audience when he has delivered a thrust, succeeded by the slow grin as the audience catches it, and tosses it around in laughter. Then I first knew the mockery which he touched off by popping his mouth open suddenly in the shape of an O. Then I first knew the emphatic rage as he lambasts his enemies" (Thomas Stokes, quoted in Moore "F. D. Roosevelt's Image," 187; see also 155–58).

87. James Agee's definition is reported in Alfred Kazin, *On Native Grounds* (New York: Anchor, 1956), 152. On American photography in this period, see Carl Fleischauer and Beverly Brannan, *Documenting America, 1935–1943* (Berkeley: University of California Press, 1988); this contains also an interesting essay by Lawrence Levine.

88. The regular corps of White House photographers once blocked a cameraman from getting a picture of Roosevelt being carried. A Republican newspaper had assigned the photographer to get the picture (Schoenherr, "Selling the New Deal," 148).

89. Moore, "F. D. Roosevelt's Image," 642; Winfield, "Roosevelt and the Press," 102, 219.

90. Moore, "F. D. Roosevelt's Image," 646.

91. The particular care Early dedicated to the presentation of FDR's image also had a direct political motivation. Because the National Democratic Committee was not generous with the appropriation of promotional funds, the press secretary was forced to exploit the official photographic portrait to the maximum (Schoenherr, "Selling the New Deal," 181–82).

92. An interesting exception was the permission to use photographs of the President to promote photojournalism itself within the trade press—a further confirmation that politics and communication legitimated and publicized one another in the 1930s (Moore, "F. D. Roosevelt's Image," 447).

93. For example, an intimate photograph entitled, "Have a Smoke Son!"—showing Roosevelt and his son seated in the rear seat of an automobile with the father helping the son light up—won third place in the 1936 first annual news picture exhibition. Pictures like this required "not only happy chance, but also an alert, friendly photographer who has been permitted considerable freedom to select his position and poses" (ibid., 449).

94. Schoenherr, "Selling the New Deal," 38; Moore, "F. D. Roosevelt's Image," 443.

95. Moore, "F. D. Roosevelt's Image," 425, 430.

96. Winfield, "Roosevelt and the Press," 213.

97. The divorces of Roosevelt's sons and some of their entrepreneurial activities provoked the criticism of the more conservative press, but they were never transformed into scandals damaging to the image of the presidential family.

98. FDR's opening speech at the fair was transmitted on closed-circuit television, his appearance at the 1940 Democratic National Convention was televised (Molella and Bruton, *FDR*, 58).

CHAPTER 2

1. The information in this chapter derives mostly from an analysis of documents preserved at the Roosevelt Library in Hyde Park, N.Y. (FDRL), integrated with information from Ronald Brownstein's *The Power and the Glitter: The Hollywood-Washington Connection* (New York: Vintage Books, 1992).

2. Warner Bros. Theatres to Marguerite Le Hand, March 23, 1933, OF 73, FDRL. The logistics of the screenings is discussed in an exchange of letters between Nancy Cook of the Democratic State Committee, Steven Early, and Donald Dailey of Kodak (March 21, March 22, May 6, 1933, OF 73, FDRL).

3. In the first draft of the article, Eleanor Roosevelt also says: "The movies really came to their present state of perfection while my husband was ill, so it was not until we went in 1929 to Albany to the Governor's mansion that we gave any thought to this as a method of relaxation . . . [for times when] the Governor was tired and his mind needed a change. In addition, in those terrible evenings when an execution was pending, life could be made a little more bearable by a movie, which could at least keep my husband's mind off the thought of the minutes slowly ticking away the hours of a man's life" (draft of article, 1938, Eleanor Roosevelt 3035, FDRL).

4. It is interesting to note that the First Lady uses the language of a "normal" spectator. For example, she calls *The Life of Emile Zola* "a film I shall never forget."

5. For a discussion of the system of self-censorship, see Chapter 4. The Hays Code was adopted two days before FDR's entry into the White House (Will H. Hays, *The Memoirs of Will H. Hays* [Garden City, N.Y.: Doubleday, 1955], 447).

6. In the period in which Eleanor Roosevelt wrote this article, Will Hays was "at home" in the White House and the First Lady's son-in-law, John Boettiger, had recently stopped working for the Hays Office (see below, under "The Roosevelts in Hollywood").

In the article, Eleanor Roosevelt discusses the possible use of cinema in the classroom, devoting most of her attention to the impact of this medium on the young: "There is great opportunity also to teach our children English and voice culture through the movies, for they can have the best teachers in the country teaching diction, recitation and expression through the medium of the talking film. This can be done in the smaller rural schools as well as in the bigger schools of the cities, for, once the school is equipped with the proper apparatus, the cost is small. . . . Finally we come to the possibility of using the motion picture as a character-building instrument."

7. King Vidor to Early, October 24, 1934, OF 73, FDRL. In addition to this letter, there are numerous records of suggestions for film showings. For example, Early re-

minds the First Lady that when George Putnam of Paramount was her guest at a luncheon she had discussed with him her "desire for better radio and motion picture entertainment for children" and he had told her that "Paramount is just releasing a picture which, because of [her] interest, he thinks she should see. The picture is called *This Day and Age,*" (memorandum, Early to Mrs. [Eleanor] Roosevelt and to Miss [Marguerite] Le Hand, August 16, 1933, OF 73, FDRL).

8. Steven E. Schoenherr, "Selling the New Deal: Stephen T. Early's Role as Press Secretary to Franklin D. Roosevelt," Ph.D. diss., University of Delaware, 1976, 121.

9. "By the late 1930s, the number of reporters covering Hollywood was exceeded only by the number covering New York and Washington (Brownstein, *The Power and the Glitter,* 75).

10. An additional association between the Roosevelts and Hollywood was the marriage of the President's son Elliott to the actress Faye Emerson.

11. Undated press clippings, Jack Warner file, Warner Collection, University of Southern California Library, Los Angeles (USCL).

12. *Motion Picture Herald,* March 11, 1933.

13. The relationship between Hollywood radicals and the New Dealers is a common focus of studies of the politics of the film community in the 1930s and therefore will not be taken up here. See Larry Ceplair and Steven Englund, *Inquisition in Hollywood: Politics in the Film Community, 1930–1960* (New York: Anchor Press, 1980); Nancy Lynn Schwartz, *The Hollywood Writers' Wars* (New York: Knopf, 1982); William Alexander, *Film on the Left: American Documentary Film from 1931 to 1942* (Princeton, N.J.: Princeton University Press, 1981); and Brian Neve, *Film and Politics in America: A Social Tradition* (London and New York: Routledge, 1992). See also my book on Hollywood politics from the 1930s to blacklisting, *La Lista nera a Hollywood* (Milan: Feltrinelli, 1979).

14. Neve, *Film and Politics,* 8.

15. Mayer believed that the studios had a responsibility to use the screen to teach respect for the values of "family, patriotism, clean living, [and] small-town solidarity" (Brownstein, *The Power and the Glitter,* 26–27). See also Bosley Crowther, *Hollywood Rajah: The Life and Times of Louis B. Mayer* (New York: Dell, 1960), and Neal Gabler, *An Empire of Their Own: How the Jews Invented Hollywood* (New York: Doubleday, Anchor Books, 1988), 80–119.

16. Gabler, *Empire of Their Own,* 114–16. Brownstein, *The Power and the Glitter,* 32.

17. Brownstein, *The Power and the Glitter,* 31. The interplay of radio, press, and movies is particularly significant in this instance.

18. Leo Rosten, *Hollywood: The Movie Colony.* (New York: Harcourt, Brace, 1941), 134–39. See also Greg Mitchell, "How Hollywood Fixed an Election," *American Film,* November 1988. "They built an industry without rules and regulations. They were brought into politics by legal problems, rules and regulations and so forth. It was a necessity, a business necessity" (Brownstein, *The Power and the Glitter,* 43). The friendship between Mayer and Hearst was finally severed because of political and film matters. Cosmopolitan Pictures went to Warner Bros., but soon Hearst went to New York, and Mayer remained in Hollywood, where he became the highest-paid executive in America.

19. Richard Maltby, *Harmless Entertainment* (Metuchen: Scarecrow, 1983), 150.

20. See Ceplair and Englund, *Inquisition in Hollywood.*

21. On Helen Douglas, see Ingrid Winther Scobie, *Center Stage: Helen Gahagan Douglas: A Life* (New York: Oxford University Press, 1992), and the comments on her work, in Scobie, "The Life of a Star: Helen Gahagan Douglas," in Sara Alpern et al., eds., *The Challenge of Feminist Biography* (Urbana: University of Illinois Press, 1992), 177–94. See also Brownstein, *The Power and the Glitter,* 48–103.

22. For a discussion of the impact of the Popular Front, see Brownstein, *The Power and the Glitter.* "On matters of ideology, the Popular Front eventually created enormous problems for the Hollywood liberals. But on matters of political tactics, it was an unsurpassed tutor. Its leaders understood intuitively that in a modern media society, celebrities were most useful as beacons to illuminate a political agenda for the public, not as prizes to dangle privately before politicians" (20).

23. Ibid., 62.

24. Scobie, "Life of a Star," 178.

25. Brownstein, *The Power and the Glitter,* 57–59.

26. Ibid., 74–75.

27. Ibid., 79.

28. Rosten, *Hollywood,* 160.

29. Like most politicians, Raymond Moley notes, Roosevelt was intensely superstitious and insisted on wearing the same hat throughout the campaign (Moley, *After Seven Years* [New York: Harper and Brothers, 1939], 54).

30. Memorandum by Early, February 19, 1941, OF 73, FDRL.

31. These names are listed in the typed program and filed with materials on the relationship between Jack Warner and Roosevelt, in the Warner Collection, USCL.

32. Brownstein, *The Power and the Glitter,* 81.

33. She gained a reputation as a leading liberal and was reelected to the House in 1946 and 1948 by increasing majorities. She lost the race in 1950 to the Republican congressman Richard M. Nixon "in a celebrated red-smear campaign" (Scobie, *"Life of a Star,"* 178).

34. Brownstein, *The Power and the Glitter,* 94.

35. Examining Orson Welles's participation in Hollywood film and political activities, Neve underlines how he had become "nationally known through radio, and his earnings of $3,000 a week from that source enabled him to decline an offer from David Selznick" (*Film and Politics in America,* 14). Welles moved to Hollywood at the end of the thirties, created a masterpiece out of a quasi-biography of Randolph Hearst—the media tycoon we have so often encountered in these chronicles, who had a failed political career, notwithstanding the support of Louis B. Mayer. (Mayer, still loyal to his old pal and afraid of a possible backlash on the industry created by *Citizen Kane,* offered the president of RKO, George Schaefer, $850,000 to withdraw the film). Like many other Hollywoodians who seem to have been on more progressive positions in politics than the rest of the country in the 1930s, Welles supported Henry Wallace. In phases of red-baiting Welles was accused of communist affiliations, but he never belonged to the Communist party.

36. Brownstein, *The Power and the Glitter,* 99.

37. Ibid., 100.

38. Ibid., 101–2.

39. Schoenherr, "Selling the New Deal," 218.

40. Ibid., 75. If it were not FDR, one might wonder if this refusal had anything to do with the institution of the *Paramount* case.

41. Special Collections, USCL, holds a folder of documents and press clippings on James Roosevelt, from which the information for this part is derived.

42. See Chapter 3, n. 52.

43. Unidentified press clippings, dated June 1941, and September 17, 1940, James Roosevelt File, USCL.

44. "Taking Part" (editorial), *Motion Picture Herald*, December 24, 1938. The inclusion of James as one of the defendants in the *Paramount* case was discussed in a memorandum by Williams to Thurman Arnold, February 8, 1939, Correspondence Files of the *Paramount* case, 1938–42, Antitrust Division, Justice Department, Washington, D.C. (AD).

45. Richard Steele, *Propaganda in an Open Society: The Roosevelt Administration and the Media* (Westport, Conn.: Greenwood Press, 1985), 158.

46. "Dispute Rights to Pastor Hall," *Motion Picture Herald*, July 27, 1940.

47. On FDR's foreign policy, see William E. Leuchtenburg, *Franklin D. Roosevelt and the New Deal, 1932–1940* (New York: Harper, 1963), 226–30.

48. Press clippings, Affari politici, 1931–45, USA, Envelope 38, Ministry of Foreign Affairs, Rome. For more on Mussolini's son, Vittorio, see p. 52.

49. Hays was asked to make the offer to Boettiger by Louis Howe, the President's secretary. See Richard Neuberger, "Young Man with Two Horns," *Saturday Evening Post*, July 8, 1939. Peter Collier, in *The Roosevelts: An American Saga* (New York: Simon & Schuster, 1994), gives another account: "He allowed Joseph Kennedy, one of the opportunists nibbling at the edges of the Roosevelt family, to use his Hollywood connections to help him get a job with Will Hays, the film industry's czar and censor" (364).

50. Hays to Boettiger, January 26, 1935, Will Hays Folder 1935–37, Boettiger, FDRL. This correspondence is preserved in Boettiger's file at FDRL.

51. Boettiger to Ken Clark, May 23, 1939, Clark Folder, 1936–39, Boettiger, FDRL. He wrote in fact an article entitled "Block Booking—A Ridiculous Bill" in the *Seattle Post-Intelligencer*, August 12, 1939. The reference to this article derives from a sample of "monitoring of the press" by the MPPDA, dated August 21, 1939 (MPPDA Folder, Boettiger, FDRL).

52. Hays to Boettiger, April 17, 1940, Hays Folder, 1938–46, Boettiger, FDRL. Hays had good contacts in the whole range of communications, including radio.

53. Collier, *The Roosevelts*, 373.

54. Hays to Boettiger, January 12, 1937, Hays Folder, 1935–37, Boettiger, FDRL.

55. Hearst put Elliott in charge of his radio operations in 1935; by 1937 Elliott had assembled four radio stations for Hearst in Texas and one in Oklahoma (Collier, *The Roosevelts*, 375–76).

56. Boettiger to Clark, May 13, 1937, Clark Folder, 1936–39, Boettiger, FDRL.

57. Neuberger, "Young Man with Two Horns."

58. Raymond Moley, *The Hays Office* (New York: Bobbs-Merrill, 1945), 48. Moley,

in the description of this department of the MPPDA, went to great lengths in supporting the representation of the Protective Department according to Hays's view: "Since this brief description immediately raises in the reader's mind the picture of lobbying, with all its sinister connotations, it may be well here and now to state plainly the policy pursued by Hays on this subject. It goes without saying that in selecting Hays, the people in the industry were aware of his political acumen. But if they expected him to follow the conventional pattern of the lobbyist, they grossly underestimated their man. A real maestro in politics, like Hays, disdains the crude and dishonorable practices of the trade. Hays knew so much about politics that he was capable of directing the public relations of the industry into channels which needed no apology and risked no evil consequences" (ibid.).

59. The boxes coded OF 73, at FDRL, that is, the section concerning cinema, include numerous examples of letters addressed to the White House from these groups. They are contained mainly in the first box, for 1933, when the censorship question was still a hot issue, or appear later, on the occasion of the block booking hearings.

60. Moley, *The Hays Office*, 49.

61. Moley, *After Seven Years*, 53.

62. Dale to Early, October 1936, OF 73, FDRL. During the hearings for the Pettingill Bill, Pettijohn said: "In the Smith-Hoover campaign we kept a record of the new reels, the film, and there was not more than 6 feet difference between the amount given to each one" (House Committee on Interstate and Foreign Commerce, Subcommittee, *Motion-Picture Films: Hearing Before a Subcommittee of the Committee on Interstate and Foreign Commerce*, 74th Cong., 2d sess., March 1936, 458).

63. The agencies of George Gallup, Elmo Roper, and Archibald Crossley conducted the first surveys in 1935; Hadley Cantril formed the Office of Public Opinion Research in 1940. On this subject see Steele, *Propaganda*, 63–64.

64. Pettijohn to Boettiger, September 24, 1937, Pettijohn Folder, Boettiger, FDRL.

65. Billi, "V. Mussolini nel giudizio di un compagno di viaggio," *Il Progresso Italo-Americano*, September 26, 1937; Italicus, "Vittorio Mussolini a Hollywood," *L'Italia*, October 4, 1937, Affari politici, 1931–35, USA, Envelope 38, Ministry of Foreign Affairs, Rome.

66. Pettijohn to Mussolini, November 19, 1935, Minculpop, Foreign Press Office, file 476, Pettijohn, Ministry of Foreign Affairs, Rome.

67. Report by the Ambassador Suvich in Washington, October 15, 1937, Affari politici, 1931–45, USA, Envelope 38, Ministry of Foreign Affairs, Rome. In a recent television interview, however, Vittorio Mussolini stated that actually FDR gave him a message for his father, with whom the American President had been, until then, on good terms.

68. That is, the Senate hearings on anti-Nazist propaganda in Hollywood cinema discussed in Chapter 4.

69. Clark to Boettiger, dated "Wednesday evening" in reply to a letter from Boettiger, February 16, 1942, Clark Folder, 1940–45, Boettiger, FDRL.

70. Pettijohn to Boettiger, February 3, 1942, Pettijohn Folder, Boettiger, FDRL. In 1944, Pettijohn was anyway sponsoring a campaign against juvenile delinquency with Roosevelt's endorsement, to be directed by J. Edgar Hoover, with the cooperation of Bob Hope, Bing Crosby, and Clark Gable (Pettijohn to Early, July 6, 1944, OF

73, FDRL). He maintained his position between the film industry and the administration, at least from the point of view of public relations, even if he had lost the power granted him by his previous role.

71. Clark to Boettiger, November 18, 1941, Clark Folder, 1940–45, Boettiger, FDRL.

72. Clark was present at the Neely Bill hearings of May 1940, representing the MPPDA office, responsible for the monitoring of the press (House Committee on Interstate and Foreign Commerce, *Motion-Picture Films (Compulsory Block Booking and Blind Selling): Hearing Before the Committee on Interstate and Foreign Commerce on S.280,* 76th Cong., 3d sess., pt. 1, May 1940, 508, 523).

73. Robert Denton of Paramount Newsreel—the firm Early had worked for—even dared to give advice on Eleanor Roosevelt's makeup, but Early's pencil notes on the letter show a negative reaction (Denton to Early, December 7, 1933, OF 73, FDRL).

74. Hays, *Memoirs,* 496.

75. Hays to Boettiger, January 12, 1937, Hays Folder, 1935–37, Boettiger, FDRL. Hays was accompanied, on this occasion, by his wife.

76. Hays, *Memoirs,* 492.

77. For example, he wired Senator Arthur Vanderberg, to encourage him to support "the President's project of reorganization of the machinery of the federal government": "The accomplishment of the President's purpose on Governmental reorganization will have results far beyond the increase of administrative efficiency and consequent economy. I earnestly urge you to help take this out of politics and use this opportunity to help get it done. The knowledge of the need for reorganization has been a personal worry to me ever since I was in the Government until office associates have suggested I might better worry about my own troubles. What I am concerned with is getting something done" (telegram, Hays to Vanderberg, January 18, 1937, attached to a letter addressed to Boettiger dated February 3, 1937, Hays Folder, 1935–37, Boettiger, FDRL).

78. After describing the various services rendered to the cinema by several U.S. Presidents, Hays mentions "the influence of American pictures abroad" during the Roosevelt administration (*Memoirs,* 510).

79. Hays to Boettiger, January 12, 1937, Hays Folder, 1935–37, Boettiger, FDRL.

80. Hays, *Memoirs,* 516–19.

81. FDR to Hays, February 7, 1941, Hays Folder, 1938–46, Boettiger, FDRL. The term "Czar" indicates the degree of control Hays exercised on the film industry.

82. Gerard to FDR, May 13, 1944, OF 73, FDRL.

83. J. F. Carter, *The New Dealers* (New York: Simon & Schuster, 1934), 255.

84. Edward R. Ellis, *A Nation in Torment* (New York: Capricorn Books, 1971), 498.

85. Carter, *The New Dealers,* 255.

86. MPTOA Folder, FDRL; House Committee on Interstate and Foreign Commerce, *Motion-Picture Films (Compulsory Block Booking and Blind Selling): Hearings Before the Committee on Interstate and Foreign Commerce on S. 280.* 76th Cong., 3d sess., pt. 2, May–June 1940, 717.

87. Parker Corning, June 14, 1933, OF 73, FDRL. The letter also said, "Cinema and radio are much more powerful than the press."

88. Hays to FDR, November 21, 1940, PPF 1945, FDRL.

89. Carter, *The New Dealers,* 257.

90. Moley proposed, "the rejection of the traditional Wilson-Brandeis philosophy that if America could once more become a nation of small proprietors, of corner grocers and smithies under spreading chestnut trees, we should have solved the problems of American life. . . . We believed that any attempt to atomize big business must destroy America's greatest contribution to a higher standard of living for the body of its citizenry—the development of mass production" (*After Seven Years,* 24).

"Ray Moley had been charged with the dreadful duties of liaison officer between the New Deal and business, and particularly since his attack on the undistributed profits tax, he had been much courted by big businessmen" (Joseph Alsop and Robert Kintner, *Men Around the President* [New York: Doubleday Doran, 1939], 104).

91. Moley, *Hays Office.*

92. Alsop and Kintner, *Men Around the President,* 103–6.

93. The high level of control on cinema exercised by the government during World War II is discussed in Clayton R. Koppes and Gregory D. Black, "What to Show the World: The Office of War Information and Hollywood," *Journal of American History* 64 (June 1977): 87–105.

94. Film producer with Pathé and FBO, later taken over by RCA, a component of RKO; Kennedy oversaw also the financial reorganization of Paramount (Rosten, *Hollywood,* 253). He was a "film historian" in that he was the organizer of a series of lectures at Harvard University on the film industry. These lectures, published as *The Story of the Films* (Chicago: A. W. Shaw, 1927), are one of the earliest texts on the economic-institutional history of the industry. Also, they served as a key moment in the legitimization process that the industry underwent in the twenties and thirties. This process eased the transition of the industry into a more advanced mode of organization—not exactly financial capitalism but a less craftsman-like manner, less so-called "family business. To achieve this legitimization, it was necessary to draw the attention of the financial world, of which Kennedy was an advanced leader.

95. Hays, *Memoirs,* 552.

96. Transcripts of the *Paramount* case trial, June 3–7, 1940, 198, A.D.

97. Allan M. Winkler, *The Politics of Propaganda: The Office of War Information, 1942–1945* (New Haven, Conn.: Yale University Press, 1978), 25.

98. Richard D. MacCann, *The People's Films: A Political History of U.S. Government Motion Pictures* (New York: Hasting House, 1973), 166–67.

99. Nick Roddick, *A New Deal in Entertainment: Warner Brothers in the 1930s* (London: BFI, 1983).

100. Ellis, *A Nation in Torment,* 141.

101. Jack Warner, *My First Hundred Years in Hollywood* (New York: Random House, 1964).

102. Ibid., 216, 220, 221, 223, 224, 239. "Roosevelt seemed to sense how keenly the moguls craved the social validation of a White House dinner or an autographed photo of the president on their desk—proof that they stood in the company of powerful and serious men, even if they were not allowed into Los Angeles's country clubs. These social benefactions didn't cost Roosevelt much, but they resonated with enormous force in Hollywood's insecure corridors. In exchange for the admiration of

NOTES

men whose cultural influence exceeded even their own understanding, Roosevelt dispensed his favor with regal grace" (Brownstein, 77).

103. Harry Warner wrote to FDR: "As you may know, the revenue derived from the distribution of motion pictures in the United States is not sufficient to return the cost of production. We depend upon a world market to support our production costs. . . . Our situation is further complicated by the fact that we have large loans from British banks, which were principally secured by our film receipts in England. With the closing of theatres in England, I am apprehensive that the British loans may be called. The loss of British and French income will weaken the financial condition of our company, and it is therefore extremely unlikely that we will be able to borrow money in this country to pay off the British loans. . . . A new and almost fatal element is present in the motion picture industry. I am referring to the Federal litigation which has been opened up on all fronts against our industry, and the multitude of private suits which have been brought against us, based upon the Federal litigation. The preparation for and the defense of these suits constitute a drain upon the financial resources of our company and, more importantly, diverts the time, attention and energy of the principal executives and managerial personnel of the company. If our company, as well as the other companies in the industry, are to work their way out of the difficulties imposed upon us by the European war, we must be freed from the overwhelming burden and non-productive effort and expense which this multitude of litigation entails" (Harry Warner to FDR, September 5, 1939, PPF 1050 Warner, FDRL).

104. The letter quoted represents a key element in the mechanism that started the reconsideration of the *Paramount* case by the White House; an analogous correspondence, signed by the Warners, appears in Chapter 3.

105. His works include *Idiot's Delight, Abe Lincoln in Illinois, Rebecca, The Best Years of Our Lives,* and *Man on a Tightrope.*

106. Sherwood deals with this activity in *Roosevelt and Hopkins: An Intimate History* (New York: Harper, 1950), 819–31.

107. Schoenherr, "Selling the New Deal," 202; Winkler, *Politics of Propaganda,* 28.

108. Winkler, *Politics of Propaganda,* 27.

109. Sherwood, *Roosevelt and Hopkins,* 819.

110. Graham J. White, *FDR and the Press* (Chicago: University of Chicago Press, 1979), 12.

111. Roffman and Purdy, *The Hollywood Social Problem: Madness, Despair, and Politics from the Depression to the Fifties* (Bloomington: Indiana University Press, 1981), 91.

112. It is interesting to remember that Howard Koch and Abraham Polonsky had been writing for Welles, on radio, before moving to Hollywood to become screenwriters (and unfriendly objects of attention by HUAC). Koch is among the writers of *Casablanca,* a celebrated piece of popularized foreign policy, produced, not by chance, by Warner Bros.)

On the role of film stars and radio, in politics, Brownstein writes: "Radio and the stars functioned synergistically. A star could reach many more people by radio than through personal appearances, and the use of a star could enlarge the audience for a political broadcast. The widespread use of radio dramatically enhanced the political value of celebrity, just as television did later" (*The Power and the Glitter*, 79–80). Frank Sinatra's radio performances in support of FDR in 1944 are a perfect example.

113. Eleanor Roosevelt, "Why We Roosevelts Are Movie Fans," 84.

CHAPTER 3

1. Italian sociologists Giorgio Galli and Franco Rositi, in *Cultura di massa e comportamento collettivo* (Bologna: Mulino, 1967), attempt to explain why the people of Germany and the United States, a few months apart, reacted to the economic crisis and to analogous socioeconomic problems by electing as their leaders Hitler on one hand, and FDR on the other. They regard as insufficient both the explanations that cite either differences in political structures (the American bi-party system and the relatively recent German multiparty system) or the "innate" cultural tendencies (American democraticism and individualism, and the "German spirit" and totalitarism). Attributing to cinema the role of "the principle vehicle of mass communication" in the thirties, they analyze the films seen and made in the two countries between 1929 and 1932, trying to go beyond Siegfried Kracauer's interpretation of an innate authoritarianism of German culture and beyond the general view of Hollywood cinema as purely escapist entertainment. For them, "through mass culture the average man was the point of arrival of a flux of images, views, models, stimuli which has no precedent in the history of humanity" (14). This broadening of the consumption of culture had a political impact, in that it gave the people models of behavior, patterns into which to fit their experiences, a vision of the world, an education on life and society and their rules, outside of, and at times in opposition to, elitist culture. The authors pay particular attention to the tension between the spheres of the private life of affections and leisure—a sphere greatly affected by the development of mass consumption in those years—and the public world. They conclude that German culture expressed a high degree of rigidity, of formalism and repression, in the former sphere. German cinema often treated "individual affectivity" with pessimism (frequent tragic endings) or indulged in optimistic stories, where there was no place for any moral conflict but only for a very simplistic and imaginary representation of life. American cinema, however, was more optimistic. It reached the ritual "happy ending" only after the resolution of some (usually moral) conflict, that is, of some confrontation between reality and desire. It embodied a kind of morality that did not entirely repress erotic drives but satisfied them at a subliminal level, functioning, in their analysis, as an antidote, to the Depression and to the latent authoritarian tendencies of American culture in the 1930s.

2. Margaret Thorp, *America at the Movies* (New Haven: Yale University Press, 1939).

3. Andrew Bergman, *We're in the Money: Depression America and Its Films* (New York: Colophon, 1971), xii; and R. E. Brauer, "When the Lights Went Out: Hollywood, the Depression, and the Thirties," *Journal of Popular Film and Television* 8, no. 4 (Winter 1981): 18–29.

4. As one infers from the Block Booking Hearings (see Chapter 4, n. 78).

5. Lary May, "Making the American Way: Modern Theatres, Audiences, and the Film Industry, 1929–1945," *Prospects* 12 (1987): 107. In this essay, May discusses the difficulty of analyzing 1930s film attendance statistics and emphasizes the particular

identification of a middle-class audience: "Pollsters repeatedly found, for example, that over 63 percent of the public expressed fear of unemployment and wishes for more security in their lives, and over 65 percent felt that businessmen and elites had too much power, and that the inequalities of wealth were wrong. Yet by no means had the people lost faith in values derived from an older progressive tradition. When asked what class they were coming from, over 88 percent felt they were among the middle class" (104).

6. "Mass media—magazines, movies, radio, television—were designed to appeal to large cross-class audiences. . . . Pessimists focus on the rise of centralized, commercial production, use the term 'mass culture,' and call the consequent corroded form of society 'mass society.' Populists tend to prefer the terms 'popular culture' or 'working-class culture,' to indicate a 'people's culture.' Over decades, fashion has favored one or another assessment" (Richard Butsch, ed., *For Fun and Profit: The Transformation of Leisure into Consumption* [Philadelphia: Temple University Press, 1990], 4).

7. "As much as one-third of the population went to the movies at least once a week at a time when the unemployment rate reached 25% of the work force" (Brauer, "When the Lights Went Out," 19).

8. At the beginning of the 1930s, film executives realized that "profits could be found only with high volume and quick turnover from groups with modest incomes" (May, "Making the American Way," 114).

9. Lizabeth Cohen, "The Class Experience of Mass Consumption: Workers as Consumers in Interwar America," in Richard Wightman Fox and T. J. Jackson Lears, eds., *The Power of Culture: Critical Essays in American History* (Chicago: University of Chicago Press, 1993), 152.

10. Butsch, *For Fun and Profit*, 16.

11. Ibid., 16–17.

12. As Miriam Hansen very pointedly argues, "The conception of the show as performance, the continued importance of nonfilmic activities, and neighborhood orientation of the smaller theaters gave local acts of reception a certain margin of unpredictability and autonomy. This made cinema an institution with relatively more diversity than later, more standardized modes of exhibition would allow. It is therefore very likely that a considerable tension remained, even *after* the final implementation of the classical codes, between the textually constructed spectator-subject of classical cinema and empirical audiences that were defined by particular and multiple social affiliations and capable of sharing culturally and historically specific readings" (Miriam Hansen, *Babel and Babylon: Spectatorship in American Silent Film* [Cambridge, Mass.: Harvard University Press, 1991], 345).

13. "The Hollywood dream machine was no monolith," Sklar argues. "The struggle over interpretation, of large issues well as small, went on at every level, from decisions made in executive suites down to daily choices on the sets, how actors dressed, their facial expressions, how they spoke a line" (Robert Sklar, *City Boys: Cagney, Bogart, Garfield* [Princeton University Press, 1992], 9).

14. May, "Making the American Way," 109–11.

15. Quoted in ibid., 99. This remodeling of American exhibition in the 1930s was facilitated by New Deal legislation. In reference to the concept of horizontality, May observes: "The spatial organization of the moderne renewed the democratic side of

the republican tradition. An innovator like [Paul] Frankl, for example, saw that the central ideals of a classless society had been realized in a perpetually expanding movement westward. On the frontier the uniqueness of America was that people organized themselves horizontally as equals. Yet with the end of free land in the 1890s and the coming of urban America arose monopolists who, like European lords, used their power over machine production to construct lavish buildings and entertainments organized on a hierarchical basis, all of which followed a vertical axis" (ibid., 101).

16. Cohen, "Screening out and Tuning in Mass Media," in *Making a New Deal: Industrial Workers in Chicago, 1919–1939* (Cambridge: Cambridge University Press, 1990), 129.

17. Butsch, *For Fun and Profit,* 16.

18. Sklar, *City Boys,* 89–90.

19. Alfred D. Chandler, *Strategy and Structure: Chapters in the History of Industrial Enterprise* (Cambridge, Mass.: MIT Press, 1969).

20. This is documented by the trade press, in particular by the *Motion Picture Herald* and Film Daily. *A* Film Daily YearBook editorial for 1938 stresses: "The Year 1937 saw the responsibility of the 'build-up' campaign definitely shift from the local theatre to the producer and the distributor" (75).

21. House Committee on Interstate and Foreign Commerce, Subcommittee, *Motion-Picture Films: Hearings Before a Subcommittee of the Committee on Interstate and Foreign Commerce,* 74th Cong., 2d sess., March 1936, 141, 168, 269.

22. May, "Making the American Way," 106.

23. Galli and Rositi, *Cultura di massa,* 18.

24. See Lawrence W. Levine, "American Culture and the Great Depression," *Yale Review* 74, no. 2 (1985): 204–5; Levine, "Hollywood's Washington: Film Images of National Politics During the Great Depression," *Prospects* 10 (1985): 169–95. Both essays are included in Levine, *The Unpredictable Past: Explorations in American Cultural History* (New York: Oxford University Press, 1993).

25. Hansen discusses the concept of "public sphere" in reference to cinema in the first decade of the twentieth century, with specific reference to the Supreme Court decision defining cinema as "a business pure and simple," and not an organ of public opinion. Hansen argues: "The cinema was excluded from dominant notions of the public by the legal discourse surrounding the question of censorship. . . . Whether because of puritanical reservation against spectacle on the grounds of the essentially private motivation of its economic existence, the cinema was refused First Amendment protection—recognition of a "public" status. . . . This decision capped numerous efforts on local and state levels, from about 1908 on, to establish control over the mushrooming exhibition of motion pictures—precisely because the dominant forces discerned in it the incipient formation of an alternative public sphere" (Hansen, *Babel and Babylon,* 15). In a sense, the implementation of the Hays Code, that is, the taking of censorship in its own hands, legitimized a self-assigned role of "public sphere" by the film industry.

26. "The photograph and the film, too, changed the nature of cultural communication in America. Unlike the printed word in newspapers and books, the photograph affected even those who could not read. . . . The film and the picture essay

brought the figures of power, in every aspect of their activity, personal as well as public, into the immediate experience of most Americans" (Warren Susman, *Culture as History: The Transformation of American Society in the Twentieth Century* [New York: Pantheon, 1984], 159–60).

27. Bergman, *We're in the Money,* 148.

28. A particularly significant instance of this strategy occurred at the 1932 Democratic Convention, which nominated Roosevelt, when the final words of the candidate's speech were saluted by the playing of "Happy Days Are Here Again!" (Arthur M. Schlesinger, *The Age of Roosevelt,* vol. 1 [Boston: Houghton-Mifflin, 1959], 293).

29. For the work of Adorno and Horkheimer, see Andrew Arato and Eike Gebhardt, eds., *The Essential Frankfurt School Reader* (New York: Urizen Books, 1978).

30. Sklar, *City Boys,* 15–16.

31. "For the purpose of diagnosis or dissection of social institutions, it is necessary to realize that what we call free will, and sin, and emotion, and reason, are attitudes which influence conduct and not separate little universes containing principles which actually control institutions. The world from the point of view of reason and free will may be compared to a highly idealized portrait of an individual which flatters him and makes him proud. It is useful to hang on the wall. It is entirely useless as a basis for diagnosis or prescription if the individual happens to be ill. The separate utility of these two points of view is seldom recognized in political or economic thinking. We are still convinced that appeals to the thinking man to choose his system of government are not ceremonies but actual methods of social control" (Thurman W. Arnold, *The Folklore of Capitalism* [New Haven, Conn.: Yale University Press, 1937], 9).

32. See Giuliana Muscio, "Gli sceneggiatori: Dei cretini presuntuosi con la macchina da scrivere," in Vito Zagarrio, ed., *Hollywood in Progress* (Venice: Marsilio, 1984).

33. Cohen, *Making a New Deal,* 128.

34. See Bergman, *We're in the Money.*

35. In *City Boys,* Sklar writes: "Considering the central importance of radicalism in the arts and intellectual life during the Great Depression, it is also true that the New Deal fostered a conservatory, if not conservative, cultural agenda in which radicals were often significant participants. Around the administration's efforts to recast popular understanding of national historical origins and development, there grew up a lively discourse about American past and its heroes in historical fiction, plays, biographies, even epic poems" (80).

36. Sklar emphasizes the "important differences between the cowboy and the city boy in American mythology and its underlying ideology. Both embody a traditional dilemma for the American male–independence and isolation, on the one hand, attachement and responsibility on the other. The cowboy, however, was and remained fixed in the past, a permanent character, a figure of constancy. . . . For the movie audiences of the 1930s, however, the city boy was a contemporary, one recognizable both in daily headlines and in daily life." Sklar also argues that "The city boys of the movies . . . were not merely a reflection of social actuality. They were, instead, social constructs: the product of genre and convention, definition of the city boy came not only from dominant practice—both in ideology and commercial exploitation—but also from . . . the products of ideologies in contention. . . . The formation and oppositional culture" (Sklar, *City Boys,* 8–9). •

37. ibid., 13. Sklar gives as an example the actor John Garfield as a city boy mirroring the city boys looking at him at the Strand theater: "There is nothing noisy, stagy, or showy about him. One can find hundreds such along Sixth Avenue, spelling out the signs in front of the employment agencies. There were also hundreds such crowding into the Strand" (ibid., 90).

38. Brian Neve, *Film and Politics in America: A Social Tradition* (London and New York: Routledge, 1992), 2–3.

39. Rogers was master of ceremonies for the parade held in Los Angeles in honor of Roosevelt in 1932. FDR, seen exploding into a laugh in the newsreel documenting the event seemed to like Roger's sense of humor. Also Shirley Temple was publicly associated with the image of Roosevelt, having visited him at the White House and being one of Eleanor Roosevelt's favorite Hollywood personalities (see her article "Film Folks I Have Known," *Photoplay,* January 1939).

40. Female stars had a direct impact on consumerism and fashion through the sale of "Hollywood fashion," tie-ups, etc. See the important essay by Charles Eckert, "The Carol Lombard in Macy's Window," *Quarterly Review of Film Studies* (winter 1978); Jane Gaines and Charlotte Herzog, eds. *Fabrications: Costume and the Female Body* (New York: Routledge AFI Film Readers, 1990); and Christine Gledhill, ed., *Stardom: Industry of Desire* (London: Routledge, 1991).

41. May, "Making the American Way," 93.

42. Becky H. Winfield, "Roosevelt and the Press," Ph.D. diss., University of Washington, 1978, 221. FDR's statement is taken from PFF 210 FDR to Paramount, August 4, 1937, Roosevelt Library, Hyde Park, N.Y. (FDRL).

43. On American newsreels in general, see Raymond Fielding, *The American Newsreel, 1911–1967* (Norman: University of Oklahoma Press, 1972).

44. Ibid., 201.

45. William Alexander, *Film on the Left: American Documentary Film from 1931 to 1942* (Princeton: Princeton University Press, 1981).

46. On *The March of Time,* see Raymond Fielding, *The March of Time* (London: Oxford University Press, 1978), and Eric Barnouw, *Documentary:* A History of the Non-Fiction Film (London: Oxford University Press, 1974), 121–22.

47. Telegram, Carl Laemmle of Universal to the President, March 6, 1933, OF 73, FDRL.

48. Telegram, Early to the editors of Pathé News, Paramount News, Fox Movietone News, Universal News, MGM News, March 12, 1933, OF 73, FDRL.

49. *Motion Picture Herald,* March 11, 1933.

50. "I am wondering whether it would not be possible for you to open your film with a silent big close-up motion picture of the president, and then introduce, by title, a talking picture of the Chairman explaining" (Winfield, "Roosevelt and the Press," 222).

51. The newsreels responded quickly, gratified by this recognition of their informative function. Emanuel Cohen of *Paramount News* offered to transmit the presidential message "without elimination of one word," stating that he was happy to "do our share in bringing the President's message home to the people." Truman Talley (for *Fox Movietone News* and *Hearst Metrotone News*) hurried to respond that these two newsreels would have spread the message as soon as possible and that he was also giv-

ing "all exchanges and exhibitors advance information regarding its importance" (OF 73, FDRL).

52. Steven E. Schoenherr, "Selling the New Deal: Stephen T. Early's Role as Press Secretary to Franklin D. Roosevelt," Ph.D. diss., University of Delaware, 1976, 153–55.

53. I conducted this analysis at the National Archives in Washington, D.C., which preserves the *Universal News* collection.

54. At the 1924 convention, "not wanting to show up in a wheelchair, he conscripted his eldest son, James, now a strong sixteen-year-old, to help him. They marked out a fifteen-foot path in the 65th Street house, the same distance he would have to travel to the rostrum, and then, gripping James on his left, and using a cane on his stronger right side, FDR worked at making the trip without appearing to struggle. To keep people from focusing on his halting progress, FDR instructed his son to make it seem that they were moving slowly on purpose and to engage him in laughing banter so that the delegates would focus on their faces" (Peter Collier, *The Roosevelts: An American Saga* [New York: Simon & Schuster, 1994], 294).

55. *Hearing on Bills to Prohibit the Trade Practices Known as "Compulsory Block Booking. . . "* (Washington, D.C.: Government Printing Office, 1936), 458.

56. William M. Moore, "F. D. Roosevelt's Image," Ph.D. diss., University of Wisconsin, 1946, 441.

57. Ibid., 464.

58. *Motion Picture Herald,* February 15 and 22, 1936.

59. See Richard D. MacCann, *The People's Films: A Political History of U.S. Government Motion Pictures* (New York: Hasting House, 1973), 43–44, one of the principal sources of information for this section. See also Charles Wolfe, "The Poetics and Politics of Non Fiction," in Tino Balio, cd., *Grand Design: Hollywood as a Modern Business Enterprise, 1930–1939* (New York: Scribner's, 1993), 351–86.

60. On Hopkins, see Robert E. Sherwood, *Roosevelt and Hopkins: An Intimate History* (New York: Harper, 1950); on Tugwell, see Bernard Sternsher, *Rexford G. Tugwell and the New Deal* (New Brunswick, N.J.: Rutgers University Press, 1964).

61. William Stott, *Documentary Expression and Thirties America* (New York: Oxford University Press, 1973), 102.

62. Barnouw, *Documentary,* 113.

63. On radical filmmakers, see, in addition to Alexander, *Film on the Left,* Russell Campbell, "Radical Cinema in the United States, 1930–1947," Ph.d. diss., Northwestern University, 1978; Michael Klein and Jill Klein, "Native Land: An Interview with Leo Hurwitz," *Cineaste* 6, no. 3 (1974); Bill Nichols, "The American Photo League," *Screen* 13 (winter 1972–73): 108–15; Fred Sweet et al., "Pioneers: An Interview with Tom Brandon," *Film Quarterly* 26, no. 5 (1973).

64. MacCann, *The People's Films,* 106.

65. Fielding, *The American Newsreel,* 269.

66. Richard Steele, *Propaganda in an Open Society: The Roosevelt Administration and the Media* (Westport, Conn.: Greenwood Press, 1985), 28–29.

67. The administration intended "to educate the city dweller to the needs of the rural population" (Rollins, "Ideology and Film Rhetoric," 39). Sensitive to the modern idea of information and promotion, this agency had a printing office, directed by the noted journalist J. F. Carter, which produced informative materials, scripts, and

radio recordings on these dramatic problems. When the New Deal's reforms in agriculture came under attack, however, this program proved to be insufficient, given the strong ideological implications that the theme of the conservation of American land assumed.

68. On the myth of the land in the political culture of the thirties, see the important work of George Mosse, *The Nationalization of the Masses* (New York: Harvard Fertig, 1974).

69. "Radio, Roosevelt and the drought were linked in many interesting ways at this time. Father Coughlin had described the drought as God's revenge on America for having elected FDR in 1932. And it was widely believed that the continuous lack of rain was actually caused by radio's interference with normal 'ether' conditions" (Robert S. Fine, "Roosevelt's Radio Chatting: Its Development and Impact During the Great Depression," Ph.D. diss., New York University, 1977, 249.

70. Peter Rollins, "Ideology and Film Rhetoric: Three Documentaries of the New Deal Era (1936–1941)," in Rollins, ed., *Hollywood as Historian: American Film in a Cultural Context* (Lexington: University Press of Kentucky, 1983), 39. On Lorentz, see R. L. Snyder, *Pare Lorentz and the Documentary Film* (Norman: University of Oklahoma Press, 1968); Barnouw, *Documentary;* and MacCann, *The People's Films.* The critical activity of the director has been collected in *Lorentz on Film: Movies 1927 to 1941* (New York: Hopkinson and Blake, 1975).

71. Lorentz had attempted to "sell" other projects to Hollywood. See documents on the film *Black Fury,* Warner Collection, University of Southern California Library, Los Angeles (USCL).

72. On the making of the film, see Alexander, *Film on the Left,* 97–102; MacCann, *The People's Films,* 62–63; and Barnouw, *Documentary,* 114.

73. Lorentz said of *The Plow,* "a melodrama of nature. Our heroine is the grass, our villain the sun and the wind, our players the actual farmers living in the Plains country" (MacCann, *The People's Films,* 66).

74. The film was shown in about three hundred movie theaters—not a small percentage of the approximately fifteen hundred active at that time (ibid., 70–71). Thereafter, *The Plow* was shown frequently, mostly in electoral years, thus confirming the possibility of an instrumental political and promotional use of this kind of production by the administration.

75. MacCann, *The People's Films,* 79.

76. At the time, this commentary received considerable critical consensus and even a favorable comment by James Joyce (Rollins, "Ideology and Film Rhetoric," 40).

77. MacCann, *The People's Films,* 75. This documentary won a prize at the Festival of Venice (surprisingly so, given that in the same year also Leni Riefensthal's *Olympia* was presented at the festival). This prize appears as a confirmation of the ideological co-extensibility of the American myth, in this phase, even with respect to fascism.

78. Fine, "Roosevelt's Radio Chatting," 254.

79. Thurman W. Arnold, *Bottlenecks of Business* (New York: Reynal Hitchcock, 1940), 217–18.

80. Condemning Hollywood, Lorentz had written: "A social revolution is in progress and crying out to be photographed while most studios grind out the same old escape stuff" (cited in Rollins, "Ideology and Film Rhetoric," 38–39).

81. "It must be admitted that the competition was not too severe, because few of the films were of the entertainment variety. But it can well be imagined that the motion picture industry looked askance at such competition. Late in 1939, 87 films were reported already put out by the New Deal administration, and a few months later the government had 373 pictures in circulation" (Will H. Hays, *The Memoirs of Will H. Hays* [Garden City, N.Y.: Doubleday, 1955], 496).

82. Senator Robinson to Howe, June 24, 1933, OF 73, FDRL.

83. Jesse Jones was a banker at the Reconstruction Finance Corporation and a financer of film theater chains in Texas (*Motion Picture Herald,* March 11, 1933). Jordan A. Schwarz devotes a paragraph to Jesse Jones, in *The New Dealers: Power Politics in the Age of Roosevelt* (New York: Vintage Books, 1994), 59–95.

84. Exchange of correspondence between Hays and Early, March 11, 1933, and between Nick Schenck and Early, March 12, 1933, OF 73, FDRL.

85. In his autobiography, Hays connected the adoption of the code to Roosevelt's election: "On March 4, 1933, Franklin D. Roosevelt was inaugurated. Two days later the emergency bank holiday was declared. That night of March 6 we in our Association held a meeting in New York that lasted until seven o'clock the following morning . . . and reaffirmed the entire pledge" (*Memoirs,* 447).

86. Early to Hays, April 24, 1933, OF 73, FDRL.

87. Early to Howson, April 27, 1933, OF 73, FDRL.

88. *Looking Forward* was adapted by Bess Meredyth from the play *Service,* by C. L. Anthony, starring Lionel Barrymore. Mayer cited Hearst at length: "It is a glorious picture, an inspiring picture. It should be of immense value in this Depression. I think," went on Hearst, "you are making a most valuable contribution toward the restoration of courage and confidence. This is the kind of picture which reflects credit on the industry and must give you pride in your profession" (telegram Mayer to Early, March 25, 1933, OF 73, FDRL).

89. Hays to Early, May 5, 1933, OF 73, FDRL.

90. Weil to McIntyre, July 26, 1933, OF 73, FDRL. On this film, see Peter Roffman and Jim Purdy, *The Hollywood Social Problem: Madness, Despair, and Politics from the Depression to the Fifties* (Bloomington: Indiana University Press, 1981), 87–88.

91. Lewyn to FDR, November 18, 1933, OF 73, FDRL.

92. In *Mission to Moscow,* for example, you see hands at work on the presidential desk. This type of self-censorship is not limited to America and to this period, but it expresses a deference toward living public figures, diffused in many cinematographies, which forbids their physical or "impersonated" representation in the context of fiction films.

93. Denton to Early, October 13, 1944, OF 73, FDRL. Various letters addressed to early during June–October 1944, OF 73, FDRL, to the use of FDR's radio messages in *Action in the North Atlantic* and in *Yankee Doodle Dandy,* both by Warner Bros., in order to obtain similar authorizations.

94. Roffman and Purdy, *The Hollywood Social Problem,* 87–88. Metro, or better the producer David O. Selznick, proposed a film project entitled *Corpse on the White House Lawn,* but, given the disapproval immediately manifested by Early, he withdrew it (Selznick to Early, April 11, 1934, OF 73, FDRL). In an electoral year, Orr of MGM proposed to Early the project of making of a sort of documentary, to be titled *A Day*

with the President, but here again the response was negative. Orr even asked for authorization to use a double, but the press secretary maintained his refusal (Orr to Early, November 11, 1936, OF 73, FDRL). "Some reports of two low-budget Republic films, *The President's Mystery* (1936) and *It Could Happen to You* (1937), written by Nathanael West with Lester Cole and Samuel Ornitz, respectively, indicate that both showed an unusual political awareness. The first film was seen in 1940 as 'outright propaganda for President's Roosevelt's re-election' and 'as undisguised sermon against the American Liberty League.'" (Neve, *Film and Politics,* 4).

95. Memorandum, Early to McIntyre, August 21, 1934, OF 73, FDRL.

96. McDermott to Early and Early to McDermott, autumn 1936, OF 73, FDRL.

97. Telegram, J.F.T. O'Connor to Early, and response, April 11, 1939, OF 73, FDRL.

98. Memorandum for Early, July 18, 1939, OF 73, FDRL. Melvyn Douglas was one of the actors most committed to the support of FDR, as we have seen in Ronald Brownstein, *The Power and the Glitter: The Hollywood-Washington Connection* (New York: Vintage Books, 1992).

99. Memorandum, Myers to Early, March 9, 1933, OF 73, FDRL.

100. Independent Theatre Owners [to FDR], June 13, 1933, OF 73, FDRL.

101. Myers to Early, Early to Myers, January 23, 1939, OF 73, FDRL.

102. This correspondence about prepublication is easily accessible at USCL. This collection is important in that it allows us to understand how the studio system operated, because, at Warner Bros., written communication was specifically requested, according to the motto that appears on the company's printed stationary: "Verbal messages cause misunderstandings and delays. Please put them in writing."

103. The shorts, an obligatory segment of the majors' production, were often used to launch new faces and experiment with new formulas, or to exploit musical rights or talent under contract, which, in the case of Warner Bros., were numerous, given the almost monopolistic control this studio exercised in the area of vaudeville and musical entertainment. The world represented in Warner Bros. backstage musicals shows the appropriation, by this studio, of this sector of entertainment, which, until the introduction of sound, acted as live "presentation" to the films in the most prestigious theaters, with its musical numbers, sketches, live variety, and so on. With sound, this form of entertainment, until then present on the stage as real bodies and real voices, was transferred onto film and distributed in many theaters, no longer a singular event (at times more spectacular than the film itself, as in the case of the performances at the Roxy) but a repeatable experience, available even in the more modest theaters.

104. *Footlight Parade* was shot between June 19 and August 5, 1933; the number "Shanghai Lil" was shot between August 31 and September 15, 1933 (Folders 681 and 2170, Footlight Parade, Warner, USCL). The production schedule had been disrupted by the IA (International Alliance of Theatrical Stage Employees) strike. "During the 1933 IA strike, *Variety* reported that . . . a forty-piece orchestra at Warners' had had to rehearse for three days to make an acceptable recording for a *Footlight Parade* song" (Denise Hartsough, "Crime Pays: The Studios' Labor Deals in the 1930s," in Janet Staiger, ed., *The Studio System* [New Brunswick, N.J.: Rutgers University Press, 1995], 232).

105. Roffman and Purdy, *The Hollywood Social Problem*, 86. Cf. Mark Roth, "Some Warners Musicals and the Spirit of the New Deal," *Velvet Light Trap*, 1 (1971).

106. Undated press clippings, Warner Collection, USCL.

107. See the notes of March 8 and 18, 1933, signed by Zanuck, in the folder 1740 Heroes for Sale, Warner Collection, USCL.

108. Exchange of telegrams, Warner-Early-Howe, April 25 and 28, 1933, OF 73, FDRL. There is no trace of these telegrams in the Warner documentation, perhaps because the request was "withdrawn," as Early had suggested.

109. Gillian Klein, "Wellman's Wild Boys of the Road: The Rhetoric of a Depression Movie," *Velvet Light Trap* 15 (1975): 3.

110. Ibid. The film was inspired by the famous Soviet film *Road to Life* by Nikolai Ekk.

111. Roffman and Purdy, *The Hollywood Social Problem*, 160.

112. From the correspondence related to the film, Folders 2064 and 2876, Warner, USCL.

113. In the film "rights have been sold to a film company to make a commercial for patent medicine with a black actor, dubbed Chief Black Star, playing an Indian" (Nick Roddick, *A New Deal in Entertainment: Warner Brothers in the 1930s* [London: BFI, 1983], 147–50).

114. Memorandum, Manny Seff to Hal Wallis, December 18, 1934, Folder 2057, G-Men, Warner Collection, USCL.

115. Cummings to Hays, March 1, 1935, ibid.

116. Hays to Harry Warner, March 1, 1935, ibid.

117. *Motion Picture Herald,* December 28, 1935.

118. Florence Amos to FDR, April 21, 1933, OF 73, FDRL.

119. Telegram, Warner Brothers [to FDR], May 20, 1940, OF 73, FDRL.

120. Memorandum on the response of Foreign Minister Sumner Welles to Representative James W. Gerard, May 1–4, 1940, PPF 210, FDRL.

121. The Pope's monitions, the work of Roman Catholic organizations in the area of film censorship in every country, the epistolary relations between families in the two Americas and Europe: it was a subtle but tight network of communications that guaranteed the homogeneous reception of American cinema in the international Catholic community. The rapport of the Democratic party with the Catholics, in addition to the inter-allied question, caused fascism to be put in parenthesis, never confronted aggressively, before American public opinion. Catholicism, Rome and Italy mixed themselves inextricably, within American politics.

122. Steele, *Propaganda in an Open Society,* 157.

CHAPTER 4

1. On the history of the American film industry, see Tino Balio, ed., *The American Film Industry* (Madison University of Wisconsin Press, 1976); Tino Balio, ed., *Grand Design: Hollywood as a Modern Business Enterprise, 1930–1939* (New York: Scribner's, 1993); Gorham Kindem, ed., *The American Movie Industry* (Carbondale: Southern Illinois University Press, 1982); David Bordwell, Janet Staiger, and Kristin Thompson, *The Classical Hollywood Cinema: Film Style and Mode of Production to 1960* (New York: Co-

lumbia University Press, 1985); and Douglas Gomery, *The Hollywood Studio System, 1930–1949* (New York: St. Martin's Press, 1986); and the recent Janet Staiger, ed., *The Studio System* (New Brunswick, N.J.: Rutgers University Press, 1995).

2. On the Hays Office, see Raymond Moley, *The Hays Office* (New York: Bobbs-Merrill, 1945), and "The Hays Office," *Fortune,* December 1938, reprinted in Balio, *American Film Industry.*

3. Hays in his autobiography describes the meeting he had with Saul Rogers and Lewis Selznick in 1922, and why he decided to accept the job. (Will H. Hays, *Memoirs of Will H. Hays* [Garden City, N.Y.: Doubleday, 1955] 323–63).

4. On the self-censorship system, see Ruth Inglis, *Freedom of the Movies* (Chicago: University of Chicago Press, 1947); Murray Schumach, *The Face on the Cutting Room Floor* (New York: Morrow, 1964); Ira Carmen, *Movies, Censorship, and the Law* (Ann Arbor: University of Michigan Press, 1967); Richard S. Randall, *Censorship in the Movies* (Madison: University of Wisconsin Press, 1970); Leonard Leff and Jerold Simmons, *The Dame in the Kimono: Hollywood, Censorship, and the Production Code from the 1920s to the 1960s* (New York: Grove Weidenfeld, 1990); Lea Jacobs, *The Wages of Sin: Censorship and the Fallen Women Film, 1928–1942* (Marison: University of Wisconsin Press, 1991); Giuliana Muscio, ed., *The Gateway to Hays* (Milan: Fabbri, 1991); and Richard Maltby, "The Production Code and the Hays Office," in Balio, *Grand Design,* 37–72.

5. Bordwell, Staiger, and Thompson, *Classical Hollywood Cinema,* 254. It would be interesting to analyze the dialectic between the studio system, as a mechanism of internal organization, and the MPPDA, an external structure that guaranteed its functioning. This analysis would allow us to define more precisely whether the film industry was an oligopoly or a monopoly.

6. On progressive reformism, see William E. Leuchtenburg, *The Perils of Prosperity, 1914–1932* (Chicago: University of Chicago Press, 1958); Morrell Heald, *The Social Responsibilities of Business* (Cleveland, Ohio: Case Western University Press, 1970); and Louis Galambos, *The Public Image of Big Business in America, 1880–1940* (Baltimore, Md.: Johns Hopkins University Press, 1975).

7. "Trade practices of the period were chaotic and savagely competitive. There were charges and countercharges of stealing and of cutthroat methods" (Hays, *Memoirs,* 326).

8. For a description of the violent character of this integration, with picturesque touches, see Benjamin Hampton, "The Battle for the Theatres," chapter 12 in *History of the American Film Industry from its Beginnings to 1931* (New York: Dover, 1970).

9. For an articulated description, department by department, of the Hays Office, see Moley, *The Hays Office.*

10. The Hays Code has been published as an appendix in Schumach, *Cutting Room Floor.*

11. The decision, *Mutual Film Corp. v. Industrial Commission of Ohio* (1915), is reprinted in Gerald Mast, *The Movies in Our Midst* (Chicago: University of Chicago Press, 1982), 136–43.

12. See Douglas Ayer, Roy E. Bates, and Peter J. Herman, "Self-Censorship in the Movie Industry: A Historical Perspective on Law and Social Change," in Kindem, *American Movie Industry,* 224–26.

13. The list of Don'ts included: profanity, obscenity, nudity, illegal drug traffic, sexual perversion, white slavery, miscegenation, venereal disease, scenes of actual childbirth, children's sexual organs, ridicule of the clergy, and willful offense against any nation, race, or creed. The list of Be Carefuls included: the institution of marriage, capital punishment, the flag, drunkenness, etc., all to be dealt with in "good taste."

14. William Uricchio and Robert Pearson, *Reframing Culture: The Case of Vitagraph Quality Films* (Princeton, N.J.: Princeton University Press, 1993), 11.

15. Ibid., 6. The authors are speaking specifically of nickelodeon audiences.

16. On this hypothesis of the "great conspiracy," see, among others, Stuart Ewen, *Captains of Consciousness* (New York: McGraw-Hill, 1976).

17. See Philip French, *The Movie Moguls* (London: Penguin, 1969), and Neal Gabler, *An Empire of Their Own: How the Jews Invented Hollywood* (New York: Doubleday, Anchor Books, 1988).

18. From the documents of the New York State Archives, Albany, it appears that, before the introduction of sound, no script was required for censorship purposes.

19. See Muscio, "Introduction," in *Gateway to Hays.*

20. Hays, *Memoirs,* 438.

21. Ibid.

22. Ibid., 447. "So a new order comes to America, to industry and the motion pictures" (Terry Ramsaye, "New Deal, Superman, and Today," *Motion Picture Herald,* March 18, 1933, 9–10).

23. The role of Roman Catholics in relation to the self-censorship system deserves a deeper examination. Catholics had both a repressive and an inspirational role. They were in fact the lever Hays used to adopt and enforce the code; they played an essential anticommunist role and hampered the movement to modify the self-censorship system in the 1950s. Their inspirational role is evidenced by the fact that the code was "written" by Martin Quigley and Father Lord, to whom the task of drafting the preamble was also entrusted. But the role of the Catholics in the writing of the code should not be exaggerated: for example, most of the articles were a re-elaboration of the Don'ts and Be Carefuls, the concept of miscegenation is typically WASP, and Hays contributed integrations and suggestions.

24. Samuel Goldwyn said: "I feel very strongly that motion pictures should never embarrass a man when he brings his family to the theatre" (Schumach, *Cutting Room Floor,* 4).

25. On the Payne Fund Studies, see Richard Maltby, *Harmless Entertainment* (Metuchen, N.J.: Scarecrow, 1983); on this subject and on the sociological interest in cinema, see Robert Sklar, *Movie-Made America* (New York: Vintage Books, 1994), 134–40. For a popularized edition of these studies, see Henry James Forman, *Our Movie-Made Children* (New York: Macmillan, 1935). This volume criticizes Hollywood cinema for not presenting life in a realistic way; for example, it does not indicate the socioeconomic roots of problems and never shows poor people or people committed to "normal" lines of work. The criticism was justified, and it coincided—symptomatically, given American reformist traditions—with certain positions of "leftist" film criticism. Granted the relation established by Michel Foucault

between power (of surveillance and punishment) and the social sciences, we can underline the emergence in the code of a more specialized knowledge about the spectator.

26. For an introduction to the work of Jacques Lacan, see Juliet Mitchell and Jacqueline Rose, eds., *Feminine Sexuality: Jacques Lacan and the école freudienne* (New York: W. W. Norton, 1982).

27. Quoted in Mast, *Movies in Our Midst,* 340.

28. *Motion Picture Herald,* February 15, 1936, 66.

29. FBI Report, n.d., *Paramount* Case Files, 1938–41, Anti-Trust Division, Justice Department, Washington, D.C. (AD), 81–82.

30. FBI report, n.d.; memorandum, Williams to the Attorney General, November 24, 1937, AD.

31. On the activities of the FTC, see Hampton "Battle for the Theatres," 276–80; Simon N. Whitney, "Antitrust Policies and the Motion Picture Industry," in Kindem, *American Movie Industry,* 162–66. The investigation was instigated by the "independent" producers of United Artists, worried about the expansion of Adolf Zukor, who was acquiring small and large companies in every branch of the industry, especially those that were recalcitrant or hostile. These producers (among them, Mary Pickford) enrolled California's Democratic senator William McAdoo, trying to protect their interests through the Justice Department and the FTC (see n. 78: Block Booking Hearings I, 472).

32. Block Booking Hearings I, 75.

33. Hampton, "Battle for the Theatres," 278.

34. Thurman Arnold, *The Folklore of Capitalism* (New Haven, Conn.: Yale University Press, 1937), 211–12. One can easily imagine that Arnold's nomination at the Antitrust Division, after he had written these pages, provoked heated polemics.

35. During the block booking hearings there were frequent references to this conference.

36. The Allied States Association had left the Motion Picture Theatre Owners Association (MPTOA), the trade organization comprising the majority of exhibitors, which included the managers of theaters "integrated" with the majors, accused of being in collusion with their interests. See Daniel Bertrand, Review Division, *NRA Evidence Study no. 25: Motion Picture Industry* (Washington, D.C.: Government Printing Office, November 1935), 52.

37. On the NRA code, see Douglas Gomery, "Hollywood, the National Recovery Administration, and the Question of Monopoly Power," in Kindem, *American Movie Industry;* and Sklar, *Movie-Made America,* 68–170.

38. *NRA Work Materials no. 34* (Washington, D.C.: Government Printing Office, 1936), 38.

39. Ibid., 38–39.

40. Myers to Early, October 13, 1933, OF 73, Roosevelt Library, Hyde Park, N.Y. (FDRL).

41. Myers to Early, December 19, 1933, OF 73, FDRL.

42. "Report to the President by the Administrator and the General Counsel of NRA," *Motion Pictures,* May 15, 1934, 6–8.

43. U.S. National Recovery Review Board, "Third Report to the President," June 1934, mimeo., Library of Congress, Washington, D.C., 50–54.

44. *NRA Work Materials no. 34*, 5, 138.

45. For a reconsideration of labor in Hollywood, see Denise Hartsough, "Crime Pays: The Studios' Labor Deals in the 1930s", in Staiger, *The Studio System*, 226–50; and Ida Jeter, "The Collapse of the Federated Motion Picture Crafts: A Case Study of Class Collaboration in the Motion Picture Industry, in Paul Kerr, ed., *The Hollywood Film Industry* (London: Routledge Keagan Paul, 1986), 78–96.

46. McGrew to McIntyre, April 1933, OF 73, FDRL.

47. Sklar, *Movie-Made America*, 171.

48. *NRA Work Materials no. 34*, 150–51.

49. The definitions of *clearance, zoning,* and *run* are discussed in ibid., 76.

50. Gomery argues that the apparent internal conflicts of the studio system have only anecdotal value; they do not constitute a form of authentic competition (*The Hollywood Studio System*, 24).

51. *NRA Work Materials no. 34*, 81.

52. Ibid., 103.

53. Ibid., 108.

54. Newsletter of the MPRC, October 4, 1933, OF 73, FDRL.

55. This suggestion was important because a federal intervention in this area required that it was a matter of interstate commerce or a question of public interest. The hearings on block booking were in fact held in front of a commission on interstate commerce.

56. Bertrand, *NRA Evidence Study no. 25*, 3.

57. U.S. National Recovery Review Board, "Third Report," 118.

58. "Reports to the President by the Administrator and the General Counsel of the National Recovery Administration," May 15, 1934, mimeo., Library of Congress, Washington, D.C.

59. U.S. National Recovery Review Board, "Third Report," 52.

60. The concept of *counterorganization* is derived from Ellis W. Hawley, *The New Deal and the Problem of Monopoly* (Princeton, N.J.: Princeton University Press, 1966), 14.

61. Douglas Gomery, "Rethinking U.S. Film History: The Depression Decade and Monopoly Control," *Film and History* 10, no. 2 (1980): 37.

62. Gomery, "Hollywood," 212.

63. Sklar, *Movie-Made America*, 169.

64. *NRA Work Materials no. 34*, 4.

65. Moley, *The Hays Office*, 8.

66. Steve Fraser, "The 'Labor Question,'" in Gary Gerstle and Steve Fraser, eds., *The Rise and Fall of the New Deal, 1930–1980* (Princeton, N.J.: Princeton University Press, 1989), 56.

67. Sklar, *Movie-Made America*, 172.

68. Hartsough, "Crime Pays," 237.

69. Ibid., 230.

70. Jeter, "Collapse."

71. Hartsough, "Crime Pays," 242.

72. Ibid.

73. See Murray Ross, *Stars and Strikes* (New York: Columbia University Press, 1941); Larry Ceplair and Steven Englund, *The Inquisition in Hollywood: Politics in the Film Community, 1930–1960* (New York: Anchor Press, 1980); Guiliana Muscio, *La lista nera a Hollywood* (Milan: Feltrinelli, 1979); and Nancy Lynn Schwartz, *The Hollywood Writers' Wars* (New York: Knopf, 1982).

74. In December 1934 Ralph Block of SWG asked Early and Howe to tell the President about the producers' refusal to obey the clauses prescribed by the NRA code on the institution of the committee with the screenwriters. The great number of letters on the NRA code sent to the President by Hollywood personalities is a clear sign of how all of the parts were trying to bring FDR over to their side: actors, producers, screenwriters, exhibitors, etc.

75. The word "friendly" became popular in the 1950s witch-hunts.

76. Jeter, "Collapse," 87.

77. *NRA Work Materials no. 34,* 97.

78. The following discussion draws from four hearings before House and Senate committees: House Committee on Interstate and Foreign Commerce, Subcommittee, *Motion-Picture Films: Hearing Before a Subcommittee of the Committee on Interstate and Foreign Commerce,* 74th Cong., 2d sess., March 1936; (hereafter: Block Booking Hearings I); Senate Committee on Interstate and Foreign Commerce, *Motion-Picture Films: Hearings Before the Committee on Interstate and Foreign Commerce on S. 280.* 76th Cong., 1st sess., April 1939 (hereafter: Block Booking Hearings II); House Committee on Interstate and Foreign Commerce, *Motion-Picture Films (Compulsory Block Booking and Blind Selling): Hearing Before the Committee on Interstate and Foreign Commerce on S.280,* 76th Cong., 3d sess., pt. 1, May 1940 (hereafter: Block Booking Hearings III); House Committee on Interstate and Foreign Commerce, *Motion-Picture Films (Compulsory Block Booking and Blind Selling): Hearings Before the Committee on Interstate Foreign Commerce on S. 280,* 76th Cong., 3d sess., pt. 2, May–June 1940 (hereafter: Block Booking Hearings IV).

79. For a full issue devoted to exhibition, see *Film History* 6, no. 2 (summer 1994).

80. Block Booking Hearings I, 28–29.

81. Report to accompany S. 280, June 1, 1939, 5–6.

82. Block Booking Hearings III, 41. It is not surprising that these groups would mention Capra, the populist director par excellence, but it should also be remembered how he was then fighting for the recognition of the role of the director "against" the producers. Because of the polemics about *Mr. Smith,* "several congressmen let it be known that the Neely Bill hearings might be rushed through the House in retaliation." In a note, however, we learn: "That *Mr. Smith* quickened interest in the Neely Bill is ironic in that all of Capra's films at Columbia between 1936 and 1939, including *Mr. Smith,* were sold individually rather than in blocks" (Charles Wolfe, *Mr. Smith Goes to Washington: Democratic Forums and Representational Forms,* in Peter Lehman, ed., *Close Viewings: An Anthology of New Film Criticism* [Tallahassee: Florida State University Press, 1990], 306, 309).

83. Block Booking Hearings IV, 996–97.

84. Block Booking Hearings III, 41.

85. Ibid., 312.

86. "Once I said to a Negro man—because we Better Filmers go down there to the colored theatres, go down to their theatres. I saw something that I thought was not so good, or I did not like very much, and I said, 'Taylor, why don't you give your people something that is educational?' He said, 'Lawdy, Mrs. Richardson, they don't want to be educated no more than the white folks do" (Block Booking Hearings IV, 878).

87. The report on the Neely Bill in 1939 (see Block Book Hearings III, 10–15) admitted: "This bill is a compromise. Some of the public groups demanding remedial legislation favored strict Government regulation, including censorship at the studios. Others favored a bill requiring the leasing of pictures one at a time after they had been completed and had been given a trade showing. This compromise was effected in order to accomplish needed reforms with a minimum interference with the industry's practices."

88. Block Booking Hearings III, 303.

89. Block Booking Hearings I, 44.

90. Ibid., 216.

91. Sklar, *Movie-Made America*, 47.

92. Block Booking Hearings IV, 505; I, 48, 118.

93. Arnold argued, "It seems to me further, that the conduct of the whole business is wasteful and extravagant. I do not like to be in the position of throwing stones, so to speak, at the gentlemen connected with the motion picture industry, but it does occur to me that this vertical trust is the greatest sort of contributor to waste. The reason is they can force their product on the market regardless of cost. The theatres cannot pick and choose" (Block Booking Hearings IV, 1011).

94. Block Booking Hearings I, 227–28.

95. The combination of block booking and blind selling was at the basis of the studio system, encouraging, for example, long-term contracts with personnel and diversification of product.

96. Ibid., 433.

97. Block Booking Hearings IV, 462.

98. Ibid., 714.

99. Block Booking Hearings III, 344–69. Substituting the "external" production of low-budget films with the institution of B-units, the industry completed the integration of every phase and aspect of film production, including in its very structure the "independent" element. An interesting work on the Bs is Brian Taves, "The B Film: Hollywood's Other Half," in Balio, *Grand Design*, 313–50.

100. This campaign was documented in the hearings by a letter sent by the MP-PDA to the directors of the studios' publicity offices, which included samples of letters that the personnel were required to write to their representatives (Block Booking Hearings III, 393–96).

101. Block Booking Hearings IV, 834.

102. Block Booking Hearings III, 396–99.

103. Block Booking Hearings II, 552; IV, 474.

104. Block Booking Hearings III, 182. This atmosphere of suspicion was noticed by Charles Pettingill, who publicly disapproved the personal attacks he had witnessed throughout the hearings. Pettijohn had tried many times to discredit Myers, calling the independents' distribution project the "Tiffany Franchise," and its five-year con-

tracts a "five year plan," reminiscent of the Soviet economic model. On their side, the independents accused the MPPDA of having unleashed a propaganda campaign against these legislative proposals, "thought out and thoroughly executed as any Hitler blitzkrieg" (Block Booking Hearings I, 238, 428, 455, 485; III, 397).

105. The prewar atmosphere of the years 1939–40 is revealed by the political overtones of the debate. While Myers argued, "There is no point in railing at political dictatorship abroad whilst condoning economic dictatorship at home," one of the film executives countered, "It does seem strange that in the midst of a world shocked, terrified, and aghast at the amazing and cruel events that have stirred even this Nation to the depths, we should be here at this time striving so earnestly about such domestic legislation as this" (Block Booking Hearings IV, 959).

106. Ibid., 893.

107. Ibid., 985. The 1940 *Film Daily YearBook*, in an article signed by the architect John Eberson, discusses this very transformation. See also Lary May, "Making the American Way: Modern Theatres, Audiences, and the Film Industry," *Prospects* 12 (1987): 89–124.

108. Senate Committee on Interstate and Foreign Commerce, Subcommittee, *Propaganda in Motion Pictures: Hearings Before a Subcommittee of the Committee on Interstate Commerce on S. Res. 152,* 77th Cong., 1st sess., September 9–26, 1941. On the HUAC, see Walter Goodman, *The Committee: The Extraordinary Career of the House Committee on Un-American Activities* (Baltimore, Md.: Penguin, 1964).

109. Senate Committee, *Propaganda in Motion Pictures,* 1.

110. Ibid., 71.

111. Ibid., 26–32.

112. The newspaper reported how Nye "deliberately, adroitly, with every trick of timing and inflection of voice, accused the motion-picture industry of fostering pro-British sentiment, and then called a list of Jewish names associated with the motion-picture industry, drolly exaggerating their Hebraic-sounding syllables, with pauses to encourage his enflamed hearers to shout and hiss" (ibid., 9–11).

113. Sklar, *Movie-Made America,* 249.

114. Ceplair and Englund, *Inquisition in Hollywood,* 160.

115. On the foreign policy of the New Deal, see William E. Leuchtenburg, *Franklin D. Roosevelt and the New Deal, 1932–1940* (New York: Harper, 1963), and Richard Dallek, *Franklin D. Roosevelt and the American Foreign Policy* (New York: Oxford University Press, 1979).

116. Leuchtenburg, *Franklin D. Roosevelt,* 312–22.

117. Ken Clark to Boettiger, September 13, 1941, Boettiger 17, FDRL.

118. Warner went on to say: "Frankly, I am not certain whether or not this country should enter the war in its own defense at the present time. The President knows the world situation and our country's problems better than any other man. I would follow his recommendation concerning a declaration of war." (Senate Committee, *Propaganda in Motion Pictures,* 338.)

119. Ibid., 339, 343.

120. This information was supplied by Leith Adams, curator of the Warner Collection, University of Southern California Library, Los Angeles.

121. Sklar, *Movie-Made America,* 250.

122. Daniel Bertrand, W. Duane Evans, and E. L. Blanchard, "Investigation of Concentration of Economic Power: Study Made for Temporary National Economic Committee," *Monograph no. 43,* Motion Picture Industry–Pattern of Control (Washington, D.C.: Government Printing Office, 1941).

123. On the TNEC, see Hawley, *New Deal.*

124. Memorandum, Doyle to Williams, February 25, 1939, AD.

125. Bertrand, Evans, and Blanchard, "Investigation," 56.

126. Ibid., 56. From the correspondence on the *Paramount* case, it is evident that the fundamental work by Mae Huettig, *Economic Control of the Motion Picture Industry* (Philadelphia: University of Pennsylvania Press, 1944), was based in part on documents from the *Paramount* case (Wendell Berge to Williams, May 28, 1940, AD).

CHAPTER 5

1. Michael Conant, *Antitrust in the Motion Picture Industry* (Berkeley: University of California Press, 1960); Ernest Borneman, "United States versus Hollywood: The Case Study of an Antitrust Suit," in Tino Balio, ed., *The American Film Industry* (Madison: University of Wisconsin Press, 1976); Simon N. Whitney, "Antitrust Policies and the Motion Picture Industry," in Gorham Kindem, ed., *The American Movie Industry* (Carbondale: Southern Illinois University Press, 1982).

2. For this chapter the primary sources have been the original Antitrust Division (Justice Department, Washington, D.C.) documents and the correspondence on the case kept at the Roosevelt Library, Hyde Park, N.Y. (FDRL). Because the files of the *Paramount* case are not catalogued, they are defined here by heading and date, followed by the initials AD (Antitrust Division).

3. Walter Adams, "Dissolution, Divorcement, Divestiture: The Pyrrhic Victories of Antitrust," *Indiana Law Journal* 27, no. 1 (fall 1951): 1–37, and Eugene V. Rostow, "Monopoly Under the Sherman Act: Power or Purpose?" in Sylvester Berki, ed., *Antitrust Policy Economics and Law* (Boston: D. C. Heath, 1966), 57–58 and 60.

4. See Howard Zinn, ed., *New Deal Thought* (Indianapolis: Bobbs-Merrill, 1966).

5. Conant, *Antitrust in the Motion Picture Industry,* viii. He specifically listed among these effects: "The public has gained many more pictures of high quality from the entrance of so many independent producers into the freer film market. . . . The decrees have also made available earlier to some city's areas by the move-up in runs and shorter clearances of some neighborhood theatres" (p. 201).

6. Rostow, "Monopoly Under the Sherman Act," 68–69. Rostow insists on the meaning of the motion picture antitrust cases in clarifying the doctrine of the Sherman Act: "Together they had a good deal of particularity to the law of the Sherman Act, in helping to identify the degree of market power the existence of which is deemed illegal; in clarifying the role of non-economic, or subjective ingredients in defining the offense under Section 2; and, above all, in asserting that where the offense is the acquisition of a forbidden degree of market power, not through loose association, but by reason of the size of business units, the normal antitrust remedy is to reduce their size" (60).

7. Alfred D. Chandler, *Strategy and Structure: Chapters in the History of Industrial Enterprise* (Cambridge, Mass.: MIT Press, 1969).

8. Adams, "Dissolution Divorcement," 5.

9. *United States v. Fox West Coast Theater Corporation et al.* (1928); *United States v. Barney Balaban et al.* (1928); *United States v. Griffith Amusement Company et al.* (1939); *U.S. v. Schine Chain Theaters, Inc., et al.* (1939); *U.S. v. Crescent Amusement Co., Inc., et al.* (1939).

10. For the *St. Louis* case, see Whitney, "Antitrust Policies," 161 and *Motion Picture Herald,* February 1, 8, and 29, 1936.

11. House Committee on Interstate and Foreign Commerce, Subcommittee, *Motion-Picture Films: Hearing Before a Subcommittee of the Committee on Interstate and Foreign Commerce,* 74th Cong., 2d sess., March 1936 (hereafter: Block Booking Hearings I), 427.

12. President of Celebrity Production to Culkin, April 3, 1935, AD.

13. *United States v. Warner Brothers Pictures, Inc.* See Block Booking Hearings I, 83–84.

14. The peculiarity of the case was represented by the need to prove the intent of monopolizing through trade practices and through the integrated structure of the industry, even in the absence of "conspiracy."

15. Memorandum, Benham to Williams, September 17, 1936, AD (my italics).

16. Memorandum, Williams to Dickinson, June 8, 1936, AD.

17. Memorandum, Benham to Williams, September 17, 1936, AD. Benham added: "The complaints of certain independent producers and exhibitors have been so persistent throughout the years that the Department should know whether there are, in fact, violations of law involved in the methods and operations of chain theatres, a matter that has never thus far been investigated by the Department. In the event that the complaints as to the chains and the other charges enumerated above could be established, it would seem that an action might be under the Sherman Act."

18. Memorandum, Williams to Dickinson, July 6, 1936, AD.

19. Rostow argues that the trade associations were the sites where monopoly was articulated in the twenties and thirties ("Monopoly Under the Sherman Act").

20. Memorandum, Williams to Dickinson, July 6, 1936, AD.

21. Later on, in the legal skirmishes of the case, the film companies, Warner Bros. in particular, boasted this specific instance of "cooperation" with the "petitioner," that is, the Justice Department: "Many compilations were prepared for petitioner by Warner employees. In the fall of 1937 for a period of approximately four months the petitioner had three, four and five men at the offices of the 'Warner' group of defendants almost daily, examining the records and contracts of the 'Warner' group of defendants. Petitioner made elaborate copies and summaries." Later, however: "Petitioner declined to give a copy of the compilation and summaries which they took off the books of the Warner defendants, and it has now become necessary in the preparation of this case to duplicate the work done by the petitioner" (Paramount Case Files, September–December 1939, Southern District Court of New York).

22. Memorandum, Williams to Dickinson, January 6, 1937, AD.

23. Memorandum by Williams, April 23, 1937, AD.

24. Ibid.

25. *Motion Picture Herald,* January 18, 1936.

26. It has not been possible to find a copy of this petition in the Antitrust Division files.

27. Memorandum, Hoover to Jackson, October 1937, AD.

28. Memorandum, Williams to Jackson, November 24, 1937, AD.

29. Whitney, "Antitrust Policies," 168–69.

30. Memorandum, Williams to Jackson, November 24, 1937, AD.

31. For a description of the scene of legal thought in the thirties, see Edward Kearny, *Thurman W. Arnold Social Critic: The Satirical Challenge to Orthodoxy* (Albuquerque: University of New Mexico Press, 1970). A very influential book at the time was Charles Beard's, *An Economic Interpretation of the Constitution of the United States* (New York: Macmillan, 1935).

32. Alan Brinkley, "The New Deal and the Idea of the State," in Gary Gerstle and Steve Fraser, eds., *The Rise and Fall of the New Deal, 1930–1980* (Princeton, N.J.: Princeton University Press, 1989), 98.

33. Ibid., p 90.

34. According to Gene Gressley, "he brilliantly refashioned an age-old concept by adding a dimension of flexibility that enabled him to widen his enforcement program. . . . The defendant would present a plan to the court, but this scheme must now not only incorporate sufficient redress of the indictment but offer a genuine reorganization of a company on a industry-wide basis that could be more beneficial to the general public than would be the results of a criminal prosecution" (*Voltaire and the Cowboy* [Boulder: University of Colorado Press, 1971], 46)

35. "Actually, it appears, the bulk of Arnold's support came not from any uprising of consumers, but from smaller businessmen, or dissatisfied business groups unable to compete successfully with their large rivals, from such groups as . . . the Allied States Association of Motion Picture Exhibitors" (Ellis W. Hawley, *The New Deal and the Problem of Monopoly* [Princeton, N.J.: Princeton University Press, 1966), 447.

36. Pare Lorentz and Morris Ernst, fervent New Dealers, expressed similar fears of the monopolization and standardization of film production by the Hollywood studio system in their book *Censored: The Private Life of the Movies* (New York: Jonathan Cape and Harrison Smith, 1930): "When two hundred men direct corporations controlling a hundred papers, or ten million radios, or 40% of the world's movies—and with the sole thought of making their companies show a profit—you can wonder how far the modern leader has run from Horace Greeley, Tom Paine, or Jefferson." These two intellectuals practiced their antimonopolism and their dissatisfaction with the Hollywood studio system, Lorentz by making non-Hollywood films, that is, his documentaries financed by the New Deal administration, and Ernst, a lawyer, working for the Antitrust Division in the later revision of the *Paramount* case.

37. Abram F. Myers, "Latest Developments Along the Movie Front," (speech delivered to the Twentieth Century Club of Boston, April 26, 1938, AD). The address also states: "Entrenched behind this efficient defensive organization, the major companies (known as the "Big Eight") have reduced the motion picture business to a degree of monopolization never achieved in any other industry. The monopolistic practices which they have devised and put into effect bear most heavily on the independent theatre owners, and that explains my interest in the subject. But they also

have created a condition that is wholly undemocratic and un-American in that it enables the Big Eight to control the production and distribution of 85% of the type of films the theatres must have to operate successfully; also, to control not only the operating policies of the 14,000 independent theatres in which they have not a penny invested. The serious side of this, from the standpoint of the public, is that, since the exhibitors are not free agents, they cannot fairly be subjected to community control regulation or influence for the manner in which they operate their theatres, their operating policies being beyond their control."

38. See Gerstle and Fraser, *Rise and Fall of the New Deal.*

39. My research justifies these charges: the Republican Hays had a very friendly relationship with the Democrats; and it would be enough to calculate time, energy, and people "invested" in the legal defense of the film industry in the *Paramount* case to prove their great means.

40. On the film project, see Peter Roffman and Jim Purdy, *The Hollywood Social Problem: Film, Madness, Despair, and Politics from the Depression to the Fifties* (Bloomington: Indiana University Press, 1981), 165, 187, 312–13.

41. See Adams, "Dissolution, Divorcement," 2 n.4.

42. Memorandum of the conference between Berge, Williams, and Arnold, July 18, 1938, AD.

43. In the block bookings hearings, Pettijohn stated that the film industry was not a public service industry but simply a private business that supplied the public with an entertainment service and therefore was not "a public interest" to the extent to justify federal controls and regulation (House Committee on Interstate and Foreign Commerce, *Motion-Picture Films (Compulsory Block Booking and Blind Selling): Hearing Before the Committee on Interstate and Foreign Commerce on S.280.* 76th Cong., 3d sess., pt. 1, May 1940 [hereafter: Block Booking Hearings III], 62 and 562–63).

44. Memorandum, Williams to Arnold, September 12, 1938, AD.

45. The FBI document is very interesting in that it enables us to evaluate legal arguments as supported by the evidence. For example, it reveals that the FBI had been able to "analyze" contracts and exhibition records covering the distribution of the metropolitan first-run 1934–35, 1935–36, 1936–37 feature pictures of the eight major companies in thirty-six key cities of the United States. All of the information was minutely described, including names and addresses, specific film titles, quotations from contracts, names of complaining exhibitors, lists of stars and creative personnel loaned among the studios, and so on.

46. Memorandum from Arnold, June 24, 1938, PSF, box 77, Justice Department, 1938–39, FDRL.

47. These remarks appeared in an article entitled "Political Trade Indicated in Federal Anti-Trust Film Suit," by Warren B. Francis, an undated copy of which is filed at FDRL. A civil suit allowed for requesting remedy while a criminal prosecution permitted only punishment, such as a fine.

48. The 1938 petition explained: "The alledged unlawful acts and violations . . . have been and are conceived, carried out and made effective, in part, within the Southern District of New York." The suit was filed in New York where the "brain" of the monopoly—the main executives—resided, confirming that in the power structure of the industry New York was the determinant.

49. This operation involved stars and studio personnel as well as real estate or concrete assets.

50. The first draft of the Explanatory Declaration is kept among the *Paramount* case documentation, at the Antitrust Division; the second draft is in PSF, box 77, Justice Department, 1938–39, undated but probably of June 24, 1938, FDRL; the third is in OF, box 4, Justice Department, May–August 1938, FDRL.

51. Lea Jacobs, in "The Paramount Case and the Role of the Distributor," *Journal of the University Film and Video Association* 34, no. 1 (winter 1983): 125–41; and Borneman, in "United States versus Hollywood," have both argued that distribution was the center of the monopoly. The Antitrust Division interpreted the role of distribution in a similar way, especially when it was still interested in arguing for the monopoly of production. But there were indeed problems in asking for divestiture of distribution, and showing that the remedy was "reasonable" in economic terms.

52. Gressley, *Voltaire and the Cowboy,* 11 and 28.

53. Ibid., 18–21.

54. Attorney General Cummings wrote to the President: "The general reaction in the press has been all that could be desired, and the prevailing opinion seems to be that it is a constructive move in the right direction. This result, I am satisfied, has been largely achieved because of the form of the statement that the Department of Justice released on the day the suit was filed" (Cummings to FDR, July 22, 1938, OF 10, box 4, Justice Department, May–August 1938, FDRL).

55. Earl Watters to Cummings, July 25, 1938, AD.

56. Press release prepared by MPPDA, May–August 1938, Justice Department, 1938–39, FDRL. From a judicial point of view, if these practices were necessary, they did not have the characteristics of intentionality and conspiracy, which would have made them illegal.

57. In a memo to Arnold, Williams states: "As a matter of corporation law, I know of no way in which Mr. Sarnoff can avoid his obligations and responsibilities as a director of the parent corporation by ascertaining that he has not been actively participating in the management of the corporation's affairs" (memorandum, Williams to Arnold, July 27, 1938, AD).

58. "Digest testimony of Hodkinson, J. E. Williams and Sidney Kent in record of Famous Players–Lasky case. Williams' testimony to be developed particularly as to reasons why First National was organized by the exhibitors. Was it the increased prices for product that Adolph Zukor and Lasky were seeking to impose upon them? Or was it their fear of his domination of the industry by placing all the stars with box office drawing power under contract to Famous Players-Lasky? These or other reasons should be carefully defined and rationalized for use in a complaint" (memorandum, Evans to Williams, November 4, 1938, AD). The Antitrust Department culled data accumulated by the government in the discussion of the motion picture NRA code and various monopoly investigations to create an economic and institutional history of the film industry that would reveal "innate monopoly tendencies." Just as we should be wary of the prejudices that permeate the film industry historiography originating from Hollywood, we should be aware that the government undertook its data collection with a view to building an antitrust case.

59. "The "shyness" of the courts in this respect stems not only from the tempera-

ment of many judges but also from a lack of training in the economic problems involved in monopoly cases" (Adams, "Dissolution, Divorcement," 32).

60. Memorandum, Evans to Williams, November 4, 1938, AD. In the memorandum Evans suggests finding evidence that, "despite high film rentals, these theatres were profitable ventures," to demonstrate that the fact that independent exhibitors were excluded from this aspect of the business damaged them from an economic point of view, thus refuting the "contention that the primary purpose in operating these theatres [was] to provide a 'showcase' for new pictures" and that they were actually "being run at a loss."

61. Ibid.

62. Thornburg to Arnold, September 30, 1938, AD.

63. Krieger to Williams, October 16, 20, and 23, 1938, AD.

64. On labor problems, see Memorandum To Be Filed on "Illegal payments from the firms to the trade unions," April 6, 1939, AD. In a statement by Mr. and Mrs. James Gruen, E. E. Paramore is "supposed to have been blacklisted by the major companies because of his activities in connection with the Screen Writers' Guild."

65. Williams' explained the majors' rationale in a memo to Arnold: "New centers of population are growing which do not contain theatres. Constant changes in residential and other neighborhoods, opening of new thoroughfares, limitations on downtown parking, etc., are constantly shifting the localities to which the public will go for entertainment. Such conditions, it is asserted, require corresponding changes in theatre locations.

It is then observed that a business catering to public patronage and involving changing ideas of comfort and convenience of a large number of people must be alert either to anticipate these changes or to meet them swiftly when they come. In view of these conditions, it is said, the proposed preliminary injunction would not preserve the status quo but would tie the hands of the defendants in the management of their present theatre holdings and would prevent them from acquiring substitute theatres to take the place of those which prudent business judgment obligates them to relinquish" (memorandum, Williams to Arnold, October 19, 1938, AD).

66. Arnold to Donovan, December 1, 1938, AD.

67. Williams to Law, July 24, 1938, AD.

68. Conant argues that "the weight of the fact makes the case against the three minor defendants questionable" (*Antitrust,* 206).

69. Memorandum To Be Filed, signed by Williams, September 8, 1938, AD.

70. Arnold to Donovan, December 6, 1938, AD.

71. House Committee on Interstate and Foreign Commerce, *Motion-Picture Films (Compulsory Block Booking and Blind Selling): Hearings Before the Committee on Interstate and Foreign Commerce on S. 280,* 76th Cong., 3d sess., pt. 2, May–June 1940, 496, 531, 541, 575. Arnold advised the industry to be "guided by the advice of [its] attorneys" because it "would be subject to continued and possibly further prosecution" if it were to continue ignoring the provisions of the consent decree (ibid., 541).

72. Krieger to Williams, January 30, 1939, AD.

73. Memorandum, Williams to Arnold, February 23, 1939, AD.

74. Memorandum, Clagett to Williams, March 2, 1939, AD.

75. Krieger to Williams, March 27, 1939, AD.

76. Memorandum, Williams to Arnold, January 25, 1939, AD.

77. "The doubts which arise with respect to the possible inadequacy of injunctive relief, even if obtained, to cope with unfair and monopolistic trade practices in the motion picture industry give rise to the question of the desirability and advisability of the creation by Congress of some of the adequate Federal authority to deal with the problems which now affect the industry" (ibid.)

78. See the case of FCC in Eric Barnouw, *The Golden Web: A History of Broadcasting in the U.S.,* 3 vols. (New York: Oxford University Press, 1974).

79. Memorandum, Williams to Arnold, January 25, 1939, AD.

80. Block Booking Hearings III, 563.

81. Harry Warner to Harry Hopkins, March 6, 1939, Hopkins no. 117, Motion Pictures, FDRL.

82. This sentence was underlined in the document.

83. This contact between Harry Warner and Hopkins and its real objective find a direct confirmation in a paragraph of a letter to President Roosevelt written by Will Hays and dated April 20, 1939 (FDRL), legitimating the suspicion that Hays had inspired Warner. After two paragraphs, very warm and complimentary to Roosevelt, he writes: "You will be interested in knowing that I had a long talk with secretary Hopkins last week in Washington before he went away and I am going to proceed with him to carry out the program as soon as he gets back. I am meeting with Frank Walker tomorrow here to discuss it all. Frank will be most useful in all constructive ways in connection with the whole matter."

84. Memorandum, Arnold to the Attorney General, June 29, 1939, AD.

85. Gressley, *Voltaire and the Cowboy,* 46.

86. Hays to FDR, November 20, 1939, PFF 1945, Hays, 1934–41, FDRL.

87. Roosevelt to Hays, November 21, 1939, PFF 1945, Hays, 1934–41, FDRL.

88. From materials preserved at the Antitrust Division, it emerges that Podell had worked for the Hays Office in the days of the NRA, but nevertheless, the department decided to use him in the case.

89. Williams to Law, February 2, 1940, AD.

90. There is no reference to the *Paramount* case, for example, in Larry Ceplair and Steven Englund, *Inquisition in Hollywood: Politics in the Film Community, 1930–1960* (New York, Anchor Press, 1980).

91. Williams to Podell, February 19, 1940, AD.

92. Podell to Williams, March 7, 1940, AD.

93. Block Booking Hearings III, 355.

94. Podell to Williams, March 7, 1940, AD.

95. Ibid.

96. The "History of the Suit to February 1, 1940," describes this phase in detail: "These interrogatories consisted of 38 questions in which United Artists sought to elicit the names and addresses of persons having knowledge of relevant facts with respect to the allegations made in certain paragraphs of the Petition, and this entire set of interrogatories was 13 typewritten pages long. From time to time the Government's time to object to these interrogatories was extended, and finally, on December 7, 1939, a stipulation was entered into extending the time of the Government to answer the United Artists' interrogatories to February 1, 1940. On January 19, 1940, however,

United Artists indicated that it was considering joining in the requests for information made in the interrogatories filed by the other defendants."

97. Arnold, Williams, and Wright appeared together again in the final stage of the case, in 1948, when the "remedy" for which they had fought for, was finally granted.

98. Memorandum, Wright to Arnold, January 12, 1940, AD.

99. Memorandum, Farnsworth to Williams, February 6, 1940, AD. Before working for the division, Farnsworth was involved in the drafting of the *Evidence Study no. 25*, related to the NRA Code.

100. Hampton, *The History of the American Film Industry*, 255.

101. Memorandum, Farnsworth to Williams, February 13, 1940, AD.

102. This definition underlines the continuity of this plan with the NRA's experience, both for the way it was reached (through government-industry negotiations that also involved many people who had also taken part in the NRA code discussion), as for its self-regulating character.

103. Memorandum, Tupper to Niles, March 11, 1940, Hopkins box 117, Motion Pictures, FDRL.

104. Myers to the Attorney General, March 26, 1940, AD.

105. Tupper to Hopkins, April 4, 1940, Hopkins box 117, Motion Pictures, FDRL. On the evaluation of the size of the parties interested in the Commerce Department plan, there is an exchange of correspondence between Hazen and Tupper, then referred to Hopkins, between May 31 and April 5, 1940, which reveals a high degree of political crudity.

106. Farnsworth to Williams, April 1, 1940, AD.

107. Williams to Podell, April 6, 1940, AD.

108. Memorandum, Hayes to Baldridge, April 17, 1940, AD. "I understand that we have taken the position that 'affiliated' means a producer who has any contractual relation with the majors, whether or not such producer is completely owned by independent capital. . . . I am skeptical of our ability to maintain this position. Carried to its logical conclusions it would mean that whenever any producer obtained distribution for a particular picture, he would not be considered an independent."

109. Stanton Griffis, "Notes for Town Hall Address," May 6, 1940, AD.

110. U.S. Southern District Court of New York, *U.S. v. Paramount Pictures, Inc., et al., Defendants,* Official Record of Stenographer Minutes, June 3, 4, 5, 6, 7, and 10, November 14, 1940, 13.

111. Ibid., 11–25,

112. Ibid., 25–105.

113. Ibid., 105–89.

114. Ibid., 198.

115. Ibid., 228.

116. Ibid., 285–322.

117. Ibid., 228.

118. Ibid., 320. Tacher viciously attacked the small independent producers, whom he considered to be "failures."

119. Ibid., 266.

120. Ibid., 284.

121. Ibid., 326. Frolich refers to *United States v. Interstate Circuit* (1935).
122. Ibid., 330.
123. Memorandum, Williams to Arnold, June 7, 1940, AD.
124. Myers to Arnold, June 13, 1940, AD; this is a detailed fifteen-page memorandum that analyses the legal aspects of the decree, rather than its contents.
125. Myers to Wright, July 15, 1940, AD.
126. Myers to the Attorney General, July 23, 1940, AD.
127. The plan for the decree was sent to Mary Bannerman and to Ray Layman Wilbur of the Motion Picture Research Council, for example, and to Harry Brandt, R. H. Poole, Albert Myers, and Ed Kuykendall, representatives of the main exhibitors associations, on August 6, 1940.
128. Memorandum, Williams to Arnold, August 6, 1940, AD. One of the division's attorneys commented: "I do not see how this consent decree can be viewed as an experiment. I do not think that any one in the Department is ever going to become excited enough once the case has been settled to carry on a crusade of the type we have been conducting. Furthermore, I do not think that we can even seriously consider the possibility of trying this case some time in the future, once it has been settled. First, the experience of exhibitors will be two or three years older. We have enough difficulty at present helping exhibitors remember what an exchange manager told them in 1934. You can readily understand how much more difficult that is going to be if we wait until 1943 to ask him that transpired years ago. Second, I doubt whether the Department three years from now will be able to arouse the enthusiasm in independent exhibitors which is necessary for the successful prosecution of the suit. The Government will never be in as good a position to try this suit as it now is . . ." (Simon to Wright, August 7, 1940, AD).
129. Telegram, Simon to Wright, August 15, 1940; Myers to Arnold, August 28, 1940, AD.
130. Memorandum, Williams to Arnold, and Recapitulation of Complaints Received on Consent Decree, August 29, 1940, AD.
131. Arnold devoted a large section of *Bottlenecks of Business* (New York: Reynal Hitchcock, 1940) to a heavy attack on industry-government cooperation in the light of the war efforts, while, in his opinion, it was a moment in which antitrust surveillance was essential.
132. Memorandum, Rowe to Roosevelt, August 15, 1940, PSF 148, Executive Office, FDRL. The alternative to the President's intervention was the contact with William Douglas, Supreme Court judge and Arnold's great friend, who could have mediated between the division and the commission.
133. Storm to Myers, August 22, 1940, AD.
134. "The Schine, Griffith and Crescent cases will be dismissed as to the distributor defendants who consent to the New York decree and will proceed against the other defendants. In the Fox West Coast case a supplemental decree will be entered . . . providing for the arbitration by any independent exhibitor. . . . Similarly, in the Balaban and Katz, . . ." (Arnold to Myers, November 5, 1940, AD).
135. During the war, the companies that owned theaters enjoyed an unmatchable prosperity, because of the great participation by the public (Douglas Gomery, *The Hollywood Studio System, 1939–1949* [New York: St. Martin's Press, 1986], 8).

136. *U.S. v. Paramount,* Official Record, 382.

137. Ibid., 438.

138. Ibid., 463.

139. Harry Warner to Arnold, November 22, 1940, AD.

140. It is important to understand the conviction with which Warner considers the decree as being a definitive solution, without understanding its provisionary nature (Jack Warner to Roosevelt, November 25, 1940, OF 73, FDRL).

141. Memorandum signed by Wright, December 30, 1940, AD.

142. Memorandum, Wright to Arnold, January 8, 1941, AD.

143. Memorandum signed by Baldridge, November 15, 1941, AD.

144. Isseks to Wright, November 26, 1941, AD.

145. Press release, Department of Justice, January 22, 1942, AD.

146. Memorandum signed by Doyle, February 19, 1942, AD.

147. *Film Bulletin,* February 23, 1942.

148. Borneman, "United States versus Hollywood," 333.

149. Ibid., 335.

150. Ibid., 338.

151. On postwar American cinema, see Robert Sklar, *Movie-Made America* (New York: Vintage Books, 1994), and John Izod, *Hollywood and the Box Office 1895–1986* (New York: Columbia University Press, 1988).

152. Petition to the Supreme Court, January 1948, signed by Philip Perlman, John Sonnett and Robert Wright, 122–24.

Conclusion

1. See Giuliana Muscio, *Hollywood/Washington* (Padua: CLEUP, 1977); Thomas Doherty, *Projections of War: Hollywood, American Culture, and World War II* (New York: Columbia University Press, 1993).

2. See Richard Steele, *Propaganda in an Open Society: The Roosevelt Administration and the Media* (Westport, Conn.: Greenwood Press, 1985).

3. See Clayton Koppes and Gregory Black, *Hollywood Goes to War* (New York: The Free Press, 1987).

4. Robert Sklar, *Movie-Made America,* (New York: Vintage Books, 1994) 249–50.

5. In 1951 Stanley Kramer agreed to direct the film. About this film project Peter Collier writes: "there were interminable discussions within the family about how the royalties would be split and who would control the script. . . . The movie would continue to be discussed over the new few years. . . . But despite often desperate maneuvering by Jimmy and John, and eventually Franklin Jr., it did not come to fruition until the play *Sunrise at Campobello* provided a vehicle that delivered handsome royalties to each of the children" (*The Roosevelts: An American Saga* [New York: Simon & Schuster, 1994], 437.)

Index

INDEX

INDEX

Warner Theaters, 36
Washington Times, 27
Washington, George, 96
WASP, 57, 76, 109, 112, 133
Welles, Orson, 23, 45–46, 67
Wellman, William, 97–99
West, Mae, 110, 115
Wheeler, Burton, 53, 104, 139. *See also* Propaganda hearings
White, Edward D., 146
Why We Fight, 102, 198
Wild Boys of the Road, 99–100
Williams, Paul, 149–171, 172, 173, 174, 176, 177–81, 182, 185, 186, 187, 190, 191, 192, 193. *See also Paramount* case
Williams, Raymond, 1
Willkie, Wendell, 139, 141, 186–87
Wilson, Woodrow, 96
Woodward brothers, 85
Working class, or workers, 3, 5, 6, 21–22, 66, 67, 69, 109

World War I, 18, 27, 59
World War II, 2, 8, 10, 26, 62, 104, 197–99
WPA (Works Progress Administration), 2, 3, 11, 82, 83, 85
Wright, Robert, 172, 173, 190–91, 192
Writers Project, 11, 82
Wyman, Jane, 46
Wynn, Ed, 23
Wynn, Keenan, 46

Y

You Have Seen Their Faces, 83

Z

Zanuck, Darryl, 45, 46, 98–99
Zukor, Adolf, 47, 116, 125, 180

Media as force for change, not just a reflection 2

Hollywood & ND
    85% of industry pro FDR   ) 44
    mgmt mostly anti FDR